exploring

INTERFACE
DESIGN

dedication

This book is dedicated to Julie, my life's love, and to Ben and Emily, my shining lights. My life is testament to their support, patience, and love.

exploring

INTERFACE DESIGN

Marc Silver

THOMSON

DELMAR LEARNING ™

Australia Canada Mexico Singapore Spain United Kingdom United States

Exploring Interface Design
Marc Silver

Vice President, Technology and Trades SBU:
Alar Elken

Editorial Director:
Sandy Clark

Senior Acquisitions Editor:
James Gish

Development Editor:
Jaimie Wetzel

Marketing Director:
David Garza

Channel Manager:
Fair Huntoon

Marketing Coordinator:
Mark Pierro

Production Director:
Mary Ellen Black

Production Manager:
Larry Main

Production Coordinator:
Dawn Jacobson

Art/Design:
Thomas Stover

Technology Project Manager:
Kevin Smith

Editorial Assistant:
Marissa Maiella

Cover Design:
Steven Brower

Cover Image:
Chris Navetta

Library of Congress
Cataloging-in-Publication Data:

Silver, Marc.
    Exploring interface design / Marc Silver.
        p. cm.
Includes index.
    ISBN 1-4018-3739-5
    1. Animated films--Technique. I. Silver. II. Title.
    NC1765.H35 2003
    741.5'--dc21
                                2003008885

NOTICE TO THE READER

table of contents

TABLE OF CONTENTS

v

preface

INTENDED AUDIENCE

When challenged to design the interface for a website or multimedia project, many designers reach instinctively for their favorite paint program or web development software. The true measure of a design's success, though, is the quality of the target audience's experience when using that product. The growing demand for better end products requires today's designers to be equipped to develop products that offer a superior user experience. Exploring Interface Design offers the solid foundation and practical advice that will enable beginning, intermediate, and advanced web and multimedia design students to acquire and practice these vital skills. Even professional designers will find plenty of useful tips and techniques to help improve the quality of their designs and professional practice.

BACKGROUND OF THIS TEXT

Although general web design books abound today, most are specialized to a particular aspect of the subject—such as critiques of existing websites or investigations of design theory. Exploring Interface Design is unique in that it treats all aspects of successful user experience design in a delightfully readable style geared to designers of all levels. It then goes a step further by providing clear examples of what to do and what not to do. Exploring Interface Design invites you to experience the foundations, techniques, decision-making, and real-world problem solving from the perspective of a successful practicing designer with a genuine enthusiasm and love for design.

TEXTBOOK ORGANIZATION

Exploring Interface Design is structured like a large Web or multimedia design project. After laying the initial groundwork, the book introduces the interface design process. The book then follows that process, starting with goal setting, task and audience analysis, and idea creation, then progressing through the steps required to solve multi-faceted, real-life design challenges. Special attention is given to the important topics of visual design, writing for the web and multimedia, and designing for accessibility. The book then covers how to communicate the design, perform usability testing, and grow a professional practice.

Chapter One, *Realizing the Power of Multimedia and the Web*, sets the stage by defining the role that user experience designers and related professionals play in web and multimedia development. It introduces powerful applications of web and multimedia technology, encouraging designers to use technology's full power to provide experiences that cannot be duplicated in any other medium.

Chapter Two, *The Art of Designing Elegant Software*, lays the foundation by exploring the underlying principles that guide the designer's work. Drawing on the disciplines of design, cognitive science, and ergonomics, real-life examples are presented that clearly illustrate the principles and concepts covered.

Chapter Three, *The User Interface Design Process*, shows how the design of the user experience fits into the overall development of a website or multimedia software project. It presents the case for adhering to a process to ensure quality and consistency of design. Several different processes in common use today, including agile development methods, are examined in light of their effect on the user experience design function.

Chapter Four, *Goal Setting and Needs Assessment*, addresses the need to evaluate and plan for the needs of the target audience for a website or multimedia software product. This chapter covers methods of evaluating existing websites and software, defining user types and tasks, creating personas to describe different user types, and organizing the functions and features of the site or software.

Chapter Five, *Creativity and Idea Generation*, gives the reader specific methods for generating promising ideas that can vastly enhance the value of a designer's work. Real-life examples are presented as challenges, and the creativity methods applied to generate innovative ideas. These ideas are then evaluated to determine which is likely to produce the most successful results.

Chapter Six, *Menus and Controls*, explores the user interface elements and controls that comprise the designer's tool kit. Each interface element and control is described and its effect on the user experience examined. The chapter presents clear examples that illustrate when and how to use and not use each element and control.

Chapter Seven, *Designing Usable Navigation*, addresses all phases of this important component of usable software and website design. The chapter starts by examining various metaphors used to define a product's navigation. It covers effective search design, menu design, hyperlink design, breadcrumb trails, and the proper use of organizational controls such as tabs.

Chapter Eight, *Solving Design Problems*, provides three real-life design challenges of increasing complexity. It then takes readers through the process of designing *workable* solutions to those challenges, examining the strengths and weaknesses of each approach. This beginning-to-end method clearly shows readers how designers work at a problem to arrive at the best solution.

Chapter Nine, *Visual Considerations*, investigates how the visual organization of a page or screen contributes to or detracts from the quality of the user's experience. Numerous examples are used to show how relatively minor changes in arrangement can contribute significantly to the usability of the screen or page. Also included in this chapter is an in-depth comparative analysis of two websites that endeavor to offer similar capabilities.

Chapter Ten, *Writing for Usability*, is a mini course in effective writing for the web and multimedia. The chapter begins by showing how web visitors require a different method of structuring web writing. It shows how the inverted-pyramid writing style is best suited to web writing and provides examples of how to reduce words and simplify the message. Since websites and multimedia software are often used for education and training applications, the topic of instructional writing is covered fully, with emphasis on context, voice, pace, and sequence.

Chapter 11, *Designing for Accessibility*, explores this increasingly important topic. The chapter begins by identifying the most prevalent types of disabilities affecting computer users, including simulations of many different types of vision impairments. The chapter then examines screen readers, screen magnifiers, and refreshable Braille displays, and presents techniques for designing websites and multimedia software that is more accessible to users with special needs.

Chapter 12, *Specifying the Design*, presents practical techniques to help designers communicate their ideas to team members, clients, and other stakeholders. A real-life multimedia website example runs throughout the chapter, and the reader can see how to specify progressive design steps via pencil sketches, software-based wireframes, storyboards, and artist's concept drawings.

Chapter 13, *Performing Usability Testing*, provides a practical approach to this important step that designers frequently overlook. Readers will explore the rationale for such tests, investigate the roles of the various participants in a usability study, then learn to set up a usability-testing lab and conduct one of several types of usability studies. The chapter also includes practical tips for writing up the results of the usability test in a recommendations report.

Chapter 14, *The User Interface Designer in Professional Practice*, addresses the needs of individuals who are planning to start a practice or who are presently in one. The chapter covers client relationships, building your business, creating effective proposals, and protecting yourself from unethical client practices. The chapter also includes plenty of tips and techniques for effectively organizing the practice.

HOW TO USE
THIS TEXT

The following features can be found
throughout this book:

▶ Objectives

Learning Objectives start off each
chapter. They describe the compe-
tencies the readers should achieve
upon understanding the chapter
material.

▶ Tips

Tips are interspersed throughout the text
and provide special hints and practical
information to the reader.

▶ Sidebars

Sidebars appear through-
out the text, offering additional valuable information
on specific topics.

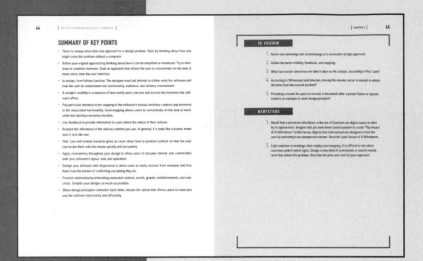

Key Points, Review Questions, and Exercises are located at the end of each chapter and reinforce material presented to allow readers to assess their understanding of the chapter.

FEATURES

The following list provides some of the salient features of the text:

- Teaches the key principles of user experience design, knowledge that is essential to creating successful, usable multimedia and web products.

- Teaches "best practices" by illustrating and critiquing state-of-the-art examples of multimedia and website designs. Provides firsthand knowledge of the logic and thought processes applied by successful user experience designers.

- Defines and clearly explains a step-by-step methodology for designing, implementing, and evaluating the user experience.

- Numerous tips, hints, examples, and techniques enable readers to quickly apply user experience design principles to real-world situations.

- A friendly, conversational writing style engages readers and renders even complex topics easy to understand and absorb.

- Poses interface design challenges and possible approaches, then analyzes the advantages and drawbacks of each approach to determine which is best.

- Covers in a single book the material typically taught in both introductory and advanced interface design courses.

- Objectives clearly state the learning goals of each chapter.

- Summary of key points and review questions reinforce material presented in the each chapter.

- Creative, engaging exercises allow students to demonstrate their skills.

about the author

ABOUT THE AUTHOR

Marc Silver has been designing innovative, award-winning websites and multimedia software for the past twenty years. His experience includes the design of more than 150 multimedia applications websites, and large-scale Web applications used for education, marketing, training, and entertainment. Mr. Silver is an inventor and designer of interactive games for Palm and Pocket PC handheld devices. He collaborates with U.K.-based Astraware Ltd., the premier developer of handheld games, for programming and worldwide distribution. Mr. Silver has written numerous trade articles and conducted workshops and seminars on design and creativity topics at national and regional conferences. He is a member of the Association of Computing Machinery's Special Interest Group in Computer-Human Interaction (SIGCHI).

THE LEARNING PACKAGE

E.Resource

This electronic manual was developed to assist instructors in planning and implementing their instructional programs. It includes sample syllabi for using this book in either an 11- or 15-week course. It provides answers to the review questions in the book, PowerPoint slides that highlight main topics and provide a framework for classroom discussion, and additional learning tools. The ISBN is 1401837417.

ACKNOWLEDGMENTS

I am indebted to many people who have helped make this book a reality.

Sincere thanks to Mark Huth, who first suggested that I write this book, and then introduced me to Jim Gish to help make it happen.

Thanks to Andrew Gardner, associate and friend, who has taught me much of what I know about conducting and organizing a business.

Thanks to David Sides and all my friends at Dolphin Inc. for the collaborative spirit that helped us create great products together for nearly ten years. Special thanks to Derek Richards, whose artistic talents and tireless effort added tremendous value to my designs and helped bring them to life. Thanks also to Dave Sugar for our many lake-based discussions of software design and engineering, among other topics.

Thanks to Eric Z. for the creativity, artistic talent, and perseverance he demonstrated creating the cover for this book.

Many thanks to the team of talented professionals at Delmar who provided the support, guidance, and encouragement that helped this book become a reality, including Thomas Stover, Project Editor, Dawn Jacobson, Production Coordinator, and Marissa Maiella, Editorial Assistant.

I am deeply indebted to Jim Gish, Senior Acquisitions Editor, who believed in the idea that became this book and contributed his extensive knowledge of book publishing and the market.

Special thanks go to Jaimie Wetzel, my Developmental Editor at Delmar, for her everyday enthusiasm, support, trust, and sense of humor.

Delmar Learning and the author would also like to thank the following reviewers for their valuable suggestions and expertise:

Rebecca Gallagher
Digital Media Department
Katherine Gibbs – New York
New York, New York

Karen Girton-Snyder
Multimedia and Web Design Department
Art Institute of Philadelphia
Philadelphia, Pennsylvania

Giraud Polite
Visual Communications Department
Brookhaven College
Farmers Branch, Texas

Paco Virella
Academic Director
Art Institute of Las Vegas
Las Vegas, Nevada

—Marc Silver
2004

QUESTIONS AND FEEDBACK

Delmar Learning and the author welcome your questions and feedback. If you have suggestions that you think others would benefit from, please let us know and we will try to include them in the next edition.

To send us your questions and/or feedback, you can contact the publisher at:

Delmar Learning
Executive Woods
5 Maxwell Drive
Clifton Park, NY 12065
Attn: Graphic Arts Team
800-998-7498

Or contact the author at:
marcsilver@comcast.net

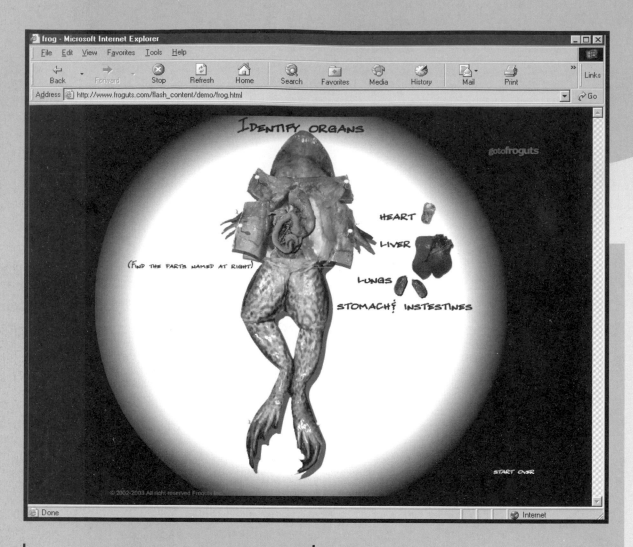

realizing the power of multimedia and web

CHAPTER 1

REALIZING THE POWER OF MULTIMEDIA AND WEB

objectives

Explain how multimedia and websites can use the power of interactivity to persuade, sell, create a sense of community, teach, and entertain

Describe the importance of researching audience requirements prior to beginning to design a multimedia software project or website

Describe why it is important to create designs on paper before beginning coding

Summarize some of the costs associated with poor user interface design

Recognize the difference between being creative and being a good designer

introduction

We live in a truly magical age. At our fingertips, on our desktops, and in our pockets, we have easy access to a universe of powerful experiences—many of them simply there for the taking. Multimedia software and websites have the power to enrich and transform us. In the home, the car, at school, in government, in small businesses and corporations, the power of software can persuade, connect, entertain and divert, challenge and teach, inform, reward, move us to laughter or tears, and compel us to take action to improve ourselves and our surroundings.

Examples of the power of this medium abound in areas as diverse as the human experience itself. Multimedia and the Web play an ever-increasing role in medicine, marketing communications, education and training, transportation, commerce, shipping, and entertainment, to name but a few. Let's take a brief look at some well-known, and perhaps not-so-well-known, ways in which multimedia software and the Web have demonstrated their true power and utility.

THE POWER TO PERSUADE

When the city of Atlanta, Georgia, decided to make a bid to win the 1996 Summer Olympic Games, most people didn't give them a serious chance of winning. Considered a dark-horse candidate, they faced stiff competition from, among other cities, Athens, Greece, the overwhelming favorite to win the bid. The Atlanta team was short on money needed to mount a serious campaign, but they made up for it in ingenuity. They decided that technology might be the most compelling means to show Atlanta's preparedness and suitability as a potential host city.

The Georgia Institute of Technology, better known as Georgia Tech, was the proposed site of the Atlanta Olympic Village. Georgia Tech's Michael Sinclair, other members of the university, and volunteers designed and pieced together two ambitious, interactive systems. The first one used a trackball and flight simulator technology to allow International Olympic Committee (IOC) officials to virtually fly around the city and tour the proposed venue sites. The second system combined a small, 3-D, plastic model of the Olympic Village Campus illuminated with computer-generated graphics. Touching one of the buildings or areas in the model displayed vignettes showing a day in the life of an athlete as it applied to the selected building or area.

A key feature of the presentations was the ability of IOC officials to interact with the presentations. Rather than simply sitting back and watching passively, the officials could control the pace and direction of the show. This must have been a welcome change, since it is likely that most if not all of the other presentations offered officials a much more idle experience. This made the Atlanta presentation stand out from other cities' presentations.

When the IOC announced that Atlanta had beaten the odds and won the bid to host the 1996 summer games, the persuasive power of the interactive multimedia presentations received much of the credit.

| TIP |

Use the power of interactivity to engage your audience. People are drawn to experiences where they can participate, and studies show that people retain more information when actively engaged than when they watch or listen passively.

FUELING COMMERCIAL ENTERPRISE

These days, it seems as if everyone has something to sell. The success of the World Wide Web is largely fueled by its ability to give even small, Mom-and-Pop operations a chance to show their stuff in the same forum as corporate Goliaths. A well-conceived, well-executed website can reap many times its initial investment in sales of the company's products or services. Of particular interest to us here are the multimedia and Web applications that raise service to a new level, extend our ability to make good choices, or increase our buying and selling power—in short, those that use the power of the medium to its full advantage.

Perhaps you are handy and are thinking about adding a deck to your house, but you are not sure you are up to the task. You drive to your neighborhood lumber or hardware store, where a sales assistant escorts you to a kiosk. With the assistant's help, you design your deck using an interactive multimedia application. You specify its shape and dimensions, including any special features such as seating, stairs, or a hot tub cutout. When you are satisfied with your creation, the assistant clicks the Print button and, in a few minutes, hands you a complete set of design drawings, construction details, and an accurate materials list for your deck. The materials list includes quantities and the store's own part numbers and prices. You purchase the materials and head home to begin construction. Figure 1-1 shows the Cad Quest Deck application.

| TIP |

Look for ways to maximize the value that your application provides to customers. Provide an experience that cannot be duplicated using any other medium.

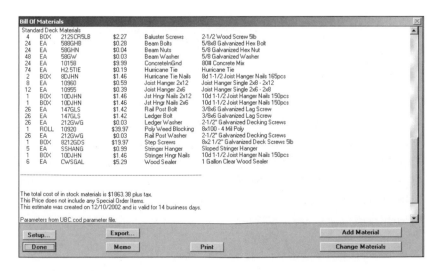

figure |1-1|

The CAD Quest Deck application allows do-it-yourselfers to design their own deck in the lumber or hardware store. The software then creates and prints a parts list complete with quantities and prices. Photographs provided by Cad Quest, Inc.

Those who purchase tickets online to events such as sports competitions or concerts are probably familiar with this next example. Before you commit to purchasing the tickets, you are shown a page that contains a graphic representation of the stadium or concert hall, with its seating sections clearly marked. You click on a section to see the actual view from that section. After checking out the view from several different vantages, you select the section that matches your budget and taste and purchase your tickets. A little later in this book, we will closely examine and compare some examples of this particular application available on the Web at the time of this book's writing. We will see how the various designers differ in their approach, including which designs result in the best experience and which miss the mark.

The Web also offers consumers the opportunity to customize the products they order to their exact needs. Computer manufacturers, such as Dell, allow customers to configure systems with exactly the features they want. Customers who place orders can watch *their* system's progress through the various steps of manufacturing and quality testing. Once the system is shipped, the customer is linked directly to the shipper's site to track the order's progress toward arrival. These sites illustrate a growing trend toward offering unprecedented levels of personalized service.

Amazon.com has been a leader in establishing a sense of community among its customers. If you choose, Amazon.com will tell you what your friend or family member would like to receive for his birthday. It can tell you what purchases your friends are making (if they choose to share this information), and it will even notify you if one of them writes a review of a particular product. Giving users a sense of community and shared purpose translates into more purchases. Figure 1-2 shows Amazon.com's Friends and Favorites options, which help customers feel like they are part of a community.

SIMULATION AND TRAINING

Multimedia software is excellent at simulating all sorts of lab experiments, surgical procedures, business situations, scientific and economic models, flight and weapons systems, and hundreds of other types of systems and processes.

Biology students who don't have (or don't want) access to frogs for dissection can simulate the experience using a virtual frog at froguts.com, shown in Figure 1-3. By offering features such as interactive anatomical part labeling, sites such as this add to the educational value of the experience.

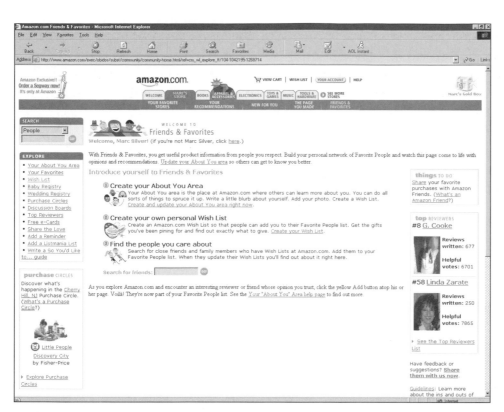

figure |1-2|

Commercial Web sites, such as Amazon.com, attempt to create a sense of community among their users.

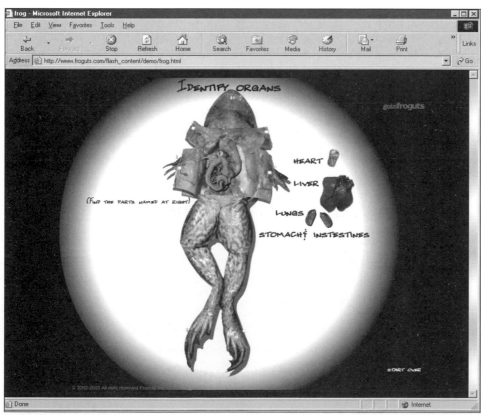

figure |1-3|

Students can dissect virtual specimens online at Froguts.com.

Chemistry students can conduct potentially dangerous experiments in a virtual laboratory—experiencing flare-ups, caustic spills, toxic fumes, and explosions as events offering learning rather than injuries requiring treatment. Similarly, apprentice electricians can practice their wiring skills in a virtual electrical laboratory without risking injury to themselves or damage to expensive equipment. Figure 1-4 shows a generator wiring activity from Delmar's *Virtual Laboratory in Electricity* multimedia software.

Surgeons can practice intricate procedures on computerized simulations that closely mimic the look and feel of real organs and tissue. The simulation itself, or human operators hidden from view, can introduce unexpected events in the "patient," testing the surgeon's ability to react quickly with the proper technique or course of action. The software can report fully on the surgeon's performance, giving specific feedback and recommending additional practice or coursework as necessary.

In classrooms, corporate and government training centers, in institutions and at home, the Web can provide accessible computerized models, simulations, animations, and interactive lessons that help people, young and old, to master diverse subjects. The Web is a community where teachers can share the ideas that work best in the classroom and where students can turn for help when they need it. Students with special needs don't have to be left behind, as more is known about how to make multimedia and Web applications available to a greater percentage of the population.

| TIP |

Use the modeling capabilities of software to simulate dangerous, fragile, expensive, rare, intricate, or unavailable machines, systems, organisms, and processes.

figure | 1-4 |

This multimedia training software allows apprentice electricians to practice wiring devices such as generators without fear of causing injury to themselves or damage to expensive equipment. Software copyright Delmar Learning and Dolphin Inc. Graphic design by Derek Richards.

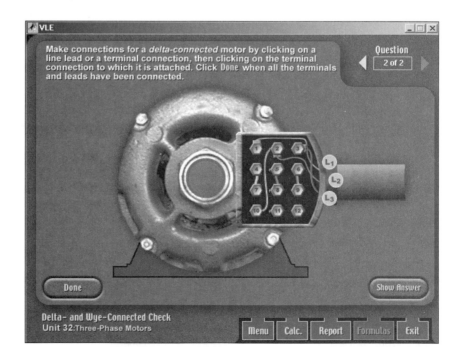

STRIVE FOR APPLICATION POWER

Designers of websites and multimedia should continuously strive to do what the applications we've described do so well—use the power of the medium to full advantage. It is disappointing to access a website or CD-ROM application that simply repurposes information originally meant for a different medium, usually paper. There is nothing wrong with paper—it achieves its purpose extremely well, but software is about interaction, engagement, and experiences.

Ensuring that this magical medium fulfills its limitless promise falls to those who craft the experiences that give the medium its awesome power—the ones who decide which combination and layout of buttons, menus, text fields, images, and other elements will best connect us with the experiences we choose. In the right hands, the interface is crafted so skillfully that it seems to disappear, allowing the power of the application to emerge fully realized. In less capable hands, the user interface is a burdensome obstacle, standing between user and intention.

DEFINING BASIC TERMINOLOGY

Before we proceed too far, we need to define the phrase **user interface**, which is often shortened to **interface**, or is sometimes called **human-computer interaction (HCI)** or **computer-human interaction (CHI)**. For our purposes, these terms may be defined as the means by which humans interact with a computer to fulfill a purpose. The term **user experience** is sometimes used interchangeably with user interface. This term recognizes that users have experiences that have been orchestrated by the designers. This term is also used to describe the entire relationship that a website user has with a company's products and services.

A note of warning: the choice of the word *user* has been criticized over the years—it is a cold, impersonal term with negative connotations for something so positive and people oriented. With no reasonable substitute and with apologies to those who object to it, we will make numerous references to *users* and the *user interface* in this text.

Throughout most of early computing history, the programmers or software engineers who wrote program code were also responsible for creating the user interface. Since the engineers were often the users of the programs they wrote, they tended to create interfaces that made sense to them. Often the interface would simply mirror the data that the system was storing internally. The screen pictured in Figure 1-5 shows a typical user interface from that time.

The programmers were the ultimate power users; they could tolerate (and even preferred) shortcuts and cryptic key sequences that, though hidden, quickly performed system functions. The user interface was an afterthought—viewed as insignificant compared to the software's functionality.

figure | 1-5 |

Early software programs focused more on function than on usability. The user interface was little more than a reflection of how the program's data was internally stored.

```
LOG=========================================================================
  Command ===>

  Welcome to PEDS V1.2.
  NOTE: AUTOEXEC processing beginning; file in \projects\peds


  NOTE: PEDS initialization used:
        real time            5.080 seconds
        cpu time             0.884 seconds


  NOTE: AUTOEXEC processing completed.

==========================================================================
  Program EDitor System
  Command ===>
  NOTE: At left side.
  01H
  02H
  03H
  04H
  05H
  06H
  07H
  08H
  09H
  0AH
  0BH
  0CH
```

Users of these early programs, justifiably awed by the promise and novelty of this new medium, mostly overlooked the fact that these systems were extremely difficult to learn and use. Programmers made the rules, and users had little choice but to follow them. When a company authorized the purchase of a new software system, it was assumed that a large part of the investment would go to teaching users how to be productive with the new software.

RISING EXPECTATIONS FOR SOFTWARE

As John Naisbitt wrote in his 1982 book, *Megatrends*, "Whenever new technology is introduced into society, there must be a counterbalancing human response—that is, high touch—or the technology is rejected." As the popularity of personal computers rose sharply during the 1980s and 1990s, users' tolerance for hard-to-use software began to decrease. This intolerance grew for several reasons. First, when the company placed one of these sleek, costly, new devices on your desk, it expected the investment in you to be rewarded with increased productivity. Early personal computer users valued software that did not require significant additional expenditures in money and time for extensive training.

Second, personal computers were perceived as status symbols as well as productivity tools. People had higher expectations for the software running on *their* computer than they had for software running on the corporate mainframe. Early in the personal computer's history, there were more companies competing for market share among the different types of software—e.g., word processors or spreadsheet programs. This competitive climate helped begin to spur improvements in how easily users could learn and use these products.

DESIGNING WITH USERS IN MIND

We use the term **user-centered design (UCD)** to describe the process and result of designing with the needs of the user in mind. The process requires that the user-interface designer adopt the mindset that the user's experience is the one that matters most. It is born out of the notion that software, like other products, is created chiefly to serve its audience. The designer's and the product's success is ultimately measured by how well it meets the needs of that audience.

To develop user-centered designs, designers must be willing to subject their work at various stages of development to selected members of its intended audience. This input helps focus the designer's efforts and highlights potential problems in the design, allowing them to be resolved before the product is released.

The Science of Usability

The creation of an elegant user interface is equal parts science and art. The science is often referred to as **usability**. The International Organization for Standardization (ISO) defines usability as the effectiveness, efficiency, and satisfaction with which specified users achieve specified goals in particular environments. The ISO further defines these terms used in the definition of usability. **Effectiveness** is the accuracy and completeness with which specified users can achieve specified goals in particular environments. **Efficiency** is the resources expended in relation to the accuracy and completeness of goals achieved. **Satisfaction** is the comfort and acceptability of the work system to its users and other people affected by its use.

We can try to distill this somewhat dry set of definitions into a simpler one: Usable software and websites are easy to learn, easy to use, easy to remember, and they enhance the user's ability to perform desired tasks. Of course, a beautifully designed interface is not usually, by itself, sufficient to attract repeat visits to a website or multimedia program. The quality of the software or website's content must be compelling as well. But users often refuse to return to a site that is hard to use, regardless of the quality of its content. It is therefore no wonder that the demand for designers who can create truly usable systems is increasing.

A related group of workers, **usability engineers**, often work with designers to help test and ensure that the products being designed and developed are usable to their intended audience. They design and conduct usability studies in the lab or field, then analyze the results of these studies to identify usability defects. They bring these defects to the attention of the designer or design team for improvement. Figure 1-6 shows a usability study being conducted at one of these labs.

figure |1-6|

Here are two views of a usability lab. The first photo shows the testing area. The second photo shows the control room with a view of the testing area through a one-way mirror. Photos provided by The Leede Group

Usability engineers often have earned advanced degrees in human-computer interaction, usability engineering, or various disciplines of psychology. In firms that do not employ usability engineers, the designer assumes much of the responsibility for creating usable systems.

The Art of Design

It is the second part of the equation, the *art* of design, which inspires and often keeps designers glued to their computers long after others have gone home for the evening. We are not speaking about art in terms of graphic art, although this certainly plays an important role in the development of the user interface. We are speaking of the ability of the designer to create a vision of what the user interface can and should be.

| TIP |

At the beginning of a website or multimedia development project, know the minimum system configuration and operating environment that will be used to run the finished application. Test your application on these minimal systems early and often during the development process.

The designer seeks and receives input from a variety of interested stakeholders, including clients, users, and other members of the development team. The designer combines that information with his or her own talent, skill, and experience to create the most beautiful design possible. A beautiful user interface design is one that ideally expresses the software's function, satisfies the requirements of its audience, and adheres to established user interface and graphic design principles. Of course, it must also be pleasing to the eye and ear, and it has to perform well on the hardware and software platforms for which it is specified.

That last point, regarding the hardware and software platforms, deserves special mention. Often, the developers who create a website or multimedia project do the development work on high-end computer systems connected by fast T1 lines or cable modems. When tested on these platforms, the project runs flawlessly. The compelling, dramatic images, video, and audio blend seamlessly, eliciting high praise from the managers and clients who are shown demonstrations of the work in progress.

Unfortunately, no one on the team bothered to determine what sort of systems the intended audience was using. In fact, many of these were low-end, low-memory platforms connected by slow, 28K dial-up lines. As a result, when the software was run or the website accessed, both the audio and video were delivered in short, choppy bursts. Since most systems lacked the plug-in that was needed to display the animation, this part of the screen simply displayed a red "X."

Express the Software's Function

We used the term *beautiful* to describe a well-designed user interface. Some inexperienced designers believe that this means calling for the latest, coolest, Photoshop® effect, or requiring the newest streaming video technique. Accomplished designers strive for a much deeper expression of beauty—the perfect matching of form to function. The graphical look supports the software's purpose, but never overshadows it.

Software development is often compared to architecture, and there are many similarities between the two. In fact, those who specialize in organizing the information of a website or software application are called **information architects**, a term that is sometimes also used to describe a user interface designer. The disciplines of architecture and user interface design share some of the same methodologies and underlying principles. Like a good building, a well-designed website or multimedia program is an extension of its users. When a designer of either buildings or software captures this elusive quality, visitors are likely to return again and again. Figure 1-7 shows the Frank Lloyd Wright-designed *Fallingwater* residence in

figures |1-7|

Frank Lloyd Wright's Fallingwater residence beautifully fits its structure to the surrounding environment. Similarly, good user interface design reconciles the functional needs of the software with the needs of its audience and environment. Photograph of Fallingwater courtesy of Western Pennsylvania Conservancy

Pennsylvania. Notice how well the structure fits into its site, complementing rather than detracting from its environment. The site receives thousands of visitors each year.

Beginning multimedia and Web developers, when faced with a software design challenge, often reach for their favorite Web development tools or professional image-editing software. Keeping with the architecture analogy, this is akin to an architect calling in the bulldozers after the first client meeting. Although it is possible to build a house or a website in this fashion, it will be painful and expensive to do so.

A better idea is to express your ideas on paper. An architect creates a set of blueprints that specify and guide the construction of the building. Likewise, the user interface designer creates a set of specifications, often in the form of wireframes or other prototype, before any coding begins. **Wireframes**, as they relate to user interface design, usually are schematic sketches of the important screens in the software or website. The images contain crude representations of the various user interface elements that appear on each screen. Explanatory text accompanies the images, describing the screens and indicating what happens when a particular control is activated. Figure 1-8 shows a sample wireframe typical of those created by the author. A **prototype** is a more general term that describes a partial implementation of a software system

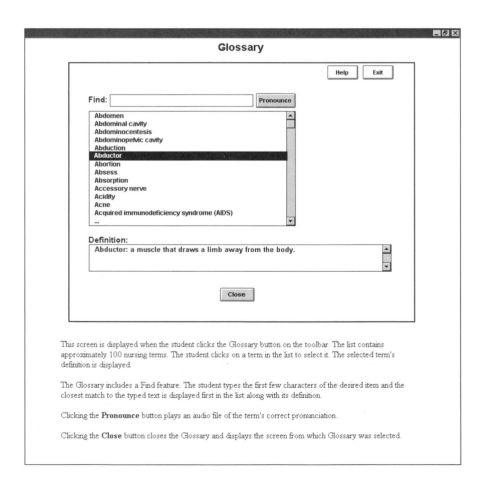

figure |1-8|

A sample wireframe, containing a schematic drawing at the top and a textual description below. The wireframe focuses on the functionality and basic layout of the screen's elements. The graphic look will be developed later.

or website. The prototype can be on paper or delivered electronically. It sometimes includes actual functionality to demonstrate how a particular feature will operate. We will discuss the specification of the user interface design, using tools such as wireframes, in Chapter 12.

When the designer must make changes to the design, the changes can be made much more cheaply to the paper version of the design than to the finished code. By contrast, the designer who begins coding immediately invests a lot of time and effort into the creation of that code. Such a designer will be less willing to make the kinds of changes that a client has the right to expect, which can lead to frustration for the developer and the potential loss of the project and the client.

The client also bears some responsibility in this process. The client's approval of the wireframes means that work can continue to the next phase of development. A client who subsequently requests significant changes to the user interface design after approving the wireframes may incur additional costs for the changes.

Satisfy the Audience's Requirements

The most important—and most often ignored—step in the development of a successful website or multimedia project is to thoroughly understand its intended audience. The people who visit your website or use your multimedia software may not think or act anything like you do. They may be older or younger, of a different gender or culture, may be hesitant to use technology, or may be in a great hurry. In their minds, they have their own model of how your site or software is set up. This may or may not coincide with your model. Figure 1-9 shows four widely different computer users.

figure | 1-9 |

Websites and multimedia software have a wide variety of users, each with his own attitudes, points of view, and requirements. The user interface designer must learn about the target audiences and design to their needs.

Watching a live user operate a software program or website for the first time can be a surprising and humbling experience for the designer. Assumptions the designer made regarding how functions should be organized, or what labels to use for choices, may not stand up to the one test that really matters—the audience's ability to use the software. When this happens, often the designer's first impulse is to blame the victim. With few exceptions, though, when users have trouble operating software, the responsibility is the designer's.

| TIP |

When someone tells you that he is having trouble operating your software or website, first thank him, then find out where you went wrong and correct the problem.

If you want to find out what the users want, there is only one way that really works—you have to ask them! Find out all you can about why they are using your software. What brought them here? What choices to they expect to see? In what environment will they be using your software? When your design is at the storyboard stage, show it to them and ask them to try to perform various functions. Try several different design options and see which one they prefer. Later, when the software or website is available for testing, invite some of them in to try it out.

Adhere to Established Design Principles

The field of user interface design, although still quite young, is rapidly developing a set of best practices. These principles have evolved through the experiences and contributions of many professional user interface designers and through usability research performed at universities and corporate lab settings. Some of these principles are specific in nature; they apply to a particular function or circumstance. Examples of these principles may be found throughout this book. Other principles are more general, covering a wider range of situations. A number of these are covered in the next chapter.

Here are two examples of user interface design principles that are specific:

1. If an element (such as an Exit button) is repeated on multiple screens, then place that element in the same position on each screen that it appears.

2. It is more difficult to read all uppercase (capitalized) letters than a mixture of upper and lower case. USING ALL UPPERCASE LETTERS ALSO MAKES IT SEEM LIKE YOU ARE SHOUTING AT YOUR AUDIENCE.

The usability principles are useful to practicing professionals and newcomers to the field, but they can be daunting. The sheer volume of study results, often critical of commonly held beliefs or often-used techniques, may lead beginning designers to conclude that *everything* they do is wrong. With experience comes the knowledge that the principles exist to improve our design skills, enabling us to better serve our audiences and clients. The more experienced you become in designing multimedia software or websites, the easier it becomes to put new findings into perspective and determine how best to incorporate them into your own work.

The Web, of course, is a great source of current information about newly emerging information regarding usability. It provides multiple forums for the nearly instantaneous exchange of usability information. Those who are interested can subscribe for free to a number of electronic newsletters containing articles and summaries of recent research. A recent Google search (http://www.google.com) of the phrase, "usability groups," turned up 311 entries.

The rapid rise of the Web has led to a growing group of professional practitioners devoted almost exclusively to website usability. This group, led by the eminent usability expert Jakob Nielsen, concentrates its efforts on what makes websites successful, especially from a commercial perspective.

Throughout this book, we will discuss user interface design principles as they relate to both the Web and multimedia software. We will pose design problems, present possible solutions, and analyze each to determine which is the best approach. These discussions will include coverage of many user interface design principles.

Graphic design principles, such as balance and sequence, are also important to the look of websites and multimedia software. Many excellent books exist that cover graphic design principles in wonderful detail. Graphic design principles are beyond the scope of this book.

THE COSTS OF BAD USER INTERFACE DESIGN

- Imagine being stuck in a room with no visible way to get out.
- Imagine being lost in a foreign country and being unable to communicate with anyone. When you finally find someone who speaks your language, he forces you to listen to his life story before giving you the directions you need.
- Imagine being forced to make a decision with serious consequences when you don't understand the choices.
- Imagine being on a highway with so many signs competing for your attention that you can't possibly pick out the one you need to follow.
- Imagine having to reintroduce yourself every time you saw your best friends.
- Imagine having to walk around the block every time you want to move from one room to another in your house.
- Imagine being incredibly hungry, but unable to figure out how to open the refrigerator.
- Imagine hiring an employee who refuses to do what you ask of him and makes you feel stupid for asking.

Experiencing any of the situations posed above might cause feelings of frustration, anger, and helplessness. Bad user interfaces subject users to similar emotions countless times each day.

- We're taken to a Web page with no visible means of getting back to a known page.

- A group of buttons is displayed with cryptic icons whose meaning or function we cannot guess.

- A Web page presents a confusing array of text choices, poorly organized links, ambiguously labeled buttons, and meaningless graphic images.

- We are forced to retype the identical user information that we provided to the same site yesterday.

- A tutorial program requires that we click the right arrow through 25 screens of information to get to the review quiz we were working on yesterday.

- We are presented with a modal dialog box that presents two undesirable choices, from which we are forced to select one. A **modal dialog** box is one that forbids the user from selecting any other buttons or other controls except those within the box. Figure 1-10 shows an example of a modal dialog box.

As you browse the Web or use software applications, begin developing your awareness of usability problems. Notice when you have difficulty navigating a particular site or understanding an icon or button label.

figure | 1-10 |

A modal dialog box, like the one shown here, requires the user's action. No other controls on the screen or page can be accessed until the user acts on the controls within this box. User interface designers are gradually reducing their dependence on modal dialogs.

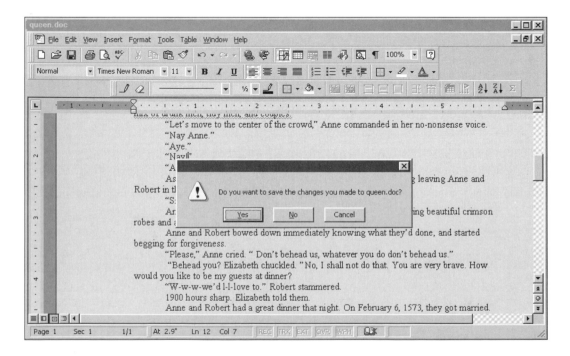

Although we know of no studies that conclusively link badly designed software to increased health risks, nearly all of us have felt our blood pressure rise and our stress levels peak as a direct result of working with software that seems unfit for human consumption.

For a long time, a particular behavior of popular applications programs has been a real stress producer. It occurs under certain conditions when a user loads a document or spreadsheet simply to print it. After invoking the print function, the user attempts to close the application, only to be prompted by a dialog box asking if the user wants to save changes to the document. This is a disturbing question, since the user did not make any changes to the document but merely printed it.

Since most users know that applications usually don't prompt to save changes unless you have made at least one, many users conclude that they must have changed their document accidentally, perhaps by inadvertently striking a key. They then carefully read through each word of their document, looking for the errant change. Of course, they never find it because they never made a change in the first place. It was the software's error in presenting the prompt to save changes to the document. But users carry around a nagging doubt that there *is* an embarrassing, undetected error somewhere in their document. With time, users learn to ignore the message, possibly resulting in embarrassing inadvertent errors in true "boy who cried wolf" fashion.

| TIP |

Practice expressing verbally the problems you encounter when accessing software or websites. Use specific language, such as, "I don't know how to get back to the screen with the menu." This will often suggest improvements that could be made to the design, such as providing access to the menu on every screen.

Creeping Features

One of the best-known contributors to unusable software is a phenomenon known as **feature creep**. Feature creep is the tendency for software products to become laden with features over time, sacrificing usability. Here's how it often occurs: A company creates a software program that is elegantly designed and well suited to its intended purpose and audience. Because of this, people buy the product and are happy with it. Eventually, influential users, such as corporate users who buy many copies of the product, may begin to request that new features be added. Or the company may simply want to gain additional revenue by encouraging existing users to upgrade to newer versions for a fee. To continue receiving upgrade revenues, there must be newer and newer versions, each with new functions not necessarily anticipated in the software's original design. The weight of these new features makes the original, vital features much more difficult to find and use. This is especially true for first-time users, who did not have the benefit of learning the product when it was small and efficient. Figure 1-11 shows a typical example of a mature, feature-laden product.

Users do not have much of a choice when it comes to buying the most widely used applications, such as word processors or spreadsheets. Without competitive pressures to make software easier to use, there is little impetus for successful software companies to completely redesign their most ubiquitous products.

figure |1-11|

A typical application menu with a bewildering array of menu options, buttons, and other controls. As a software product matures, it becomes heavily laden with features. This makes it more and more difficult for new users to learn and become productive with the software.

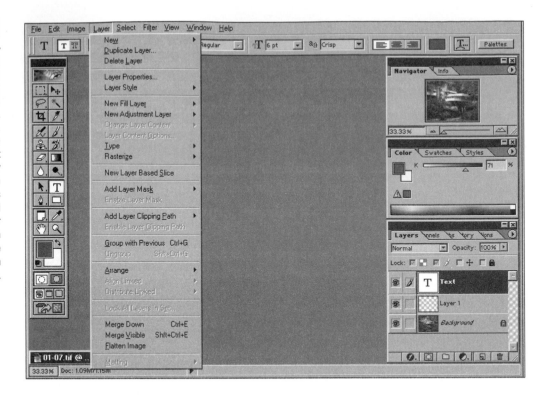

Computer-Aided Difficult-by-Design

In some cases, whole industries have emerged to compensate for software that is difficult to learn and use. Traditional computer-aided design/computer aided manufacturing (**CAD/CAM**) software is used by companies such as architectural firms and manufacturing companies. The software requires a major investment in time and effort to master. Hundreds of companies have been established that specialize in providing training and consulting in the use of this software. An easy-to-use CAD/CAM product might not only revolutionize the way buildings and products are designed, it might completely change the nature of many of these consultants' business.

Although we know of no litigation being brought against perpetrators of user-unfriendly websites or multimedia software, people's tolerance to things they perceive as harmful to their physical or mental health tends to decrease with time. In fact, a number of companies have collaborated to create a software users' bill of rights. The document covers such topics as general software product quality, accurate delivery schedules, explicit pricing, development accountability, technical support, and full disclosure of software vendors' business practices. Although usability remains a more subjective topic, its issues continue to gain publicity and momentum. As we learn to quantify and qualify what constitutes a satisfactory experience from a software user's perspective, we hope that usability will also become an integral part of the software users' bill of rights.

Counting Hits and Misses

There is another, more measurable cost associated with difficult-to-use software and websites. That cost is money, and it results when users who want to make purchases from commercial websites are frustrated in their attempts. The frustration may arise for a number of different reasons. Sometimes an online merchant has the exact item a shopper is looking for, but the potential customer simply cannot find it. Or a merchant may make it difficult for customers to figure out how to pay for their purchases. In other instances, a merchant may insist that a customer fill out a lengthy information form before they can proceed to checkout. The customer may not wish to give additional information to the merchant and may abort the purchase.

Luckily, commercial websites give us an excellent opportunity to measure the effects of user-centered design. Products such as HitBox and WebSTAT can track important website information, such as how many visitors have viewed each page of the site, how many potential customers have abandoned their purchases before completing them, and which are the most common navigational paths used by visitors. Figure 1-12 shows a WebSTAT report on the visited pages of a website.

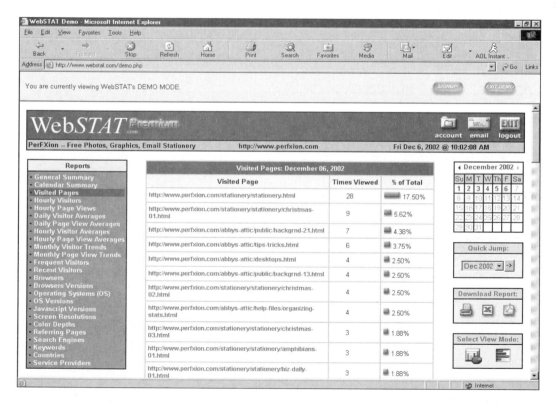

figure | 1-12 |

A screen capture showing page visits to a website. Notice the left-side menu showing the wide variety of information that is available about the users and usage of the site.

Owners of busy commercial websites track usage information such as this closely and use it to improve sales generated by the site. If statistics show that many shoppers abandon their purchases after viewing one of the pages of the checkout sequence, designers can analyze the reasons for the problems with the page, change the design, and get almost instantaneous feedback on the change's effect on visitor behavior at the site.

Obviously, online merchants want to put as few obstacles in the way of purchasers as possible. A site that is successful in selling products must certainly be easy to navigate. It must allow potential customers to see the range of products that exist and to search for a particular product by name or product type. Visitors should be able to see a close-up photo or drawing of the product as applicable. There should be well-written, compelling text that clearly and succinctly describes each product's features and benefits.

Most sites that sell products use a shopping cart symbol as the means to enable visitors to see what items they have selected for purchase. The shopping cart symbol is a **metaphor**, which is a familiar image used to make an unfamiliar idea, experience, or process understandable. Online vendors often use shopping metaphors that correspond to what shoppers do in an actual, or bricks-and-mortar, store. Since people know what a shopping cart is for—it holds the items they intend to purchase while they continue shopping—it is an effective metaphor. Online boutique stores may substitute a shopping bag for the shopping cart symbol.

Those who get too creative with well-understood metaphors do so at their own peril, especially when it affects the process used to enable shoppers to buy goods online. For example, if I am a seller of baby products, I may think it cute to call the shopping cart a "shopping stroller." Some users will appreciate such cleverness; many others will miss it entirely, concluding that this has something to do with shopping for a stroller. Frustrated with their inability to find a way to see which items they have selected for purchase, they may abandon their purchase and search for a friendlier site to shop.

Shoppers know what to do when they are in a bricks-and-mortar store when they have finished selecting the items they want—they proceed to the checkout counter. Likewise, a link that is worded "Proceed to Checkout" is a clear way of telling online shoppers what to do when they are ready to complete their purchase. Here again, although a vendor may be tempted to choose a catchy metaphor that reflects the store's products or character, it is best to resist. Figure 1-13 shows typical Shopping Cart and Proceed to Checkout controls.

A WISE CONSISTENCY

A step toward creating more usable software and websites is to understand human behavior and to apply this information to the user interface design. When faced with a new situation, people usually try to apply what they have learned from similar situations in the past. Car owners who have been faced with driving a rental car know how frustrating it is when the controls that adjust the temperature, windshield wipers, and lights are not in their familiar places.

figure |1-13|

The use of well-understood metaphors such as a shopping cart and checkout make it easier for shoppers to complete their purchases. Designers are wise to conform to these helpful conventions and apply creativity elsewhere.

Web surfers have begun to expect conventions in the placement of elements on Web pages. The identifying logo of the site, often the company logo, is usually positioned at the top left. In many sites, clicking this icon on a page (other than the home page) displays the home page. A text entry box for typing search text is often near the top right. The main menu of choices often appears along the top or down the left side.

These consistent placements have become *de facto* standards in web-site design. Designers are wise to take advantage of their existence. If we know that most users expect a particular element to be located in a particular spot, we should be happy to comply. It is one more thing we can do to make a site easy for users to understand and navigate. Some designers consider such conventions an affront to their creativity. Deviating from expected conventions certainly has its place, such as when the goals of the site are to defy such conventions.

However, what if the gas pedal, brake, and steering wheel in our rental car were similarly at the whim of such creative designers? Perhaps the control that looks like a steering wheel is actually the accelerator. Rotate it clockwise to pick up speed, and steer by shifting your weight in the seat. What looks like the horn is actually the brake. A car with such features would be considered creative, although not very useful.

Creativity is useful in interface design when it adds to the user's experience, rather than detracts from it. Often, this entails making the site or software more usable, thereby making the user more efficient. Most people prefer that their automobile controls behave just the way they always do. And most site owners appreciate it when their visitors can forget about the site's design and focus on its content. That said, if a designer can demonstrate a true advantage to a new technique, one that is easily grasped and far outweighs the benefits of a time-tested approach, then by all means use it.

SUMMARY OF KEY POINTS

- Design multimedia software and websites that take advantage of the true power of computers. Do not create software that simply delivers information originally intended for another medium such as paper or video.

- Making website visitors feel like they are part of a community will keep them coming back to your site. Do not try to force them to participate, however.

- Use computing power to simulate hazardous, expensive, or inaccessible systems and processes. Design websites that access real data to provide answers to questions that your audience is asking.

- Understanding the needs of your target audience is the single greatest determinant of the success or failure of your design.

- The field of user interface design has been growing rapidly in popularity as users' demand for usable software has increased. The related field of usability engineering concentrates on measuring the ease with which users are able to use software and websites to accomplish their goals.

- To be effective, designers must become familiar with user interface design principles. There are a number of channels that designers can use to keep current with the latest usability research.

- As software applications mature, they become more and more heavily laden with features, making them harder and harder for new users to learn and become productive with them.

- Poor usability design has been blamed for significant sales losses due to online shoppers aborting their purchases. Using Web traffic reporting software allows designers to ferret out such problems and instantly see the results of the improvements they implement.

in review

1. What is user-centered design?

2. What term is defined as the means by which humans interact with a computer to fulfill a purpose?

3. Define the terms effectiveness, efficiency, and satisfaction.

4. What are some advantages to specifying the user interface on paper before it is developed?

5. What is a modal dialog box?

6. How can hit tracking software be used to determine problems in a website's product ordering process?

exercise

1. Steven Jobs, founder of Apple, sought new ideas and solutions that were "insanely great," meaning they exceeded everyone's expectations. What computer applications have you used or customer experiences have you had that could use a complete overhaul? List one such experience and discuss how you might use the power of multimedia and/or the Web to make it insanely great.

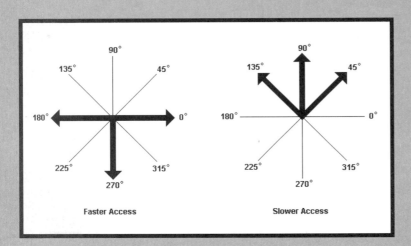

Faster Access   Slower Access

the art of designing elegant software

objectives

Analyze a simple design problem

Examine several solutions to the design problem and describe their advantages and disadvantages

Describe the importance of design principles to user interface design

Examine design principles made famous by Donald Norman, including visibility, mapping, feedback, and affordance

Describe Fitts' Law and its application to user interface design

Analyze other design principles important to user interface design

introduction

Great multimedia software and websites don't just happen. They are the result of the user interface designer's careful research and planning, strict attention to detail, and occasional flashes of inspiration. When working on the design of a particular screen, page, or function, you continuously weigh one consideration against another. Often the solution to one problem causes a different problem, and you must persist, applying creativity and sweat, until you find that better solution.

This process is repeated dozens of times during the design of each project. With experience, you will learn to quickly eliminate many potential solutions in favor of those approaches that are most likely to succeed.

In many cases, you must make compromises among the various approaches, prioritizing the strengths of each to arrive at the most satisfactory solution. There is some truth to the axiom, perhaps coined by a frustrated designer, that "Design is deciding how you want to fail." Young designers can take comfort in knowing that every user interface problem has at least one solution.

THE ART OF DESIGNING ELEGANT SOFTWARE

THE DESIGN OF A MILES/KILOMETERS CONVERTER

To help illustrate the thought process that accompanies design, here is an assignment:

Design an interface that enables adult users to quickly convert miles to the equivalent number of kilometers or to convert kilometers to miles.

Try to solve this problem yourself before reading further. Make a sketch of your design on paper. Although we have not yet discussed all of the various screen controls and widgets at your disposal—buttons, menus, checkboxes, text entry fields, and the rest—most of you have seen and used these common elements dozens of times. The next part of this chapter will explore some possible solutions to this problem.

How might you approach such a problem?

| TIP |

When you are trying to solve some types of user interface problems, start by thinking about how you would solve the problem by yourself without a computer.

| Convert Miles to Kilometers |

| Convert Kilometers to Miles |

figure | 2-1 |

A simple menu of two buttons allows the user to select which type of conversion to perform. This approach mirrors our first attempt to create a conceptual model of the problem. We will try to improve it later.

Converter Design Attempt One

How would you perform such a conversion without a computer? First, you would probably need to know if you were converting miles to kilometers or kilometers to miles. Your design must provide some means for the user to make this choice as well. Figure 2-1 shows a pair of push-buttons that might be used for this purpose.

Let us assume that you want to convert miles to kilometers. In our example, the user will click the first button, Convert Miles to Kilometers. This might display a screen with a text-entry box where the user can type the number of miles to be converted to kilometers. The user will type the number of miles, then perhaps click a button labeled Convert to Kilometers to perform the conversion. We'll assume that the software will be programmed to perform the proper conversion. The result will be displayed to the user. Figure 2-2 shows the completed screen for this approach.

When looking at this approach, it is apparent that the user could perform more conversions of miles to kilometers by entering different values for the number of miles, again clicking the Convert to Kilometers button, and viewing the new result. However, what if the user wants to do a conversion from kilometers to miles? There is currently no way to get back to the original screen—the one with the two buttons labeled "Convert Miles to Kilometers" and "Convert Kilometers to Miles." Since we will need to add a control for this purpose, we have added a button labeled "Return to Menu," shown in Figure 2-3.

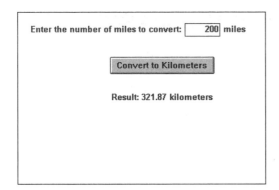

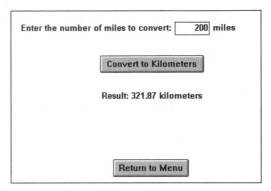

figure |2-2|

In this miles-to-kilometers conversion screen, the user enters the number of miles, then clicks the button to perform the conversion and display the result.

figure |2-3|

The Return to Menu button allows the user to return to the menu to convert kilometers to miles.

To complete this rough design, we would create the screen that is displayed if the user clicks the Convert Kilometers to Miles button. This would look much like the Figure 2-3, except that all instances of the word "miles" will be changed to "kilometers" and "kilometers" will be changed to "miles." The formula used in the code to perform the conversion will also be different.

Note that there are a number of adjustments we might make to this screen to make it clearer and easier for users. For example, we might include a title on the screen to identify its purpose. This discussion of minor improvements to the design, although valid, is premature. At this stage, we should be asking questions about the approach itself. Are users likely to be able to figure out how to operate the screens to perform conversions? The answer is probably "yes." Is there a simpler way to approach this problem, perhaps avoiding the complexity of multiple screens? Perhaps. There is only one way to find out—by setting this as our goal and experimenting to see if we can achieve it.

Converter Design Attempt Two

We designed the sequence of screens to mirror the way we would approach the problem if there were no computer. First, we had to decide if we wanted to convert miles to kilometers or kilometers to miles. Our initial design provided a menu of two buttons to allow the user to make this choice. What if we provided text-entry boxes for both types of conversions on the same screen? This would allow us to reduce the number of screens from three to one, a definite improvement.

One way to accomplish this is shown in Figure 2-4.

| TIP |

Once you have sketched out a workable solution to a user interface problem, think about how the design could be simplified by combining, reorganizing, or removing elements, or perhaps by rethinking the approach entirely.

figure |2-4|

In this version, both functions have been included on the same screen, simplifying the design by eliminating the menu and separate screens for each conversion function. The conversion occurs as the user enters the value to be converted.

| Convert Miles to Kilometers: | 200 | miles | Result: 321.87 kilometers |
| Convert Kilometers to Miles: | | kilometers | Result: |

The user types the known value into either the miles or kilometers text-entry box. The software converts the value "on the fly," meaning that a conversion value will be displayed as soon as the user begins to type values into the box. For example, if the user wants to convert 10 miles to kilometers, he will click the text-entry box labeled miles and begin typing the number "10" into it. As soon as the number "1" is typed, the kilometers field on the same line displays "1.609," corresponding to the number of kilometers in one mile. When the user types the "0," the kilometers field changes to 16.093, the number of kilometers in 10 miles.

Even though the conversion value is changing as the user types the complete number, most people will not have difficulty understanding this. If test users have trouble with the value changing as characters are typed, the program could briefly delay the display of the converted value once the user begins typing. The display of the converted number can be delayed until the user has not typed additional numbers for one or two seconds.

It should be apparent that a user interface designer can benefit from programming experience even if she is not the one assigned to code a particular project. Without such background, the designer is dependent on developers or engineers to say which parts of the design can and cannot be coded readily. A designer who does not have this experience will have difficulty gaining the respect of her teammates.

Minimalist Design of Converter

Figure 2-5 shows a way to solve our design problem using very few screen elements. Such an approach is known as a **minimalist** approach.

The problem is reduced to its simplest terms. The text-entry boxes appear on either side of an enlarged equal (=) sign. The user simply types whichever value is known in the appropriate box, and the converted value is displayed in the other box. The simplicity of this solution feels very satisfying to most designers. All extraneous elements such as buttons and labels are removed, and only the bare essentials remain. We have reduced the function of converting

figure |2-5|

This minimalist approach reduces the problem and solution to its simplest form. The user enters a number in the appropriate text-entry box, and the converted value is displayed in the other box.

| | miles **=** | | kilometers |

miles and kilometers to five elements. Nothing further can be eliminated from the screen without the basic functionality being lost.

Designers in other disciplines, such as architecture, industrial design, and fashion design, also practice **minimalism**. What minimalist designers share in common, regardless of what they are designing, is that they use as few elements, materials, or parts as possible. Experienced designers are often drawn to minimalist approaches because of their cleverness and apparent simplicity. However, just as some minimalist chair designs skimp on comfort, care must be taken to ensure that users can understand and use minimalist screen designs. If the testers of our minimalist solution are having difficulty understanding how to use the design, we may add a simple instruction line. Users may well appreciate such an addition, but it will never sit well with the minimalists!

Was your solution similar to the ones we presented or was it different? Most importantly, would your solution, once coded, be easy to understand and use for most adults? Try showing a friend the sketch of your solution without explaining it. Can your friend figure out how to operate your converter based on your sketch?

THE PRINCIPLES OF USER INTERFACE DESIGN

User interface designers are guided by design principles that have proven their value over many years. Some of these originated in other design professions but apply to user interface design. Others have their origins in software and Web design.

Form Follows Function

Louis Sullivan, the famous late architect and mentor of Frank Lloyd Wright, is credited with coining the phrase, "Form follows function," one of the most important of all design principles. This is a simple, elegant way of expressing the idea that an object's or entity's form—that is, its shape or appearance—emerges from its purpose or reason for being.

Forms that are based on function are beautiful because they have integrity; their beauty emanates from within. Passenger jets are mostly devoid of ornamentation, yet their sleek lines perfectly represent the clean expression of their function. This is not to say that the function, by itself, *is* the design. We can program the buttons and text fields in the examples above just as they appear. Although we can make the software operate perfectly, the user's experience would be significantly improved if the talents of a graphic artist were applied.

Designers who emphasize an object's form at the expense of its function are more likely to create an unusable object. This is not to say that an object's form cannot be determined independently of its function. You may decide that your dream house *must* look like a giant pint of Ben and Jerry's Cherry Garcia ice cream. If so, you can probably find an architect who is willing to make your dream come true. The predetermined form, however, may well constrain the architect's ability to create a house that will function well as a living space.

In the previous chapter, we discussed why it is important to view the design of multimedia software and website user interfaces as a process that begins with understanding the needs of the project's features, its intended audience, and the environment in which it will run. With this thorough understanding of the project's function, we can proceed confidently with the development of its form.

In his book, *The Design of Everyday Things* (Currency/Doubleday, 1990), Donald Norman describes the relationship of visibility, mapping, and feedback to the design of usable objects. Although Norman is primarily interested in the usability of tangible items, such as refrigerators, swinging glass doors, and slide projectors, the principles he describes are applicable to user interface design.

Visibility

Have you ever approached a cabinet that was so sleekly designed that you couldn't figure out how to open its doors? You may have been looking for a handle—something to pull the door open—but no such control was visible. Perhaps you discovered (or were told) that you had to simply push in slightly on the door to release the catch. Although you may have felt foolish while you were struggling to open the door, you were simply victimized by a design with poor visibility.

In software design, the principle of **visibility** describes how easily the user can find the functions that the program or website offers. When the user cannot find a needed function, even though it exists in the software, poor visibility is the culprit. The function may not be visible because it is hidden deeply in the software or website. Perhaps it is accessible only from a single screen or page. The user has to remember the exact path to that screen or page to locate the needed function.

Poor visibility can also result when too many elements are presented to the user at once. Word processors, graphics manipulation software, and other applications are particularly susceptible to this type of visibility problem. The sheer number and complexity of functions available through menus, multiple toolbars of buttons, and other controls makes finding the one needed control much more difficult. Such applications are especially daunting to new users.

Some application designers have tried to ease visibility problems by limiting the views of menus to most-often used items and items that the user has recently selected. Figure 2-6 shows a File menu with hidden items. The user accesses the additional menu items by holding the mouse down on a menu item, by clicking the down-arrow control at the bottom of the menu, or by taking no action for about five seconds. Figure 2-7 shows the expanded File menu, with all choices displayed.

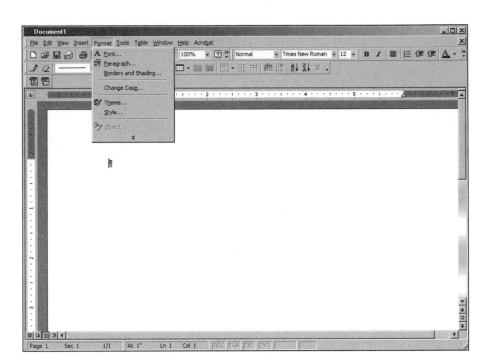

figure |2-6|

The unexpanded menu displays common items and the most recently accessed items. The menu's appearance varies according to usage. This may inhibit users from learning the software by remembering only the position of menu items in the list.

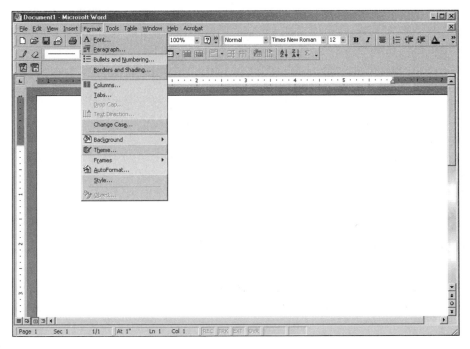

figure |2-7|

The expanded menu uses lighter shading to show items that were hidden. This pattern of dark and light bars decreases the menu's visibility.

In this case, solving one visibility problem seems to cause another. Limiting the number of menu choices that the user sees does ease the problem of too many choices being presented. The trade-off with this approach is that the menu looks different depending on what has recently been selected. Besides confusing users, it forces them to figure out how to access hidden functions.

There is another problem with these dynamic menus. Users learn to recognize a given menu choice by its name and its position in the list. If that position changes depending on usage, the user must depend solely on the choice's name for identification. It is true that the expanded version of the menu shows all of the choices in fixed order. Notice, however, that when expanded, the recently accessed items are displayed with a different background color from those items not recently accessed. The resulting pattern of dark and light bars further reduces the menu's visibility.

Figures 2-8 and 2-9 further illustrate the disorientation that can result when we change the position of items in a set. The screen contains a **tab control**, which organizes pages of options or information of similar types. In this example, the tabs are used to hold controls for setting the various system options.

In Figure 2-8, the Edit tab has been selected. Notice that it is displayed in the bottom row of tabs. Now let's say the user wants to click on the Compatibility tab to see or change its options. Figure 2-9 shows the result when the user selects the Compatibility tab. Notice that it and its entire row of tabs has shifted from the top row to the bottom row. The effect is very disorienting, especially when seen for the first time. The control has acted in an unpredictable manner, and the user loses confidence in the software as a result.

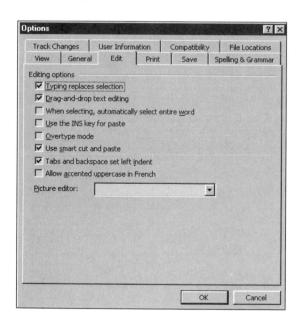

figure |2-8|

Users depend on the consistent location of elements such as tabs to understand the software interface. This interface works fine as long as the user selects tabs on the same row as the currently selected tab.

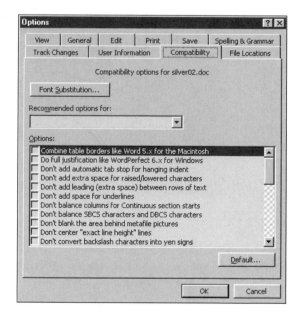

figure |2-9|

If the user selects a tab on the other row, the entire row jumps, damaging the user's confidence in the interface.

Why do the top-row tabs shift to the bottom row when selected? The reason is that the top row pages would cover the bottom row tab choices, preventing them from being seen and selected. The top row of tabs shifts to the bottom row to ensure that all tab choices are visible.

The real problem is that the wrong control was selected for this function. A tab control should only contain one row of tabs. This enables the tabs to stay rooted in place no matter which one is selected. This builds the user's confidence in the application. Figure 2-10 shows a schematic drawing of an alternate design that eliminates the double row of tabs and helps solve this problem.

Compatibility
Edit
File Locations
General
Print
Save
Spelling & Grammar
Track Changes
User Information
View

Edit

☐ Typing replaces selection
☐ Drag-and-drop text editing
☐ When selecting, automatically select entire word
☐ Use the INS key for paste
☐ Overtype mode
☐ Use smart cut and paste
☐ Tabs and backspace set left indent
☐ Allow accented uppercase in French

Picture editor: MS Paint

Save Changes   Cancel

figure |2-10|

This schematic drawing shows a suggested alternative to the double-row tab control. The user selects a category on the left, then views or edits the settings for that category.

Sound-only applications, such as voice response applications, enable users to make menu choices and enter information using the telephone keypad or their voice. We'll use the term **audibility** to describe the ease with which users can locate desired functions in these types of applications. These types of applications also can benefit from user interface design, as many of us who have gotten lost in these complex systems can attest.

Mapping

Have you ever had trouble figuring out which light switch operates which set of lights in a large classroom or conference room? If so, then you understand the effects of poor mapping. **Mapping** is the relationship between a control, the thing it affects, and the outcome that results when the control is operated. Examples of poor mapping are common in the physical world. Which circuit breaker controls the outlet in the bathroom? Which knob operates which burner on the stove? Which valves do I press to play a "C" note on the trumpet?

| TIP |

When creating a toolbar, group the buttons logically by function and include space between each group to help increase its visibility.

Designers have also created examples of excellent mapping. Norman cites the seat control of Mercedes-Benz automobiles as such an example. The clever Mercedes designers manufactured the seat control in the shape of the real automobile seat. To adjust the actual seat, you simply perform the same operation on the control. To slide the seat backward or forward, you grab the control and slide it backward or forward. To adjust the seat upward, you pull the control upward. To tilt the seatback back, you tilt the control's seatback back. This strong association of the control to the resulting action is what Norman calls **natural mapping**.

Controls that require text labels to convey their meaning often indicate poor mapping in objects. For example, the labels that tell us which knob controls which burner on a stovetop indicate a failure in mapping. Often these labels are ignored, and the user simply uses trial and error until the desired result is obtained.

Mapping plays an important role in software design. Poor mapping forces the user's attention on the interface, instead of on the task where it belongs. Good mapping in software can take the form of buttons that clearly and simply indicate their function. Buttons often contain symbolic pictures, called **icons**, to convey meaning. Unlike physical objects, buttons that contain both icons and well-written text labels often provide clearer mapping to their associated functions than buttons that just contain icons. Icons without text labels sometimes convey a meaning that is different from what the designer intended. And sometimes the icons that are chosen can seem downright silly—such as using a life preserver icon to represent a "Save" function.

Figure 2-11 shows a row of icons that were captured and altered from a travel website. In this case, the icons were included on tabs. Clicking one of the tabs displayed a set of controls for selecting or entering information such as a destination city or departure date. See if you can figure out the meaning of each of the icons shown.

When you have made a guess at each of the icons, look at Figure 2-12, which shows just the text labels that correspond to each icon on the tabs. How many of the icons were you able to accurately guess?

Finally, look at Figure 2-13, which shows the combination of icons and labels, as they were displayed on the website.

What observations can you make about these three figures? The icons, as shown in Figure 2-11, do a reasonably good job by themselves of suggesting their meaning. Most people who were visiting this travel site would be able to figure out what most of these icons mean. One exception is that you might not think to click the car icon to access rail options. Another exception is the last icon, the Deals icon, which is more difficult to decipher. The combination of a clock and an exclamation point does not immediately suggest its meaning. Some might conclude that it has something to do with being late. Actually, it is supposed to connote "last minute." Since most people associate deals with saving money, perhaps showing a crossed-out

figure |2-11|

We removed the labels from these icons taken from a travel site. Although most of the icons are clear, it takes time to figure out some of them.

figure |2-12|

Text labels by themselves are clear, but they do not add any visual interest to the site.

figure |2-13|

The combination of icons and text labels offers clarity and visual interest.

and reduced dollar amount would have worked better. The point is, as good as they are, the icons in Figure 2-11 still are not sufficient to convey their full meaning.

There are other factors to consider when judging the usability of icons alone. For example, if the site is intended for use outside the United States, will the symbols have the same meaning for people of different cultures and backgrounds? Most Americans associate a palm tree with a vacation, but what do tropical residents associate with this symbol?

What about the text-only labels in Figure 2-12? They do a better job of indicating their function than the icons. Notice how much more quickly we can read and understand a text label than we can look at an icon, even a well-chosen one, and decipher its meaning. Reading a text label is almost always faster. The clarity comes at a price, however. The text labels look quite dry and uninteresting compared to the tabs with icons. Clients generally want their site to be visually attractive and compelling. Most would not be satisfied with such a spare treatment as shown in Figure 2-12.

The combination of icons and text labels shown in Figure 2-13 offers the best combination of clarity and visual interest. The icons are pleasing to the eye, and the text labels enable fast interpretation.

Feedback

When you step into an elevator and push the button that corresponds to your destination floor, the button you press often glows. The light serves as **feedback**, which is information that the system provides to a user that indicates the status of her action. When you press the button on the elevator, the button's glow tells you that your button press has registered with the elevator's electrical system. What happens when you push a floor button and it doesn't light up? Most of us usually push it again. We expect feedback, and we often believe that a system is not operating properly when feedback is absent.

Feedback in multimedia and website design takes many forms. One example is in website **hyperlinks**, which are short sections of underlined text that the user clicks to display a new page, text section, image, or other element. When you roll the mouse cursor over a hyperlink, the cursor usually changes to a hand with a pointing finger. The pointing finger cursor gives you feedback that the text can be clicked. Browsers provide further feedback by displaying the uniform resource locator (URL) address of the clickable element down in the status bar.

Likewise, when you roll the mouse cursor over a button in many websites and multimedia software, the button's appearance may change slightly. It may take on a 3D effect that makes it appear to lift to meet your cursor, or the button colors may change. This effect is called **glow**, and it provides feedback that the button is active and that clicking it will perform some function. You can see examples of glow in the toolbar buttons of most browsers and application programs.

Feedback can be audible as well as visible. The click that you hear when you press down on a mouse button is no accident. It is designed to provide feedback that you have pushed the button sufficiently far to send the corresponding message to the software.

Because it often takes more than a few seconds to process a user's request, applications and operating systems often change the cursor to an hourglass symbol to indicate that the system is busy. Does this provide adequate feedback? The answer depends on the length of the delay between when the action is initiated and when it is complete. For delays of just a couple of seconds, the hourglass symbol works fine, especially if it is animated to show that the system is still operating.

If the delay is longer than a few seconds, use a different strategy. Have the software estimate the time remaining and display that to the user. You can also display an animated progress indicator to show the operation's progress toward completion.

Figure 2-14 shows the progress indicators used by a standard commercial software installer. The installer shows multiple progress bars that are intended to give users more information about the installation process. These additional bars cause more confusion than clarity, however. The single horizontal bar with the completion percentage and name of the file currently being copied is sufficient to convey the necessary information.

The user's expectation is that when a single horizontal progress bar is completely filled, then the task is complete. The progress bars in some applications violate this expectation. They fill up the horizontal bar, then show an empty bar and begin filling it up, repeating this process for each step in the task. This leaves the user feeling deceived and with no idea how close the task is to completion.

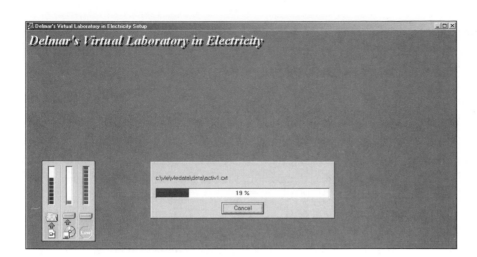

figure |2-14|

In this commercial installation software, the horizontal progress indicator in the center provides useful information, but the vertical bars on the left are confusing and partially redundant.

Web applications have a more difficult time displaying meaningful progress indicators. This is because the progress rate may be tied to factors such as server traffic and the user's connection speed. We have all seen indicators that remain fixed at about 10% completion for a long time. Just as we begin to worry that the system is hung, the indicator jumps in a single bound to 100% completion. Perhaps future technology innovations will give us better ways of predicting and displaying progress status information.

In the meantime, look for simple ways to give users status information to increase their comfort with the software or website.

Affordance

Donald Norman uses the term **affordance** to describe the perceived function of an object, based on our cultural understanding of that object. For example, we know that buttons are for pushing, knobs are for turning, switches are for flicking, and strings are for pulling. We have learned these conventions through repeated exposure and use. When approaching a door with a vertically oriented handle, we assume that we are supposed to grab the handle and pull. If we see a horizontal bar across the door, we assume that we should push it.

Note that the object itself may give us clues as to its operation, but don't confuse that with its affordance. If we all had learned from an early age that you rub your nose against a doorknob to open a door, then that is exactly what we would expect whenever we saw a doorknob. Practically speaking, though, a well-designed control *does* give us clues about its purpose. The concave shape of a button face seems to invite the touch of our finger. As usual, form follows function.

Designers quickly get into trouble when they ignore or violate affordance conventions. To users of websites and multimedia software, if a

| TIP |

When you are displaying pages in sequential order, give your users feedback about where they are in the sequence. Instead of displaying Page 4, display Page 4 of 8. Otherwise your users won't know if there are 4 or 104 pages remaining to be viewed.

figure |2-15|

The controls shown here are a sham. The entire image is a single bitmap that links to another page. Violating a control's normal function is bound to confuse users.

control looks like a button, it had better act like one! Users are sure to be confused when they encounter something that looks just like a universally accepted control, but operates differently.

For example, Figure 2-15, borrowed from a different travel website than our earlier example, seems to provide users with various controls for comparing prices on hotels, rental cars, and airline tickets. There are text boxes for typing city names and dropdown lists for selecting departure and return dates. In this case, however, appearances are deceiving. The controls are not really controls—they are all part of a single image. When you click on one of the "controls," it links to a different page instead of behaving as expected. Such deception causes users to quickly lose confidence in the site. In this example, either the controls should be true, active controls, or this entire image could have been replaced with a "Compare Prices" text or graphic link.

FITTS' LAW

Paul M. Fitts conducted early experiments (around 1954) that led to our current understanding of people's ability to select targets using a mouse or other pointing device. In one experiment, Fitts had his subjects quickly tap a center metal plate while avoiding tapping the plates that flanked it on either side. In other experiments, Fitts' subjects quickly moved rings from one peg to another or fit pegs into variously positioned holes.

Fitts' Law states that the time it takes to reach a target depends on the distance and size of that target. Users have more difficulty pointing to small objects that are far away from the current position. Designers of user interfaces use Fitts' Law to size and position objects such as buttons so that they can be located and clicked quickly and easily.

Interestingly, the four edges of the viewing screen are considered very large target objects, since the user cannot move the mouse cursor past them (unless the user has two or more monitors configured on his system). The Apple Macintosh computer takes great advantage of the largeness of the screen edges by butting the menus of the currently selected window against the top edge of the screen. Figure 2-16 shows how the menu is positioned directly against the upper screen boundary.

The user can move the mouse cursor very rapidly to this target, knowing that the cursor will stop automatically when it hits the screen edge. In operating systems that position the title bar at the top edge of the screen and the menu bar directly below it, the user must be much more precise. The mouse cursor must either be slowed down so that it does not fly past the desired menu, or it must be moved to the top edge, then slid back down to precisely hit the target.

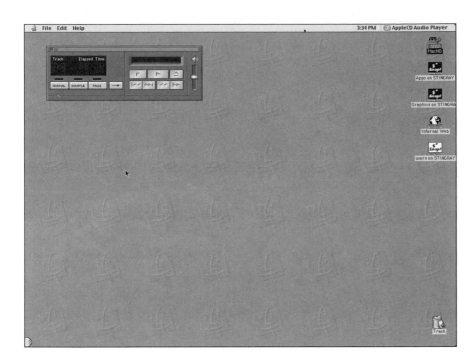

figure |2-16|

The Macintosh operating system places its menus at the extreme top of the active window. This means the user does not have to carefully locate menu names with the mouse.

Fitts' Law also tells us that larger buttons are easier to locate than smaller ones. We stated previously that buttons that contain text labels and icons are usually easier to use than buttons that contain only icons. Besides being more understandable to users, their larger size makes them an easier target to locate with the mouse.

Further research has been conducted to study the time it takes users to reach targets. A study performed by Thomas Whisenand and Henry Emurian at the University of Maryland suggests that the position of a target relative to the current cursor position is also important. Users can most easily move the mouse cursor horizontally from the current position. Moving to the right is more efficient than moving to the left. Next in efficiency is moving straight downwards. In general, upward moves are slower than downward ones. Diagonal moves are generally slower than horizontal or vertical ones. Figure 2-17 illustrates this point.

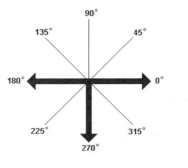

Faster Access

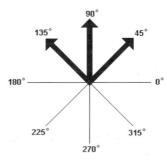

Slower Access

figure |2-17|

Experiments conducted by Thomas Whisenand and Henry Emurian show that users locate targets faster when moving the mouse horizontally or downward than when moving the mouse upward.

Designers can use this information when positioning elements that are frequently accessed or require speed. For example, position navigational controls that move backward and forward through content at the bottom of the screen rather than making them part of the toolbar at the top of the screen. They will be easier to find, since the toolbar usually contains other buttons. They will also require less time to locate, since the user will move the mouse cursor down rather than up to point to them.

CONSISTENCY

Consistency means doing the same things the same way. Designers apply consistency to the user interface to promote familiarity with the software or website. Consistent designs increase users' comfort, allowing them to focus on their work rather than the interface. Users of application software learn that the Save command is always in the File pulldown menu, and that a particular sequence of keys bolds the selected text. These conventions apply to virtually all applications, so users don't have to relearn basic functions each time they use a new or different application. Web browsers provide a consistent set of functions, such as the Back and Forward buttons, which work on most websites.

Good designers apply consistency wherever possible within a multimedia software program or website. For example, toolbars, menus, and content areas occupy the same location on each screen or page. A particular control, such as a menu button, maintains the same look and location on each screen that it is displayed. The designer decides which fonts will be used for titles, headings, general text, button captions, etc., and applies those conventions throughout the design.

Consistency applies to the software's operation as well as its appearance. Clicking the same button performs the same function throughout the software. If the designer calls for a particular animation technique to display menu items, that technique is applied whenever menu items are displayed.

Some software developers make the mistake of trying to apply consistency late in the coding stage. Programmers sometimes believe that they must create the functional code first and leave "cosmetic" changes for the end. This approach frequently results in a product that is inconsistent and perceived as lacking in quality. It also imposes unnecessary burdens on everyone involved in the development process.

For example, the designer will waste time debating with the programmer (if they are different people) which conventions can be applied and which will require too much programming effort, because of the way the screens or pages have been coded. The programmer will recode many sections to make them consistent, potentially introducing errors and certainly duplicating work. The graphic artist may have to recreate buttons and other graphic elements to match other elements. Quality assurance engineers or software testers will spend significant time trying to find every instance of text that is in the wrong font or style. This need to focus on consistency issues may prevent them from finding more significant errors in the software or site.

The time to begin determining style and operation conventions is as soon as the functional requirements are understood. You can and should make many of these decisions before you start designing individual screens or pages. Create a **style guide**, which is a document that defines the style conventions that will guide the design and development of the software. See Chapter 12 for a discussion of style guides. Distribute the style guide to everyone on the development team and make sure they follow it!

Website designers and developers can take advantage of **cascading style sheets** (CSS), which are collections of instructions that specify display elements such as fonts, font sizes, font colors, background colors, and images to a Web browser. Cascading style sheets can also control the positioning of elements on the page. They help ensure that design conventions are applied consistently throughout the site. A cascading style sheet can be set up as a separate URL, rather than including it within the HTML code for a page. Each page that uses that style sheet contains a reference to the style sheet's URL. A change made to the style sheet is then automatically reflected in all pages that refer to that style sheet.

Multimedia software designers can apply conventions normally associated with websites to their designs. For example, users know that underlined text that is colored differently from the surrounding text is a hyperlink. Users have come to understand and expect this convention regardless of whether it is used in a website or in multimedia software. For the same reason, conscientious designers now avoid using colored, underlined text as a non-linked heading style, since users are likely to try unsuccessfully to click it.

FORGIVENESS

Software should be designed to help keep users from making serious mistakes, and it should help them recover from the mistakes they make. Such software promotes **forgiveness**. Implementing forgiveness features, such as auto-saving documents, can help ensure that users don't lose work because they forgot to explicitly save their document.

Most people who do a lot of their work on computers have learned to save their work constantly, often several times per minute. Although this sounds excessive, most of us have learned through misfortune that it is no fun to have to recreate even a small amount of work.

When we write or draw on paper with pencil or ink, our work is automatically saved. We don't have to worry about the print quickly fading from the paper if we don't manually save it. We can devote all of our energies to the creation of our work.

A handheld device's operating system, such as the Palm, combines features of computers and paper and pencil. It saves work as the user creates it, rather than requiring manual saves. You

| TIP |

Make it easy for users to figure out how to navigate to any screen or page of the software or site. Then make it easy for them to return to a known location or system state. This will encourage them to explore the software, gaining experience and taking advantage of all that it has to offer.

can be in the middle of creating a calendar entry when you turn off your Palm. When you power it back up, it displays the screen you last accessed, with all of your information saved. In addition to being forgiving, this feature allows users to concentrate on their work instead of on the process of saving.

Allowing users to easily recover from their mistakes pays other dividends as well. If we provide a means for users to recover accidentally deleted items and documents, then we don't have to design in all of those confirmation dialogs that can slow users down. Messages such as "Are you sure you wish to delete this?" could be a thing of the past.

The design of many commercial websites fails to adequately take forgiveness into account. This can result in lost sales for sites that offer goods for sale. For example, online shoppers usually want to know the shipping costs for their items before committing to a purchase. Many sites, however, don't make it clear that the shopper will be able to review the total price for the order, including shipping, prior to committing to the purchase. These users may prefer to abort the purchase rather than risk being charged for items that they don't want due to high shipping charges.

It should be noted that the vast majority of these sites were not charging users excessive shipping costs. It was only the fear that these costs would not be revealed until it was too late to cancel the order that made users abandon their purchases.

As one of the first large, online shopping sites, Amazon.com had to develop design strategies to deal with hesitant shoppers such as this, many who doubted that they would even be sent the items they purchased. To ease shoppers' fears of prematurely committing to an online purchase, Amazon displayed the message, "Don't worry, you can cancel it later." This simple addition helped increase sales by building users' confidence in the site. Even today, Amazon reminds its customers when they are placing items in the shopping cart that they can remove them later.

Forgiveness can also be applied to the menu items or navigational features of a software program or website. Some software is so difficult to navigate that users are discouraged from ever deviating from the path that leads to the completion of their task.

MINIMALISM

Minimalism is a term adopted from movements in art and music. In user interface design, minimalism can be defined as a deliberate reduction in complexity for the user's benefit. Less is more. Taken literally, it means eliminating everything from the software or website that isn't absolutely essential.

When designing interactivity, minimize the number of clicks the user must make to complete a given task. Don't require two clicks of the mouse if the task can be accomplished in one. Don't require the user to scroll to get to the important information on a particular page or screen. Use one-click controls whenever practical. Reduce the amount of distance the mouse must move to access the most often-used controls.

For screen design, consider the advice of Edward Tufte, the renowned information designer and Yale Professor Emeritus, in his classic book, *The Visual Display of Quantitative Information* (Graphics Press). Tufte recommends eliminating graphic clutter—in fact, removing every single pixel that isn't used to convey necessary information. Although such visual extremism runs counter to the instincts of many graphic designers and wishes of many clients, the point is clear and valid: when designing the visual display, reduce decorative embellishments. Let the information tell the story and allow visual elements to accent rather than overwhelm.

DUELING PRINCIPLES

As you work on your own designs, you will quickly realize that the design principles often conflict with one another. In trying to be consistent with other parts of a design, I might cost my user a couple of mouse clicks. Which is more important, consistency or minimalism? Each situation must be judged on its own merits. When you consider the needs of the user first, a clear answer usually emerges. The principle that wins out is the one that makes the software or website easier to understand and more efficient to use. When we sacrifice one principle for another, we do so with eyes and minds wide open.

For example, let's say we are designing the settings page for a complex Web application. We must accommodate two types of settings. There are settings that are commonly used and "advanced" settings that are used much less frequently, but must still be included.

The principle of visibility might influence us to keep all controls visible on the same page. This will ensure that users will see them when they access the settings page. The principle of minimalism might send us in two contradictory directions. On one hand, we will minimize screen clutter if we remove the rarely used settings and make them accessible by clicking an Advanced Settings button. On the other hand, we will force users to make an extra click to access these settings.

In this case, the fact that the settings are rarely needed tips the scales clearly in favor of removing the advanced settings from the normal settings screen and requiring a button click to access them. The settings section of the software will be much easier for new users to learn, and advanced users won't be unduly penalized by the required extra click.

SUMMARY OF KEY POINTS

- There is always more than one approach to a design problem. Start by thinking about how you might solve the problem without a computer.

- Refine your original approach by thinking about how it can be simplified or minimized. Try to eliminate or combine elements. Seek an approach that allows the user to concentrate on the task at hand rather than the user interface.

- In design, form follows function. The designer must not attempt to define what the software will look like until he understands the functionality, audience, and delivery environment.

- A design's *visibility* is a measure of how easily users can see and access the functions the software offers.

- Pay particular attention to the *mapping* of the software's various interface controls and elements to the associated functionality. Good mapping allows users to concentrate on the task at hand, while the interface becomes invisible.

- Use *feedback* to provide information to users about the status of their actions.

- Respect the *affordance* of the various controls you use. In general, if it looks like a button, make sure it acts like one.

- *Fitts' Law* and related research gives us clues about how to position controls so that the user can locate them with the mouse quickly and accurately.

- Apply *consistency* throughout your design to allow users to become familiar and comfortable with your software's layout, look, and operation.

- Design your software with *forgiveness* to allow users to easily recover from mistakes and free them from the burden of confirming everything they do.

- Practice *minimalism* by eliminating unneeded controls, words, graphic embellishments, and user clicks. Simplify your designs as much as possible.

- When design principles contradict each other, choose the option that allows users to learn and use the software most easily and efficiently.

in review

1. Name one advantage and disadvantage of a minimalist design approach.

2. Define the terms visibility, feedback, and mapping.

3. What two factors determine the time it takes to hit a target, according to Fitts' Law?

4. According to Whisenand and Emurian, moving the mouse cursor is easiest in which direction from the current position?

5. Providing a means for users to recover a document after a power failure or system crash is an example of what design principle?

exercises

1. Recall that a perceived affordance is the set of functions an object seems to offer by its appearance. Imagine that you have been commissioned to create "The House of Ill Affordance." In this house, objects that look normal are designed to fool the user by operating in an unexpected manner. Describe your House of Ill Affordance.

2. Light switches in buildings often employ bad mapping. It is difficult to tell which switches control which lights. Design a new kind of switchplate or switch mechanism that solves this problem. Describe the pros and cons of your approach.

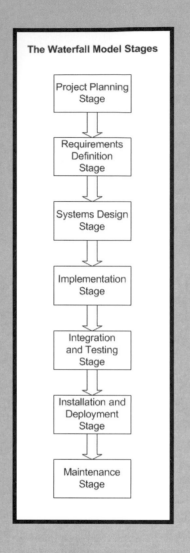

The Waterfall Model Stages

Project Planning Stage

↓

Requirements Definition Stage

↓

Systems Design Stage

↓

Implementation Stage

↓

Integration and Testing Stage

↓

Installation and Deployment Stage

↓

Maintenance Stage

the user interface design process

objectives

Summarize the reasons for adhering to a user interface design process

Examine the steps of the Waterfall development model

Examine the steps of the Repeating Waterfall development model

Examine the steps of the Spiral development model

Describe the characteristics of agile software development methodologies

Analyze which development models work best in which circumstances

introduction

Once you've been hired to develop the user interface for a website or multimedia software project, it's time to begin the important job of planning and organizing your work. How will you ensure that the website you design meets your client's needs? How will you keep the project on track so that you complete it in a timely fashion? How can you be sure that your design includes all of the necessary functionality?

Successful website and software designers and developers follow a process that guides their work on all projects, large or small. The type of process used depends on the scope of the work, the client's understanding of their own needs, the size and experience level of the development team, and other factors.

A large, complex, website or multimedia software project requires a more rigorous design and development process than a small, simple project. The processes we present in this chapter are designed to accommodate a range of projects, including the most complex ones you are likely to face. Time and experience will help you determine which process best fits each project.

The process of designing the interface is part of the larger process of developing the software or website. Many software development methodologies have emerged over the years, but they share the same goal—to produce functional software in a timely manner.

THE USER INTERFACE DESIGN PROCESS

WHY HAVE A PROCESS?

But why have a process at all, especially if the project is a small one? Won't following a process just add time and complexity to the development of the software or site? Wouldn't it be quicker and easier just to let the designer do what comes naturally?

In fact, adhering to an interface design process invariably saves the designer and developer time, money, and effort. It also increases the likelihood that you will create a successful end product, one that meets the functional and usability requirements of its audience and the budgetary and scheduling needs of your client. Here are some reasons why a process is essential.

It Increases Efficiency

Following a design process helps ensure that you perform all of the associated tasks in the proper sequence. If you perform tasks out of sequence, then the information needed for each task is likely to be incomplete or missing, resulting in the unnecessary repetition of those tasks. For example, the processes we will introduce in this chapter call for the consideration of audience needs early on. Delaying this step until after the software is developed will likely result in costly reorganization, addition, and deletion of screen elements and features to satisfy the audience requirements. Adhering to the process minimizes the need for constant maintenance, redesign, and repair of the finished product.

Designs created by following the process are better able to accommodate unforeseen changes. If the change is a minor one, the design can handle it easily. If the changes are extensive, perhaps involving the addition of new features, you will know exactly which steps need to be repeated to accommodate the changes.

It Produces Consistently Better Results

Adhering to a process helps ensure that your design is cohesive and complete. For example, if you attempt to lay out elements on the various screens before compiling and organizing the software's functions, your layout is likely to omit some of the functions. When you try to back-fit those functions into your existing design, the results are likely to be haphazard, with pieces that don't fit together well.

Without a process, you may get lucky enough to produce a usable website or software product, but it is unlikely that you will consistently achieve such results. Following a process makes success predictable. You can tailor the process to fit unusual situations, increasing your efficiency and likelihood of success. You can examine the process thoroughly over multiple projects, enhancing its strengths and eliminating

| TIP |

Keep a "Design Process" file. As you work on a project, jot down notes regarding how well your process performed on the project. Record any ideas you can think of for improving the process next time. Be sure to include the name of the project with your notes, so you can refer to them if you work on similar projects in the future.

its weaknesses. Without a process, though, there is nothing to examine, nothing to measure, and therefore no way to substantially improve your work.

It Validates the User Interface Design Function

Finally, we create and follow processes for functions that we deem important enough to want to complete successfully. We wouldn't attempt to build buildings, introduce and pass laws, or try and convict criminals without following an accepted, rigorously tested process. Designers who follow a process when designing the user interface are, in effect, acknowledging that the interface is important enough to warrant such attention.

SOFTWARE DEVELOPMENT PROCESSES

The Waterfall Model Stages

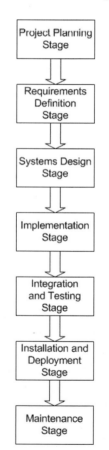

Hopefully, you are convinced that it is unwise to begin designing or developing a website or multimedia software project without having a process to follow. There are a number of different software development processes, also known as **systems development methods** (SDMs). The classic methodology is known as the **systems development life cycle** (SDLC) model. This methodology includes models with names like the Waterfall, the Spiral, the Fountain, and Synchronize and Stabilize.

Perhaps the oldest software development model is the **Waterfall**, a step-by-step process for analyzing, planning, designing, developing, and testing software. Once the process gets going, like falling water, it flows forward and never in reverse. Figure 3-1 shows a diagram of the basic steps of the Waterfall model. These steps are explained in further detail below.

The client approves the output from each step, which then serves as the input for the next step. The Waterfall model is the most time-tested methodology for developing software. Similar to processes used in manufacturing, it works best when the requirements are well known at the beginning of the project.

figure | 3-1 |

The Waterfall model always flows forward. The output from one step becomes the input to the next step.

The SDLC Waterfall Model

The Waterfall model consists of the following basic steps:

1. **Project Planning Stage:** This stage establishes the goals for the software or website. If the software or website already exists and will be enhanced or improved, then analyze the existing system and identify its deficiencies. At this stage, you may speak with the users of the system, support personnel, management, and other interested stakeholders. This step often includes an analysis of competing or similar websites or software.

2. **Requirements Definition Stage:** This stage defines the new system requirements, including corrections for the deficiencies identified during the first step. Develop the feature set for the new system, considering such factors as the audience, hardware and software operating environment, security, and the programming or development environment.

3. **Systems Design Stage:** This stage describes the new system in detail. Design the user interface for the new system, accommodating the system requirements developed during the previous step.

4. **Implementation Stage:** The new system is developed during this stage, including the creation of all program code, graphical elements, and multimedia elements.

5. **Integration and Testing Stage:** During this stage, all of the pieces are brought together and tested.

6. **Installation and Deployment Stage:** During this stage, the client accepts the software or website, which is brought into production and runs with live users.

7. **Maintenance Stage:** During this stage, the running system is evaluated, errors are fixed, and maintenance is performed as necessary.

Although many groups continue to use the Waterfall model and produce excellent results, it has fallen out of favor with some development teams. Three valid criticisms of the Waterfall model are:

a. The model reduces the role of users to simply specifying requirements. If we want to design and build truly user-centered software, then the user must be a more integral part of the design and development process.

b. The model assumes that all of the requirements for the system are known in advance. Today's reality is that project requirements often evolve while the system is being developed.

c. The client does not get to see working code until relatively late in the development process. Clients who are unable to visualize the finished product from the documentation may be in for an unpleasant surprise when they finally see the software or website.

One way to increase the role of end users during the design and development process is to invite them to evaluate the various deliverables along the way. Rather than waiting to solicit user feedback until the system is nearly complete, invite users to evaluate the project plan, wireframe diagrams or wireframes, and early software builds. The results will help ensure that the finished product meets the needs of its users.

The Repeating Waterfall Model

If a substantial percentage of the project requirements cannot be well defined at the project's inception, then a different development strategy or model may be required. Some teams use a variation of the Waterfall, in which the stages beginning with the systems design stage and proceeding through the integration and testing stage are repeated for each group of features as they are approved for inclusion in the project. The project is thus handled as a series of small waterfalls. A diagram of this variation is shown in Figure 3-2.

The Spiral Model

An extension of the Repeating Waterfall model is the Spiral model. This model, first introduced in the 1980s by Barry Boehm and discussed by Roger Pressman in his book, *Software Engineering: A Practitioner's Approach* (McGraw-Hill, 2001), is represented as a spiral-shaped line that passes as many times as necessary through planning, risk assessment, development, and feedback stages. The first couple of laps around the diagram may produce a product specification or functioning prototype. Subsequent laps represent features that are added to the emerging software. Figure 3-3 shows a diagram of the Spiral model.

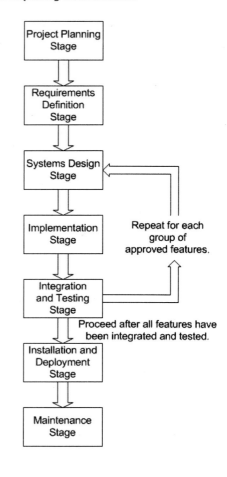

figure | **3-2** |

The Repeating Waterfall model handles changing requirements by repeating the systems design, implementation, and integration and testing stages for each group of new features.

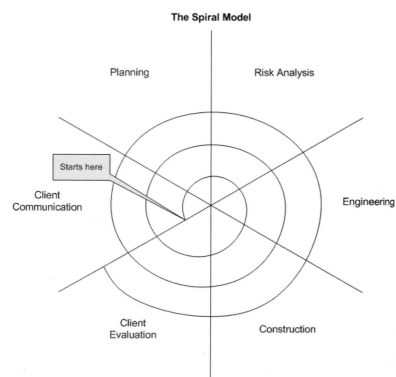

figure | **3-3** |

The Spiral model represents development as a spiral-shaped line that passes repeatedly through six planning and development stages.

The stages of the Spiral model are:

1. **Client Communication:** Establish effective communication between the development team and the client
2. **Planning:** Define resources and schedule and budget constraints, analyze audience and other project factors
3. **Risk Analysis:** Assess the technical and management risks
4. **Engineering:** Build one or more representations of the software
5. **Construction:** Construct, integrate, test, and install the system, and provide user support
6. **Client Evaluation:** Obtain client feedback based on evaluation of the software created during the engineering stage and implemented during installation

A limitation of the Spiral model from a user interface design perspective is that, although it includes a planning stage, it does not provide adequately for a cohesive user interface design for the system as a whole. This topic is discussed further during the discussion of agile development methodologies, below.

An alternative to the Waterfall model and its variants are the so-called **agile** software development methodologies. These are gaining popularity in situations requiring more flexibility during the design and development process, such as when the requirements are not well known at the beginning of the project. We'll take a closer look at the benefits and liabilities of these emerging methodologies.

Agile Software Development

Agile software development methodologies, which include models such as eXtreme Programming (XP), Adaptive Software Development, Scrum, and Crystal, use an iterative (repeating) approach. This is in contrast to a linear, step-by-step approach such as the Waterfall. Using agile methods, the development team designs, creates, tests, presents, and modifies a series of quick prototypes. Once the client approves each prototype, it is integrated into the project.

The agile methodologies emphasize verbal communications with the development team and client instead of formal specifications. In eXtreme Programming, the coders team up in pairs—one person does the actual coding while the other reviews the work, asking questions and making suggestions for revising the coding approach as needed. The user analysis takes the form of "user stories," which are requirements captured in the users' own words. These user stories form the basis for estimating development time and determining what goes into each release.

Agile techniques are intended for situations where either the project requirements or the technology used in development is not well known or evolving. They are also used when the client is not sure if the project will be approved for full development. Agile methodologies require that at least some of the developers on the team have significant project experience.

Here are the basic steps of agile software development methodologies:

1. During the requirements-definition phase, the client gives the development group whatever information is known about the functionality and requirements.

2. Establish an overall design for the project. During the development cycle, the design will be modified iteratively, with more detail and modifications made as necessary.

3. Develop working prototypes that reflect the emerging design, using the programming language or development environment.

4. Submit the working prototype to the client for suggestions and modifications.

5. Revise the prototype to reflect the client's changes.

6. Repeat steps 3 through 5 for additional parts of the system, modifying as necessary and integrating with the project as a whole.

Some software engineers have embraced agile methodologies because they want to get working software into the hands of clients as soon as possible. The argument goes something like this: If the client is going to be changing the requirements anyway, why not trade up-front planning and documentation for quick code delivery and a culture that embraces rather than fights client changes.

Such flexibility comes at a price, however. The Waterfall model allows for the creation of a cohesive user interface design that can be applied consistently throughout the software or website. When features must be changed, added, or deleted, the designer can refer to the wireframes to determine how to make the revisions while maintaining the cohesiveness of the overall design. By contrast, the agile development methodologies emphasize smaller bursts of design, development, testing, and client comment. Such an environment makes it more difficult to establish and adhere to an overall design vision.

These two methodologies have advantages and disadvantages, which must be weighed carefully. Rather than make a blanket recommendation of one method over another, it is more useful to see how each methodology relates to factors that are common to the design and development of a website or software project. Table 3-1 analyzes important characteristics of each of these two methodologies.

table | 3-1 | Comparison of Waterfall model and Agile methodologies.

ITEM	WATERFALL MODEL	AGILE METHODOLOGIES
Feature set (the features to be included in the website or software)	Best suited when the features are known prior to beginning design and development.	Best suited when feature set is not fully known and will be determined during development.
Communication of project specifications	Relies heavily on paper-based documentation, including feature specifications and user interface design descriptions.	Requires less documentation, but requires extensive communication between the team members and the client.
Ability to predict completion dates and project costs	High, assuming that project features and the design do not change radically during development.	Lower, since the product features and design can evolve over time.
Development costs	Lower, assuming that project features and the design do not change radically during development. If significant changes occur, costs can rise quickly.	Higher, due to the uncertainty of changing client requirements. On projects with frequent changes and high uncertainty, costs will be lower using this method.
Client approval	Required at each stage of specification and development before the next step can begin.	Required in stages as parts of the project are integrated into the whole.
Client sophistication level required	High, due to the need to read and understand product feature descriptions and user interface specifications before seeing actual working software.	Lower, since the client will have working prototypes rather than paper specifications to review.
Potential client relationship problems	If the client deviates from the approved approach, the developer may need to ask for additional time and money. The client may believe the developer is "nickel-and-diming" him.	Prototyped software may look complete, but internal functionality may be missing, causing unrealistic client expectations. The client may believe that the developer is responsible for late deliverables or cost overruns.
When client sees working code	Late in the development process, a disadvantage.	Early in the development process, an advantage.
Quality of user interface design	Potentially higher, since the features are known and more easily accommodated. Developers work from an approved set of specifications.	Potentially lower, since newly added features may force continuous redesign of screens. Multiple prototypes may make it more difficult for consistent interface design across the project.
Quality of finished product	Depends on the quality of specification documents and adherence to them by the developers.	Depends on communication among the development group and the client. Requires experienced, motivated developers.

A CLOSER LOOK AT THE WATERFALL MODEL

Now let's take a closer look at the stages of the Waterfall model. As we've stated, the answer to the question, "Which model is best?" is complex, since it depends on so many factors—the type of project, the development team, the client, etc. We have chosen to analyze the Waterfall model because it is still successfully used and because it is the basis for so many other development models.

We are most interested in those steps that contribute to the design and development of the user interface. As we review these steps, we will emphasize the interface designer's role and its relationship to other team members and the client. Most of the steps summarized here are covered in greater detail in subsequent chapters in this textbook.

1. Project Planning Stage

The project planning stage answers the question, "Why is this website or software being developed?" The project may represent a new effort, or it may be an upgrade to an existing one. In some cases, the software or website has been successful, and the client simply wishes to add features or otherwise upgrade the product.

Sometimes a new developer is asked to work on a project because the existing product or its original developer failed to live up to expectations. The existing product may have been ill conceived from the start. Perhaps no market exists for the product. It may have been underfunded or rushed to market before it was ready. Or perhaps the product was well positioned and adequately funded, but the developer did not fulfill his obligations. Perhaps the developer went out of business, leaving the client with an unfinished product. The list of possible scenarios goes on and on.

Different clients expect different levels of development team input on different projects. In some cases, the clients know exactly what they want to accomplish and are simply looking for a development partner who will implement their plan. More often, the development team works with a client to help set goals and priorities for the new system.

If the new system is being built from an existing one, then the development team must gain a thorough understanding of the system. One way to gain this understanding is to create a site or software map that graphically shows all of the major screens and indicates how these screens are accessed. A text-based site or software outline can serve a similar purpose.

Creating such a map or outline is an efficient way to become familiar with an existing system. It also helps establish the scope of the project for you and your client. Sometimes clients don't fully understand the capabilities of their own systems until they are catalogued and presented.

Figure 3-4 summarizes this first stage of the software development process—the project planning stage.

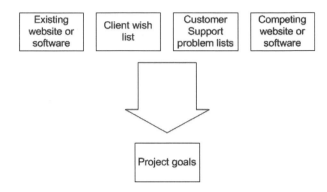

Project Planning Stage

Primary Deliverable:
    Statement of project goals

Other Possible Deliverables:
    Existing site/software map
    Existing features list
    Competitive analysis
    Sample user interface design improvement sketches

figure | 3-4 |

The project planning stage seeks to establish the goals of the project.

2. Requirements Definition Stage

During the requirements definition stage, you combine what you learned during the project planning stage with information about the audience, the functions to be included in the software or website, the hardware and software requirements, the programming or development environment, and any other information that might affect the design and development of the new system.

If possible, you also finalize the features that will be included in the new system. If the project is an upgrade to an existing system, you revise the feature list you developed during the analysis phase, deleting features that the client no longer wants and adding any new features.

Although some websites merely present information, like an electronic brochure, most sites and multimedia software offer some form of functionality. This may be an e-commerce application, product comparison feature, search function, interactive portfolio, or other interactive capability. Creating the user interface for such functions requires that you understand the various tasks that comprise them, and there are techniques that help you analyze and document them.

Another important part of this stage of the process is to analyze the target audience of the website or software. The information for this analysis may come from the client or other sources, but there is no substitute for observing and interviewing the end users themselves. If the project is a website, the interview questions are designed to determine the users' expecta-

Requirements Definition Stage

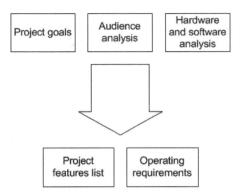

Primary Deliverables:
 Project features list
 Hardware and software operating requirements

Other Possible Deliverables:
 Task cases (essential use cases)
 Audience analysis report
 Technical analysis report

figure | **3-5** |

The goal of the requirements definition stage is to establish the list of features to be included in the project and to specify the operating environment.

tions for the site, including what information the users seek from such a site, the types of questions they are likely to ask, and the features that they find most useful or valuable. The designer also analyzes the cultural needs of the audience.

Figure 3-5 summarizes this stage, the requirements definition stage.

3. Systems Design Stage

The systems design stage is the user interface designer's prime time. Considering the requirements defined in the previous stage, the goals that have been set, your knowledge of the target audience's needs, and the delivery hardware and software platforms, you develop the conceptual design, which is the overall design approach to the project. From the conceptual design, you create the individual screen or page designs for the new system.

Conceptual Design

During this stage, you develop the conceptual design of the system, seeking ways to add value and enhance the user's experience. The conceptual design of multimedia software may be a metaphor or story line that is carried through the entire project. For example, in children's educational software, the audience might help the characters in the story find their way home by solving problems along the way.

Original thinking is particularly valuable during this stage. The team may use one or more idea-generating techniques to spur the creative process.

Gathering and Organizing Ideas

Gather the best of the conceptual ideas, and it's time to begin creating the screen designs. Different designers have their own favorite methods. Some like to begin their work with an outlining tool, gathering and categorizing ideas. Others prefer to start on paper, sketching home pages or main menu screens. Still others begin creating screen elements using a drawing tool.

Specifying the Design

When this early work has been completed, it is time to specify the design, using wireframes, storyboards, or other types of specifications. The specification method you select depends on the type of information you want to convey and the primary audience for that information.

The developers on the team are a key part of the design process. Before you show preliminary wireframes to the client and sample audience members, you must distribute them to the developers, who comment on their technical feasibility. When the wireframes are nearing completion, submit the entire set to the developers for technical review. The developers will make suggestions and suggested revisions as necessary, and you then revise the wireframe images and explanatory text as required.

After you have reflected the developers' feedback in the wireframes, distribute them to your client. The client will review the wireframes, making revisions and edits as necessary. The team reviews the revisions and, when they are approved, you update the wireframes accordingly. The revised set of wireframes serves to guide the team throughout the development of the software or website.

The designer stays in touch with the client throughout the design process. The designer may send the client preliminary wireframes to ensure that the client agrees with the project's design direction. The client also helps answer the designer's questions and can serve as a sounding board for new ideas. Equally important, usability testing should be ongoing during this stage to help ensure that the emerging design is usable by its target audience.

Creating a Style Guide

When the wireframes are complete, you or a lead graphic artist may create a style guide. The style guide provides information to the development team about the use and appearance of various fonts and graphical elements. These brief documents help ensure the consistency of elements in the finished software or website. The style guide usually includes information such as which fonts, font colors, and font sizes are used for headings, instruction text, and content text. It may also contain information such as the RGB values of background colors, cell shading, and other elements.

Creating Sample Artist's Concept Screens

As the wireframes are being completed, the graphic artist may create one or more sample concept screens. These color renderings are designed to show the client the finished graphic look of the software or website, based on the user interface specified by the wireframes. This deliverable can range from one or two sample images that are sent to the client with the wireframes to full nonfunctional prototypes that show the look of all of the major screens of the software or website.

The graphic artist often creates two or three different graphic looks for the project, without spending too much time on any one concept. These concepts are shared with the client, who will choose a favorite or provide additional feedback to the artist, and the artist then incorporates the feedback into the development of additional concept screens or actual project elements during the implementation stage.

Notice that the wireframes are separate from the concept screens. This allows the client to evaluate the wireframes for their organization and usability and the concept screens for their graphic look. Since the choice of colors and overall graphic look of a project tend to be more subjective than the functional layout and organization, it is usually best to allow the client to evaluate it separately from the more functional elements.

Just as the developers review wireframes before they are distributed to the client, they should also review concept screens to ensure that the graphic ideas presented are programmable. Clients are likely to get upset if they fall in love with an artist's concept, then find that the actual website or software falls short of the original concept due to engineering constraints.

Figure 3-6 is a diagram of this stage, the systems design stage.

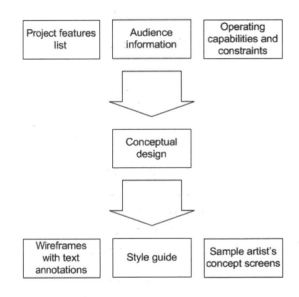

Systems Design Stage

Primary Deliverables:
Wireframes
Style guide
Sample artist's concept screens

Other Possible Deliverable:
Conceptual design document

figure | **3-6** |

The systems design stage is where the majority of the user interface design work is accomplished.

4. Implementation Stage

The implementation stage includes the creation of the program code, graphics, and multimedia elements (audio, video, etc.) that make the system functional. Sometimes the designer also assumes other roles, such as working as the developer or graphic artist. The interface designer who created the wireframes is usually the keeper of the project vision. It is this designer's responsibility to ensure that the system being developed remains true to the design.

If there are specialists handling the code development, graphic design, and creation of multimedia elements, then the interface designer becomes the primary consultant to this group. Although the wireframes and style guide will answer many questions, no set of specifications is able to foresee every situation that may arise. The designer resolves inconsistencies, provides additional design details if necessary, tests the emerging code, and modifies the design as necessary, such as when a particular screen element or function proves difficult to code or implement.

Figure 3-7 shows a diagram of this stage, the implementation stage.

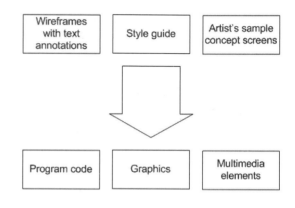

figure | 3-7 |

The implementation stage produces the code, graphics, and multimedia elements that will be integrated to form the complete software.

5. Integration and Testing Stage

During this stage, the interface designer's primary responsibility is to test the developing system. Although there may be full-time quality assurance testers on the team, they may not catch the types of errors that the designer is likely to notice. Anyone who has developed software knows that having more testers checking the software results in a higher-quality end product.

The software or website is nearly always delivered to the client in stages. If the project is a multimedia software program, the development team sends interim releases. Although these definitions vary with the development group, the term **alpha release** often represents a system with partial functionality. A **beta release** often has full functionality, but the software will not have been fully tested and may have some rough spots. Large, complex projects may have several alpha and beta stages.

The final release may be called the *gold master, production master, final version*, or similar term. It represents the finished software, fully tested and ready for distribution.

Websites may follow a similar release schedule. Often, however, the development team will post the emerging website in a secure location accessible only by password. The client can review the progress and forward comments to the team. Once the site is complete and has undergone thorough testing, it is moved to its permanent, publicly accessible Web location.

Figure 3-8 summarizes this stage, the integration and testing stage.

The interface designer maintains consulting responsibilities throughout the installation and deployment stage and the maintenance stage.

Now that we have explored how the design of the interface fits into the software and website development process, our next step is to examine how to set goals and assess needs for the websites and software we are designing.

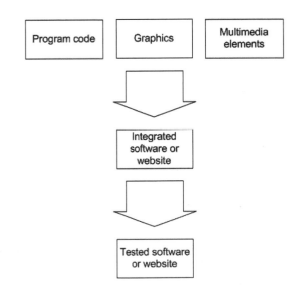

Integration and Testing Stage

Primary Deliverables:
    Interim releases (Alpha, Beta)
    Gold master or final release
    Installation routines (if any)
    Support documentation
    Help files

Other Possible Deliverables:
    QA reports

figure | 3-8 |

The integration and testing stage leads to the complete, tested website or multimedia software.

SUMMARY OF KEY POINTS

- Design and development processes help ensure that the correct steps are performed in the proper sequence.

- Adhering to an interface design process saves time, money, and effort, while increasing the quality of the finished product.

- The classic software development process is called the systems development life cycle. It includes the Waterfall model, a step-by-step process that includes client reviews at each step of the process.

- The basic stages of the Waterfall model are project planning, requirements definition, systems design, implementation, integration and testing, installation and deployment, and maintenance. Variations of the Waterfall model, including the Repeating Waterfall model and Spiral model, help get code in the hands of clients at earlier stages of development.

- Agile software development methodologies, such as eXtreme Programming, can be useful in situations where project requirements or the intended development technology is not well known. In these methodologies, the development team designs, creates, tests, presents, and modifies a series of quick prototypes which, once approved, are integrated into the project.

in review

1. Why is it important to follow a development process when creating a website or multimedia software product?

2. Which process works best when the system requirements are relatively well known and stable at the start of the project?

3. Which processes are designed to handle projects with changing requirements?

4. Why do agile development methodologies make it more difficult to control the user interface design of a project?

5. What is the primary role of the user interface designer during the implementation stage of the Waterfall process?

exercise

1. The eXtreme Programming method involves pairs of programmers working together to create program code. What if user interface designers also paired up to create their designs? Create a list of potential advantages and disadvantages to such an arrangement. If feasible, try pairing up on a design assignment, and see if your expectations matched reality. Are you able to create better designs than if you worked alone?

Three Personas

Adam I. Yard
68 years old
Retired Air Force Captain
Divorced

Avid birder with many home feeding stations

Planted trees and shrubs to attract particular species

Tracks the number of different species he has attracted to his feeders

Purchases different kinds of seed to attract different birds

Purchases seed in bulk to save money

Likes to share his knowledge with others

Uses a computer for e-mail and occasional web browsing. Has purchased books from online sources

Pet peeve is squirrels that decimate his feeders and cats that attack birds as they feed

Harriet Up
35 years old
Mother, Part-time dental hygienist
Married with three children, ages 13, 10, and 8

Pressed for time, looking for last-minute gift for her mother, who is difficult to shop for

Her mother speaks fondly of hearing birds outside her window

Races up every aisle before selecting a clock that plays different bird songs on the hour

Adds her name to store mailing list

Avid computer user. Uses computer frequently for e-mail, web browsing, online purchases, and personal finance

Dislikes wasting time racing from store to store and not finding what she wants

Urbana Family
Father Fred, 41 year-old software engineer
Mother Carol, 39 year-old marketing manager
Two children ages 10 and 7

Live in urban area

Want children to learn to appreciate nature

Purchase a number of items designed to get them started on bird feeding and identification

Parents interested in educational and spiritual benefits to the kids

Hoping this is a hobby they can enjoy together

Fred and children use the computer daily. Carol uses occasionally for e-mail and web browsing

Parents are concerned that they don't have sufficient time to spend with their family

goal setting and needs assessment

objectives

Describe how to gather ideas to help formulate goals for a new or revised system

Analyze and represent existing websites or software using site/software flow diagrams and site/software maps

Represent the steps of a process using a flowchart

Create personas to represent different user types

Examine how contextual inquiry is used to gain insight into an employee's work

Analyze tasks using essential use cases

introduction

The first three chapters of this book were designed to introduce you to the principles of user inter-face design and to help you understand its place in the software development process. In this chap-ter, we will roll up our sleeves and begin the actual work of interface design, including setting goals, analyzing an existing website or software program, and defining the requirements for a new or revised system. Defining requirements means understanding the users and analyzing the tasks that they will use the system to perform.

SETTING GOALS

What is it that our client wants the website or multimedia software to accomplish? Some companies will have very well thought out goals, while others may have only the vaguest goals. Nearly every owner of an e-commerce website wants to increase traffic and sales at the site. Other goals may be to create a sense of community, to perform a public service, or to increase brand recognition.

Some clients may have specific features that they want implemented in the site or software. They may want to introduce a new product or service, build a mailing list, or provide a forum for making announcements. The website or software may be one of a number of different strategies that the client is implementing to accomplish their goals.

As designers, we often find ourselves encouraging our clients to establish ambitious goals for the websites and software they ask us to create. There are several reasons for this. First, most of us want to be involved in the creation of something special that brings true value to people. A project that sets out to do something unique and exciting can recharge our creative batteries and energize everyone who comes in contact with it.

Ambitious projects stretch us in ways that we cannot anticipate. They add significantly to our skills and give us great additions to our portfolio. They are also generally worth more financially to us than more modest undertakings and keep us gainfully employed longer.

Too often, a client's budget and schedule constraints stand in the way of a project being all it can be. If we can get our clients to think strategically now, though, we increase the chances that they'll invest the time and money later to help the system achieve its potential. By thinking long term from the start, clients allow us to create designs and make early decisions that anticipate and accommodate future growth.

A great way to help you and your client get ideas that can support the client's goals is to analyze the website or software offering of competitors or organizations similar to the client's. Are there ideas worth considering adding to the client's system or improving in some way? What are these competitors doing to attract and hold visitors? How are they using the unique capabilities of the Web and interactive multimedia to accomplish their goals?

When considering which new features to add, think about how they will directly help accomplish the client's business goals. It makes no sense to spend money and effort to create and maintain a terrific new capability if it does not help achieve the client's goals in a measurable way. By keeping the proper business perspective, you can help ensure the success of the new system.

ANALYZING EXISTING SYSTEMS

If you have been hired to redesign a website or multimedia software program, your first step may be to analyze this system to understand its capabilities, structure, and interface. We analyze an existing system prior to redesigning it to accomplish the following:

- Understand the client's perspective. You will accomplish much more at the initial client meeting if you are prepared with a thorough understanding of the current system.

- Understand the present system's scope and breadth. This is only possible by analyzing the functions and features of the existing system.

- Understand its layout and navigation system. This allows us to keep alert for complex site organization, poor navigation, or confusing screen elements, all of which we can improve as part of our redesign efforts.

- Look for other factors that reduce the effectiveness of the site, such as poorly written text.

| TIP |

The first time you look at a website or software program is the last time you can view it objectively. Therefore, be alert for your first impressions and record them diligently.

Creating a Flow Diagram

Many designers prefer to create a visual representation of the existing system. This often takes the form of a site or software **flow diagram**, which uses rectangles and lines to show the system's structure and key screens at a glance. To create a flow diagram, use any tool capable of drawing rectangles, connecting lines, and text. Beginning at the home page of a site, or the top-level menu screen (or first functional screen) of a software product, you create one rectangle for each key screen or function. Use arrows to show the navigation path from one screen to another. A flow diagram of a very simple website is shown in Figure 4-1.

Flow Diagram of a Website

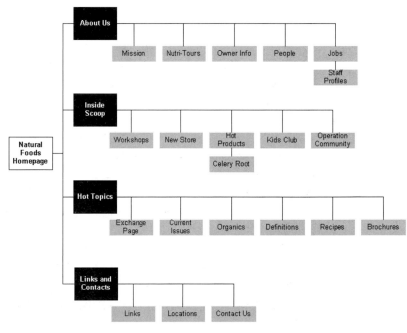

figure | 4-1 |

A website flow diagram for a simple website reveals the site's structure at a glance. The box shading helps differentiate primary functions from secondary ones.

The reviewer's notes and ideas can be recorded in a separate document. If you are creating a flow diagram of a very complex website or software product, you may need more than one page to show the entire structure. If so, you can create a "super" page that shows the main sections of the system, then use additional pages to show the detailed flow diagrams for each of the sections.

Creating a Site/Software Outline

The flow diagram that we just discussed uses boxes and lines to show an existing system's structure at a glance. By contrast, a **site or software outline** uses text in an outline format to show the structure of an existing system. Although site or software outlines do not show navigation paths as well as flow diagrams do, they offer several advantages:

- You can create and revise them quickly and easily.
- They do not require separate insert pages or other special treatment to map complex systems.
- You can include your own notes, recommendations, and other information within the outline.

Table 4-1 shows a site outline for the same website shown in the flow diagram in Figure 4-1.

In the website outline, the highest level item is the home page. Indented one level from the home page are the primary pages—those that are accessible from the home page. The next indented level corresponds to pages or functions that are accessible from the primary pages, and so on.

Also notice that the reviewer has included his preliminary observations within the outline, set aside in square brackets. The quick analysis of the website has revealed that the contact information is duplicated and that it might be better placed in the About Us section. The title of one link, Exchange Page, is unclear. There are also a couple of dead links that should be updated or eliminated.

| TIP |

When analyzing an existing software application, augment your own screen-by-screen analysis by reading the online Help system and the documentation. They often will reveal the software's more obscure features.

The outline and these notes are especially useful to refer to in client and team meetings and conversations. If the client begins talking about the Hot Products section, it just takes a moment to glance down and see that this is within the Inside Scoop area and currently contains a mystery product, which is celery root. If possible, take the time to study and memorize the various sections and their current content. Then apply your knowledge to help improve the system.

table ▎ **4-1** ▎ A website map for the same site shown in Figure 4-1 shows its outline format. This type of map is the easiest to create and revise.

A SIMPLE WEBSITE OUTLINE

I. Natural Foods Home Page

    A.   About Us

        1.   Mission

        2.   Nutri-Tours [call to sign up for one-hour on-site tours]

        3.   Owner Info [benefits of becoming an owner]

        4.   People [photos of staff and customers]

        5.   Jobs [one current posting with link to meet staff member]

            a.   Staff member profiles [photos and text]

    B.   Inside Scoop

        1.   Workshops [currently a dead link]

        2.   New Store [text and photo]

        3.   Hot Products [mystery product with link to identification and information]

            a.   Celery root information and recipes

        4.   Kids Club [text information about benefits and how to join]

        5.   Operation Community [text]

    C.   Hot Topics [this name may be too similar to Hot Products]

        1.   Exchange Page [describes a food and wellness magazine; unclear title]

        2.   Current Issues [this page is displayed when Hot Topics is clicked]

        3.   Organics [text and several links]

        4.   Definitions [currently under construction]

        5.   Recipes [text]

        6.   Brochures [text excerpts from brochures; seems more like definitions; move?]

    D.   Links and Contacts

        1.   Links [about 20 links to other sites]

        2.   Locations [text, includes link to New Store page; move to About Us?]

        3.   Contact Us [same information as Locations; move to About Us?]

Creating a Flowchart

Anyone who analyzes processes or designs any type of software should know how to create a **flowchart**. It is one of the most useful tools for illustrating the steps and flow of a process. A flowchart includes specialized symbols whose shape carries meaning. It usually consists of a number of shaped symbols connected by lines with arrowheads. Each symbol shape indicates its purpose. Figure 4-2 shows some of the most common shapes used in software flowcharts and their meaning.

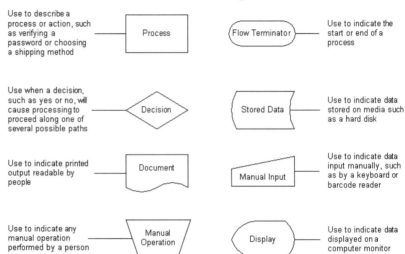

Common Flowchart Symbols

Use to describe a process or action, such as verifying a password or choosing a shipping method — Process

Flow Terminator — Use to indicate the start or end of a process

Use when a decision, such as yes or no, will cause processing to proceed along one of several possible paths — Decision

Stored Data — Use to indicate data stored on media such as a hard disk

Use to indicate printed output readable by people — Document

Manual Input — Use to indicate data input manually, such as by a keyboard or barcode reader

Use to indicate any manual operation performed by a person — Manual Operation

Display — Use to indicate data displayed on a computer monitor

figure | 4-2 |

Here are some of the commonly used flowchart symbols. Flowcharts that consist of just a few symbols (such as process rectangles and decision diamonds) are easiest for clients to understand.

| TIP |

You may find it useful to flowchart the "normal" path through the process first, then add exception paths. Using our example in Figure 4-3, we might create the normal check-out procedure, then add steps for allowing the user to abort the check-out process.

When creating a flowchart, you connect the various shapes with arrow-headed lines that indicate the direction of flow. Figure 4-3 shows a simple flowchart of a website's e-commerce process.

The process begins at the terminator labeled "Begin," then proceeds down to the process labeled "Browse for Items." After this step is a decision diamond labeled "Add Item to Cart?" If the user decides not to add an item, then flow follows the "No" line, which goes back up to the "Browse for Items" step. If the user decides to add an item to the cart, then processing follows the "Yes" path down to "Choose Shipping Method," and so on.

This flowchart shown in Figure 4-3 is oversimplified. To make it more accurate, we would add steps for indicating whether or not the credit card number was validated. We would also include paths for allowing the user to abort the check-out process before it was completed.

Flowchart of Simple E-commerce Website

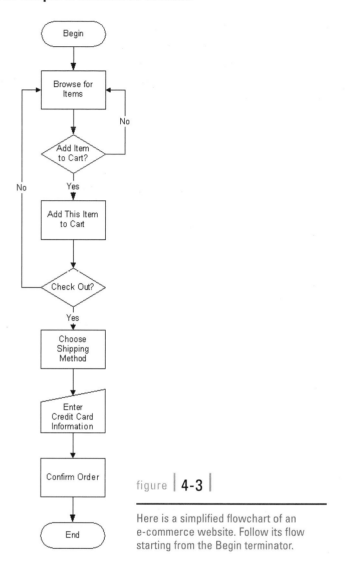

| TIP |

Always create your own flow diagrams, flow outlines, and flowcharts of a system, rather than relying on an existing one supplied by the client or obtained through other means. You will learn valuable insights in the process of creating your own. After you have created your flow diagram or outline, then it may be useful to review one from a different source, if one exists. It might reveal a part of the site or software that your analysis missed or show functionality that was originally part of the system but later eliminated.

figure | **4-3** |

Here is a simplified flowchart of an e-commerce website. Follow its flow starting from the Begin terminator.

Use any combination of the flow diagrams, outlines, and flowcharts to analyze websites and software. You might use the examples shown in Figures 4-1, 4-3, and Table 4-1 as starting points, then add features that make them more useful to you and your clients. We'll provide an example of this suggestion later in this chapter. Just keep in mind that simple is better when it comes to diagrams and other explanatory materials.

Besides analyzing a client's existing site or software, it is often useful to analyze your client's competition as well. Often your client will mention competing companies' products or websites in your initial meeting. If your client doesn't raise the subject, consider bringing it up yourself. Try to gain as much information as possible about your client's opinion of each of these major competitors. What does your client like and dislike about their websites or software? This information can prove extremely valuable when you begin designing your solution.

After the goals for the new system have been established and any existing system analyzed, the next step is to define the site or software's requirements. During this step, you will identify the various types of users of the system and assess their needs.

ANALYZING THE AUDIENCE

The audience analysis phase is where you dispense with all of your assumptions about what your users want or how they prefer to perform tasks. Ignore this step and you risk designing a website or software program that misses its mark. Perform this step well and you will be rewarded with accurate, first-hand observations and information that will increase the value of the systems you design.

Designers use a number of techniques to develop a thorough understanding of users, including surveys, interviews, direct observation and inquiry, and personas. Which techniques you use depends on the nature of the project and how accessible the audience is to you.

Surveys

One direct way to analyze the needs of an existing website's users is to solicit feedback from them. Often this takes the form of an online feedback **survey**. Although this is a valuable source of information, it can be challenging to get busy people to take the time to fill out the survey. Some companies offer prize drawings or discount coupons as incentives to users who take the time to respond to questions online.

Be sure that your survey asks questions that yield useful answers. For example, some surveys ask users to rate their sites on a scale from 1 to 10 for a variety of factors such as ease of use and ability to find what they are seeking. Such questions may tell you how users rate your site, but what specific actions can you take with such information? It is better to ask open-ended questions such as the following:

- "Why are you visiting our site today?"
- "What item or information did you *not* find that you were looking for?"
- "What should we do to improve this site?"
- "What features would you like to see added to this site?"

| TIP |

Provide a place for survey respondents to include their e-mail address, but don't require them to provide this. People value their anonymity and may quickly flee from a site that requires them to identify themselves needlessly.

Site Visits

Conducting a site visit gives you the opportunity to both observe and interview users and potential users of the software or website you are designing. This step is particularly important when you are developing applications, but is also useful for website design. Let's say that we are working on the redesign of a website for a local store that offers wild bird feeders, bird food, and associated items. The website includes e-commerce capabilities to sell its items to customers throughout the country.

One of the best ways to learn about the shopping habits of people who purchase items from such a store is to actually visit one and speak with them firsthand. Watching users (with or without interacting with them) is based on the anthropological discipline of **ethnography**. When practiced by anthropologists, it means studying the life and activities of a group of people, often by living with them for a period of time. We can learn a lot about users by, in effect, living with them as they perform their jobs or tasks.

If you are lucky enough to have a nearby client with a bricks-and-mortar store, you might be able to ask questions of shoppers about their shopping styles and intentions. Perhaps your client will be willing to offer customers a discount on their purchases in exchange for their valuable time and information.

You spend several days at the client's store observing and interviewing customers, hearing the stories they tell you, and learning about their goals and their experiences meeting or not meeting those goals. Your observations indicate that most of the store's customers seem to fall into several distinct categories:

- Some are adults who feed birds year-round. Many of the people in this group have an in-depth knowledge of birds, their identification, and their habits. A number of them are retired people with time to devote to their hobby.

- Some are parents who want their young children to develop an appreciation and fascination with birds and nature.

- Some are people who are looking for unique gift ideas for friends or family members. About half of those who make such purchases don't feed birds regularly or know much about them.

Creating Personas

Often there is more than one type of user in the target audience. Some designers use **personas**, a term coined by Alan Cooper, inventor of the Visual Basic programming language and a pioneer in the field of user interface design. A persona is an imaginary person whose characteristics match a particular type of user of a website or software product. If a website or software product will serve different user types, then the designer creates a persona to represent each

---

| TIP |

If it is absolutely impossible for you to observe and analyze the behaviors of actual users, then speak with whoever handles sales or marketing for the client. These people are the ones who are most likely to hear what customers want, don't want, like, and don't like. Client support people are also a good source of information, since they field customer complaints daily. Keep in mind, however, that such second hand information is no substitute for first hand customer observation and interviews.

user type. These personas are discussed as if they were actual people during the design phase. They help ensure that the interface will accommodate the full range of users that make up the system's audience.

You create three personas to represent the major types of users you expect to reach with your website. You name them Adam I. Yard, the Urbana family, and Mrs. Harriet Upp. Start by creating a story that describes each persona.

> Adam I. Yard is a 68-year-old retired armed forces officer. He has numerous bird feeders situated around his back yard, where he has planted shrubs and trees that provide additional food and shelter for the birds. From inside his family room, Adam can observe the numerous species that are attracted to his feeders, which are filled with a variety of different types of bird foods. He purchases seed in bulk, since it saves him money over the long run. Adam likes to share his knowledge of birds with others, and he keeps track of the number of different bird species that he has attracted to his yard. He is nearly obsessed with keeping the squirrels and neighbor's cats from decimating his feeders.

> Harriet Up is in a bit of trouble. She is pressed for time, as always, trying to find a last-minute birthday gift for her mother, who is difficult to shop for. Harriet doesn't know much about birds, but she has heard her mother speak with joy about the birds she hears singing outside her window. After racing up and down every aisle of the store, Harriet selects a gift clock that rings in each hour with a different bird song. She adds her name to the store mailing list. As she is walking out, she is trying to remember if she is supposed to pick the kids up at soccer or if it's band practice day…

> The Urbana family consists of wife Betty, husband Barney, and their two school-aged children, Jack and Jill. The Urbanas are concerned that their children don't experience much nature in the city, so they want Jack and Jill to get to know and appreciate the wild bird species that live in their urban neighborhood. They purchase a number of items—a feeder, several different kinds of food, and an illustrated bird identification book to get them started on their new hobby. They are interested in the educational benefits that the children can derive from the experience, and they hope this is something that they can do together as a family.

The personas are composites, created after speaking with a number of different people and observing their shopping behavior in the store or asking basic questions. Each persona represents a potentially enormous number of actual users, but focuses on the motivations that drive a single type of shopper. The more people you observe and interview, the more accurate your personas will be.

Finally, we add details to flesh out the personas and give them life and meaning. When complete, your personas may include the following items of information:

- The persona's name. This can be totally fictitious or provide some insight into the persona's description or point of view. Don't choose names that will cause the design or development team to poke fun at or look down on the group represented by the persona.

- The persona's age.

- A clip-art "photo" of the persona.

- An indication of the persona's familiarity and comfort with computers.

- A list of distinguishing characteristics of the persona that could impact the design of the website or software.

- A pet peeve or concern of this persona related to the completion of the task you are studying.

Our three personas are shown in Figure 4-4.

Three Personas

Adam I. Yard
68 years old
Retired Air Force Captain
Divorced

Avid birder with many home feeding stations

Planted trees and shrubs to attract particular species

Tracks the number of different species he has attracted to his feeders

Purchases different kinds of seed to attract different birds

Purchases seed in bulk to save money

Likes to share his knowledge with others

Uses a computer for e-mail and occasional web browsing. Has purchased books from online sources

Pet peeve is squirrels that decimate his feeders and cats that attack birds as they feed

Harriet Up
35 years old
Mother, Part-time dental hygienist
Married with three children, ages 13, 10, and 8

Pressed for time, looking for last-minute gift for her mother, who is difficult to shop for

Her mother speaks fondly of hearing birds outside her window

Races up every aisle before selecting a clock that plays different bird songs on the hour

Adds her name to store mailing list

Avid computer user. Uses computer frequently for e-mail, web browsing, online purchases, and personal finance

Dislikes wasting time racing from store to store and not finding what she wants

Urbana Family
Father Fred, 41 year-old software engineer
Mother Carol, 39 year-old marketing manager
Two children ages 10 and 7

Live in urban area

Want children to learn to appreciate nature

Purchase a number of items designed to get them started on bird feeding and identification

Parents interested in educational and spiritual benefits to the kids

Hoping this is a hobby they can enjoy together

Fred and children use the computer daily. Carol uses occasionally for e-mail and web browsing

Parents are concerned that they don't have sufficient time to spend with their family

figure | 4-4 |

Personas such as these help keep the needs of the audience foremost in the designer's mind, providing both information and inspiration.

Here are some ways designers use personas to keep the needs of users foremost in their minds as they design a website or multimedia software program:

- Bring them to design meetings and brainstorming sessions.
- Mount the personas on large poster board and display them where they and the design team can easily see them.
- Surround the personas with objects that represent the persona's needs and wants.
- If the software or website being created is an application, they add the tasks that each persona is responsible for completing.

Converting Personas to Design

What clues do the personas give us about the shopping habits of these types of people? Adam I. Yard is a potential repeat customer who continues to invest time and money in his hobby. He may be attracted to unusual bird foods and articles or information that contribute to his ability to attract new kinds of birds to his feeders. When new, innovative products become available, Adam may be interested in hearing about them. He may also be interested in links to professional ornithology organizations or local bird-watching groups. We can brainstorm potential ideas for attracting Adam's type of user during the concept development phase.

As we've seen, Hariett Up looks for unique gifts that she can purchase on the go. We might consider creating and putting in place tools that make shopping for gifts (including gifts for oneself) easy, fun, and efficient. For example, we might provide the means for shoppers to quickly locate gifts based on various criteria such as price range, recipient's age, and gift type, such as funny gifts, useful gifts, or artistic gifts. We might even develop a service that allows customers to enter the first name and birth and anniversary dates of the people for whom they buy gifts. When the date nears, we might automatically send the customer an e-mail reminder along with some gift suggestions or discount offers.

The Urbana family, although new to bird feeding, wants to get started as quickly as possible. Mr. and Mrs. Urbana are most interested in the educational and family benefits of the hobby. This type of user may be attracted to a complete starter's kit, including everything one needs to attract, feed, and identify birds. If building a sense of community is among the goals for the website, the Urbanas might be interested in online projects, such as "build a bird feeder from a bleach bottle," or kits that a family can build and complete in a day. We might make a note to brainstorm some additional educational and family ideas for attracting customers such as the Urbanas.

The value of personas is that they focus your efforts on solving the problems and meeting the needs of actual users. Creating a persona gives life to the needs of your audience. As you flesh out your designs, you may find yourself saying things like, "Boy, Hariett is really going to appreciate *this* feature." With experience, you will learn not to waste time creating personas for user types whose needs are out of step with the majority of your audience. You may not be able to meet everyone's needs, but creating personas will help you anticipate and design for a large percentage of users.

Although we used a wild bird website as our example, create personas for any type of website or multimedia software that you are designing. Perhaps you are creating a multimedia application for a hotel kiosk that helps visiting guests decide which restaurant to choose for dinner. You can develop personas to address the different needs of people who might use such a facility, such as conference attendees, out-of-town business people, and vacationing couples or families.

Designers of business applications may create personas to represent each type of worker who will access the system. The personas summarize each type of employee's primary reasons for accessing the system, the work conditions under which they use the system, and other information that affects the system's design. Such designers often use a technique called **contextual inquiry** to gain understanding of the needs and experiences of these users.

Contextual Inquiry

The goal of contextual inquiry is to provide designers with accurate information about users' application needs. The information gathered is accurate because the designer or usability expert observes workers while they perform their tasks, rather than relying on a worker's memory or opinions about those tasks.

A contextual inquiry is different from a survey. When conducting a survey, the interviewer has a list of questions to ask the subject directly. In a contextual inquiry, the observer usually has a list of topics, which are explored within the context of the subject's job duties. As the worker performs tasks, the observer probes with questions designed to expand the understanding of those tasks.

For example, the subject of a contextual inquiry might be a help desk support specialist who is sent problems or questions about a specific software application via e-mail. The employee then researches and provides the appropriate solutions or answers. As the employee searches the database of known problems and solutions, the observer watches and may ask questions about how easy or difficult it is to find the information using the tools provided.

The observer must exercise a great deal of skill and sensitivity to observe and ask questions without hindering the employee's ability to do his or her job. Sessions often last one to several hours, and the observer takes accurate notes of the session and the employee's responses to questions. The designer uses the insight gained to create personas and provide ideas for improving the usefulness of the application.

ANALYZING TASKS

There is a very old story about a fighter jet assembly process. At one point in the process, a worker attaches a particular component to the jet. Later in the jet's assembly process, another worker removes the same component and discards it. This extreme example of inefficiency illustrates the need to periodically step back and look at processes as a whole to see how well they work.

Task analysis is the process we use to examine the functions performed by someone using a computer application. **Tasks** are the specific functions that a user wants or needs to accomplish using the application. Examples of tasks are logging in to a system, checking your e-mail, opening a file or initiating some transaction, and checking a report.

Although many websites exist only for informational purposes, more and more companies are delivering applications on the Web or via a company's intranet. An **intranet** is a private network within an organization that allows employees to share company information and resources.

The main advantages of network-based applications are ease of installation, ease of updating, and accessibility to many people. Because these applications are installed on the Web or company intranet, all of its users are spared the burden of having to install and maintain them on individual PCs or workstations. Administrators can update the applications as often as necessary without having to ship new disks to users. And anyone who has access to the Web or intranet can use these applications.

In many cases, processes that originally worked well become overburdened with add-ons and revisions. We have already seen how a software product can become nearly unusable due to feature creep. Sometimes the people in charge of administering an application are too close to it to see how its processes can be simplified and improved.

Designing or reengineering applications is one of the most challenging and rewarding jobs that a user interface designer is called upon to do. Here are the basic steps required to understand users' tasks:

1. Identify the various types of users
2. For each user type, identify the tasks and the context in which they are performed
3. Create essential use cases to break down each task
4. Create flowcharts to illustrate all or selected tasks

We'll take a look at each of these steps in further detail, and illustrate the points by looking at an example application.

Identify the Various Types of Users

In this step, we identify all of the types of users who will have contact with the application. Even if a particular type of user's access to the system is very limited, we still include it in our list of user types.

For Each User Type, Identify the Tasks and the Context in Which They Are Performed

When we analyze tasks, we need to understand them in the context of the users (often workers) who perform them within the environment in which they are performed. Specifically, we seek answers to the following questions.

What tasks does each type of user perform?

List each task that the user performs using the application.

The user's actual tasks may be different than represented by someone else in the organization. Therefore, it is important to make your own observations and question users yourself.

How often is each task performed?

Determine which tasks are accessed most often. This will help you decide how to prioritize features when creating menus or other navigational elements. If possible, assign a percentage to each task to determine which tasks are accessed most often. Determine what events are likely to cause increases in certain types of tasks.

Which tasks do users find most difficult to learn and perform?

The answer to this question may tell you where you need to focus your design skill to make complex or difficult procedures simpler or more intuitive.

In what environment are the tasks performed?

Determine if there are dusty or hazardous conditions or other environmental considerations that might affect the user's ability to perform the task. Observe what other factors compete for the user's attention while on the job.

| TIP |

Once you have recorded the list of tasks for each type of user, you can create a useful table that shows all of the tasks that all of the user types perform. Including information about how often each user type accesses each task (next item), you will have a complete view of the tasks and their usage.

How does the user learn to perform the tasks?

Determine if the user has a mentor, reads manuals, or just muddles through. Where does the user turn for help when things don't work as expected? If there is a mentor, try to arrange to speak to her to determine which tasks seem to cause users the most difficulty.

What other resources can the user access to perform tasks?

Some users have created "cheat sheets" or other informal job aids to help them complete certain tasks. These can provide a great source of ideas for online performance support tools. Here is the list of tasks for the three types of users we have identified: students, instructors, and the administrator.

A Simple Online Educational Delivery System Example

To illustrate the steps used to analyze tasks, we'll use a simplified college online educational delivery system as an example. The purpose of this new system is to allow students to take classes online via the Web. There are three types of users for this application: students, instructors, and an administrator. In our application, an instructor may also be the administrator. However, since the roles are different, we include them both as distinct user types.

| TIP |

Identify distinct user types for any group whose situation or needs is unique. For example, if there were students who accessed the course in a classroom setting and those that accessed it from home, we would create two separate types: classroom students and remote students.

Student Tasks

- Self-register for one or more courses
- Log in to the system
- Select which registered course to access or study in a given session
- Review instructor assignments for each registered course
- Communicate with the instructor of each registered course
- Complete assignments such as readings, online practices, and exams
- Review grades for graded assignments
- Review final grade for each course
- Chat with other students about course materials and assignments
- Log out of the system

Instructor Tasks

- Log in to the system
- Review the roster for each class to which they are assigned

- Assign readings, practice, and exams to students
- Grade exams and projects as necessary
- Communicate with the class or individual students
- Post each student's final grade for the course
- Communicate with the administrator to resolve issues
- Communicate with other instructors
- Change student information, including password
- See grades and reports for each class and student
- Log out of the system

Administrator Tasks

- Log in to the system
- Create classes
- Change class information
- Add instructors to system
- Assign instructors to classes
- Change instructor information
- Delete instructors
- Register students for classes (for those students who do not self-register)
- Transfer students from one class to another
- Communicate with instructors
- See reports for each class, instructor, and student
- Change student information, including password
- Delete students
- Clear classes at end of each semester
- Log out of the system

System Tasks

We have created task lists for each of the user types of our system, but there are a number of other tasks that we have not yet listed. Those are the tasks that are the responsibility of the system itself. These may include such areas as security, accessibility to users with specific disabilities, support for languages other than English, performance requirements, and other responsibilities.

To ensure that we don't forget these important considerations, consider including them in a task list called "system." This is not a user type, such as the student, instructor, and administrator listed above, but is a repository for system responsibilities. Include in this list the tasks that the system will need to accomplish, such as the following:

- Keep all system passwords secure
- Keep all personal information secure
- Keep all student performance data secure from other students and outsiders
- Keep students from viewing each other's performance data
- Make lessons accessible to hearing and sight impaired students

Create Essential Use Cases to Break Down Each Task

To fully understand a complex system's functions, designers often break each task down into its component actions. Larry Constantine and Lucy Lockwood, in their book, *Software for Use: A Practical Guide to the Models and Methods of Usage Centered Design* (Addison-Wesley, 1999), use the term **essential use case** to describe a method for recording such an analysis. The analysis shows the user's intentions and the system's associated responsibility. It makes no assumptions about what the user interface will be. In fact, it is free of any mention of technology, focusing instead on the actions themselves (see Tables 4-2, 4-3, 4-4).

If we were actually creating this application, we would create an essential use case for each user task listed above. To show this technique, we'll select one of each user type's tasks and create an essential use case for it. We use one card or one piece of paper for each essential use case. Notice that each essential use case covers a single task. For example, students, instructors, and administrators will each have to log in to the system, but the log-in procedure is covered in its own essential use case. Therefore, it is not included in the tasks in Table 4-2.

These essential use cases will be most useful when we design the individual screens of the new application. We will refer back to them to ensure that we are accommodating the necessary functionality for each task. Since the number of essential use cases for a complex application can become quite large, some designers like to store them in separate stacks, organized by user type.

table | **4-2** | The essential use case shows only the necessary user intentions and system responsibilities. This essential use case breaks down the steps of the student completing an online practice exercise.

ESSENTIAL USE CASE FOR STUDENT: COMPLETE ONLINE PRACTICE

User (Student) Intention	System Responsibility
	Show courses for which the student has registered
Select course	
	Offer assignments menu
Select online practice activity	
	Display questions of practice activity
Provide answers for practice activity	
	Score student's work
	Prescribe reading assignment in textbook based on student's areas of difficulty
View score and prescribed readings	

table | **4-3** | This essential use case breaks down the steps of the instructor changing a student's password.

ESSENTIAL USE CASE FOR INSTRUCTOR: CHANGE STUDENT PASSWORD

User (Instructor) Intention	System Responsibility
	Show classes to which instructor is assigned
Select class containing student to change	
	Show list of students for selected class
Select student to change	
	Show menu of student choices
Select change student information	
	Display student information
Change password	
	Save changes

table | 4-4 | This essential use case breaks down the steps of the administrator assigning an instructor to a class.

ESSENTIAL USE CASE FOR ADMINISTRATOR: ASSIGN INSTRUCTOR TO CLASS	
User (Administrator) Intention	**System Responsibility**
	Show list of classes
Create class if not on list	
Select class	
	Show list of instructors in system
Add instructor to system if not on list	
Assign instructor to class	
	Save changes

Create Flowcharts for All or Selected Tasks

After you have created essential use cases for the tasks you have identified for each user type, the next step is to create flowcharts for these tasks. Some designers prefer to flowchart all of the tasks to ensure that they understand them completely, while others flowchart complex tasks—those that contain one or more decision points and many steps.

One of the most important diagrams to create is one that shows the overall flow of the website or software from a high-level perspective. This will help others to understand the system and sets the stage for more detailed diagrams. When we actually create this flowchart, however, it makes the flow seem complicated. One limitation of the standard flowcharts is that they don't handle menus of choices very well. Figure 4-5 shows a flowchart of the high-level student view of the system.

Notice that a series of decision diamonds attempts to convey that the student has various options to select from. Unfortunately, the diamonds give the appearance of a hierarchy. They make it seem as if the student must first choose whether to complete an assignment before deciding whether to e-mail the instructor or chat with other students. In fact, these might be menu options or buttons on a toolbar.

Our goal is to make the chart simpler and to more accurately convey that these options will be presented to the student all at once. To accomplish this, we have modified the flowchart by replacing the series of decision diamonds with a bar. The choices are shown as rectangles connected to the bar, which is very similar to how options are shown in the flow diagram we examined in the beginning of this chapter (Figure 4-1). Notice that the lines that connect the bar to the rectangles are drawn without arrowheads, since we do not want to imply any directional flow.

Figure 4-6 shows the results, a diagram that is less formal than a flowchart, but easier to read and understand.

Flowchart of Student Functions

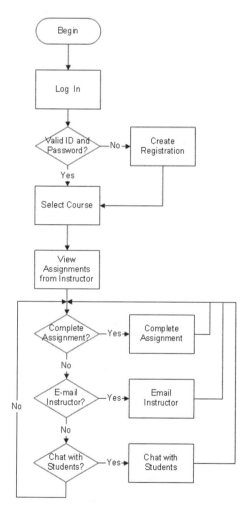

Simplified Flow Diagram of Student Functions

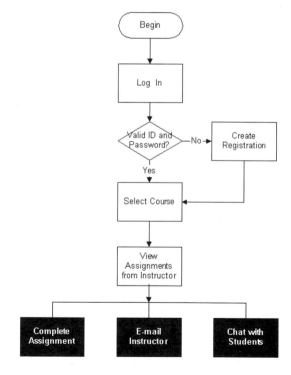

figure | 4-5 |

This high-level flowchart of student functions seems overly complex. The series of decision diamonds also implies a hierarchy of functions that is misleading.

figure | 4-6 |

Here is a different way of showing the functionality of Figure 4-5. Options that may be presented simultaneously to the user are shown as rectangles attached to a bar. Major functions, shown in black, are differentiated from interface elements, such as choosing a class.

Combining the power of the flowcharting symbols with the simple look of the flow diagram gives us the benefits of each of these methods. Keep in mind, however, that this method of combining techniques works best with charts that show a system's functionality from a high-level view. For more detailed studies, a flowchart is the preferable tool.

Figures 4-7 and 4-8 show the simplified high-level flowcharts for the instructor and administrator views of the system.

Notice in Figure 4-8 that lines without arrowheads show relationships between functions. For example, if the administrator wants to assign an instructor to a class that has not yet been created, we will provide an easy means for the administrator to access the create-class function, then return to the assign-instructor function.

Once you have finished creating flowcharts, flow outlines, and/or flow diagrams to show the organization and flow of tasks, you will have completed the requirements-definition stage of the process. You will have gained sufficient knowledge about your users and their tasks to begin grouping the various tasks in a way that will lead to a navigation structure for the website or software.

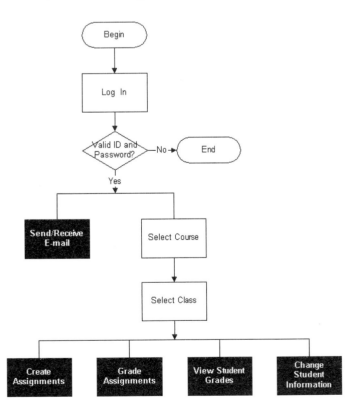

Simplified Flow Diagram of Instructor Functions

figure | 4-7 |

Here is the simplified flow diagram of instructor functions.

Simplified Flow Diagram of Administrator Functions

figure | 4-8 |

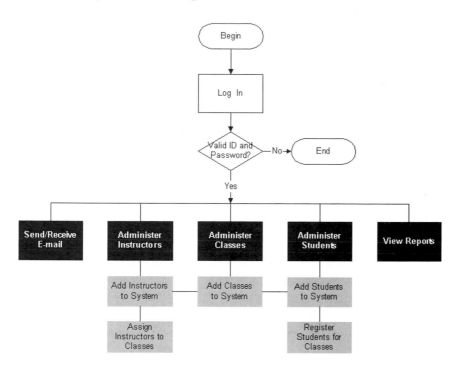

Here is the simplified flow diagram of administrator functions. The black rectangles indicate primary functions, while the gray rectangles indicate secondary ones.

GROUPING AND PRIORITIZING TASKS

Our next step is to organize the list of tasks for each user type so that they begin to suggest a navigational structure, keeping in mind the needs of our audience. Designers approach this organizational step in different ways. I find it useful to first group tasks, then prioritize them by criteria such as the order in which functions are likely to be accessed and the frequency that they will be accessed.

Grouping Tasks

We'll start by grouping tasks by function, using the administrator tasks listed earlier in this chapter as our example.

Administrator Tasks

- Log in to the system
- Create classes
- Change class information

- Add instructors to system
- Assign instructors to classes
- Change instructor information
- Delete instructors
- Register students for classes (for those students who do not self-register)
- Transfer students from one class to another
- Communicate with instructors
- See reports for each class, instructor, and student
- Change student information, including password
- Clear classes at end of each semester
- Log out of the system

Interviews with the intended administrators of the system indicated that they expect to use the system heavily at the beginning of each term, but more sporadically once this initial period is over. The interface must allow them to quickly locate the necessary function. The administrators we spoke with like to have functions organized by group—i.e., instructors, students, classes, etc. Therefore, we will begin by arranging tasks according to their constituent groups.

Class Tasks

- Create classes
- Change class information
- Clear classes at end of each semester

Instructor Tasks

- Add instructors to system
- Assign instructors to classes
- Change instructor information
- Delete instructors

Student Tasks

- Register students for classes
- Change student information, including password
- Delete students
- Transfer students from one class to another

Miscellaneous Tasks

- Log in to the system
- Communicate with instructors
- See reports for each class, instructor, and student
- Log out of the system

It is not difficult to see how these groupings might suggest a flow and menu structure for the administrator view of this application. The administrator will begin by accessing a particular Web page, where he will be required to log in with a user identification and password. The next page displayed could display a primary or main menu with the following choices:

1. Student Functions

2. Classes Functions

3. Instructor Functions

4. Reports

This is just one way that this application could be organized—it is by no means the only way. We will discuss navigation more thoroughly in Chapter 7. Although not extremely critical in this application, we should give some thought to the order of menu items on the main menu. If we consider the order in which the administrator is likely to use these functions for the first time, the administrator could either first create classes, then assign instructors to those classes or add instructors first, then classes. Students can self-register, but the administrator can also add them to the system. Therefore, there is no clear order suggested by the sequence of access.

As for frequency of access over time, the instructor may be called upon to help students who are having difficulty logging in to the system. The instructor will have the ability to change student information, including passwords, but the administrator may have to assist with these tasks. At the end of each term, the administrator will have to clear out each class to prepare for the next term. Once again, no task emerges as the clear most-frequently-accessed winner.

We have shown the order as Student Functions, Classes Functions, and Instructor Functions, since this is a logical way to think about the tasks. Students are the smallest "unit" of the system. Students are grouped to form classes. Instructors are assigned to classes. Assuming that no better alternative is forthcoming, this menu order should be tested on users in the early stages of design to determine its fitness.

The administrator is likely to want to be able to communicate with instructors from any page of the application, so we should plan to include it throughout the application. Similarly, we

| **TIP** |

Some designers prefer to write down system features on index cards, one function per card. They develop the organization of the new system by sorting the cards into piles, moving cards from one pile to another as needed. Such a system may also be used during usability testing to enable users to indicate which functions they expect to be grouped together. This information is used to develop the navigation system for the software or website.

will probably include a Log Off link or button on every page, rather than forcing the administrator to return to the home page in order to log off.

As we have seen, analyzing the intended audience and tasks of a website, multimedia software, or application leads the designer to a more complete knowledge, which directly influences the quality of the design. In the next chapter, we will shift gears a bit and turn our attention to the exciting topics of creativity and idea generation.

SUMMARY OF KEY POINTS

- Flow diagrams, website and software maps, and flowcharts are useful tools for communicating the structure of an existing or proposed website or software product.

- Designers use surveys, interviews, direct observation and inquiry, personas, and user stories to learn about the target audiences for websites or software. The type of project and accessibility of the target audience determines which techniques to use.

- Surveys are useful for collecting users' opinions and recommendations. Carefully worded questions yield useful information.

- A site visit gives you the opportunity to observe and interview users as they perform tasks or jobs.

- Designers sometimes create personas, which are fictional people who represent the different types of users of a website or software product, to keep the needs of their audience in mind throughout the design process.

- A contextual inquiry gives the designer the opportunity to observe workers as they perform their tasks and to ask questions based on these observations.

- A designer performs a task analysis to understand the steps a worker or system performs to accomplish goals. The task analysis is often used in redesigning the task to make it easier or more efficient.

- Grouping and prioritizing tasks often suggests a navigation structure for the new or redesigned application.

in review

1. Of site/software outlines and flow diagrams, which can most easily accommodate the designer's notes?

2. What are the major advantages of a site/software map?

3. What are some examples of valuable survey questions to ask a site's visitors?

4. What is a persona, and how can it help us design better sites and software?

5. Why is it important for an essential use case to avoid references to technology?

6. How does a designer manipulate a task list for a user type to suggest a navigational structure?

exercise

1. You have been asked to create a website that offers Web design students a community for interacting with each other and with instructors and professionals in the field. Develop two different personas representing students who are likely to use the site. Interview one or more of your classmates to help develop the personas.

creativity and idea generation

objectives

Examine obstacles to creativity and how to break them

Analyze and practice useful techniques for generating new ideas

Apply these techniques to solve interface problems and add value to software

Evaluate ideas to determine which offer the best chance of success

Describe how to conduct and participate in group brainstorming sessions

introduction

Once we have analyzed the needs of our audience and the tasks that they perform, the temptation is very strong to dive right in and start drawing screens. But hold on a minute! The business of designing websites and multimedia software is all about solving problems and adding value for the benefit of the audience. As a designer, you have many opportunities to contribute ideas that have direct impact on the user experience. With so much potentially at stake, how can you consistently come up with these insightful, problem-solving ideas?

To find out, first stow all your troubles away, put on your big red clown's nose, and get down to the seriously wacky business of creativity! All of us are born creative. Watch a four-year old invent games with a leaf and some dirt. Listen to a seven-year old sing a song she just made up about her brother's eyebrows. You have a wonderful imagination that was designed for coming up with useful new ideas.

By the time we reach adulthood, though, many of us have forgotten that we ever had a creative spark inside us. Instead, we've learned to internalize the judgements and criticisms that the world heaps on us, perhaps believing that we have nothing new or valuable to contribute. Now it's time to fight back and tap into that creative child inside all of us.

I'M NOT CREATIVE, SO DO I HAVE TO DO THIS?

Perhaps your previous attempts at creative problem solving have been less than successful. When faced with the need for clever, new ideas, do you respond to the challenge by vacuuming your room? Are you convinced that *lateral thinking* requires a football? Do most of your group brainstorming sessions end when someone calls the police?

Never fear! Equipped with some handy techniques and a little practice, anyone can learn to tap into his own creative wellspring. We will start our journey by looking at what keeps us from being as creative as we can be. Then we'll introduce some proven techniques for breaking down these obstacles and letting our creative energy flow. Along the way we'll show how creative problem solving techniques can add real value to the websites and software we design.

OBSTACLES TO CREATIVITY

The fact that you are reading this book proves that your are a survivor. To this moment, you have managed to handle all that life has thrown at you, and your very existence is living proof of your success. How did you manage to make it this far?

Conformity

One answer to this question is *conformity*. We were all taught from an early age to follow the rules. Go along to get along. Don't touch that! Stay out of the street! Keep your hands to yourself! Get back in line! Anyone who ever walked in front of a moving car knows that rules aren't all bad. Conforming to standards and norms of safety and health keeps us from hurting ourselves and others, while allowing us to live reasonably harmoniously in society.

But over time, our emphasis on following rules keeps us from expressing our creative selves. Creativity runs counter to convention. By definition, to innovate is to create something new and different from what preceded it. Therefore, in order to escape from our "normal" thought patterns, *we* have to be willing to act a little differently. Thinking better requires that we think differently.

Single Best Solution Orientation

We are programmed to find the single best solution to a given problem or challenge. Buy this product instead of that one because it works better. Take this route instead of that one to avoid the traffic and arrive sooner. Ask Alice, because she always knows the right answer. We are always alert for the single best solution to any question or problem. Likewise, we are expert at judging possible solutions in order to eliminate those that don't make the grade.

This is a fine and necessary strategy for solving simple, everyday problems. But solving the really tough problems or coming up with truly creative ideas requires a totally different approach. To think creatively is to begin by embracing wrong answers as much as right ones. In fact, to be creative, we apply techniques specifically designed to produce wrong, inappropriate, outlandish, nonsensical, and impossible solutions to our problem. This helps us find practical solutions that we never would have considered otherwise.

Going Directly from Here to There

Look at the difference between the way adults and children get to where they are going. Adults race to get from point A to point B as quickly and directly as possible. Children, though, are accomplished meanderers, stopping to explore anything and everything that catches their interest. They seem to look for reasons not to get where they're going.

Creative thinking requires that we act more like children by taking our time and choosing the less-traveled road. Great ideas aren't found by racing down the wide avenues. It is the small, hidden paths that lead us to unexpected and enchanting destinations. It may take us a little longer to get there, but the journey and the potential results are worth it.

Fear of Failure

The single greatest impediment to creativity is the fear of sounding or appearing stupid. Although it is sometimes true that you won't fail or be ridiculed if you don't take a risk, you also won't get very far. It takes courage to express your ideas out loud. You have to be prepared to hear, "That isn't practical," or "We tried your idea before, and it didn't work."

The key to creative success is not confusing your ideas with your self. A rejection of your idea is not a rejection of you or an indictment of your creative abilities. There are many reasons why ideas are rejected, many that are completely beyond your control. It might not be the right timing, the right situation, or the right solution. Learn from the rejection and keep trying. If your idea doesn't pan out, don't worry! You can always come up with new ideas. Just going through the process of innovating, choosing workable ideas, and showing your idea to others is beneficial. And you never know when one of your ideas will prove to be truly magical.

| **TIP** |

If you can't think of a single idea, then think of a hundred ideas. Sometimes our search for the perfect idea keeps us from thinking of *any* ideas. A great way to get unstuck is to force yourself to write down lots of ideas, even if many of them are just mediocre. Allowing yourself to be less than brilliant will help nurture your creativity.

Thinking You Were Born Uncreative

When Robert K. Merton, the late sociologist and professor, coined the phrase *self-fulfilling prophecy*, he could well have been describing people who declare themselves uncreative. It's true. If you think yourself uncreative, then you will be. If you declare your brain incapable of original thought, then it will do its best to comply.

For those who fall into this category, at least *try* some of the techniques described in this chapter. Don't just read about them, but apply them to a problem that you would like to solve. Relax and have fun with them. If you were wrong and you really *do* have a creative bone in your body, then you will have learned something very valuable about yourself. On the other hand, if you are still unable to generate a single creative idea after trying the techniques discussed listed here, you will at least have the satisfaction of saying "I told you so."

TECHNIQUES FOR GENERATING NEW IDEAS

For years, creativity enhancement techniques have been used successfully by those whose livelihood depends on their ability to generate new ideas. Inventors, advertising people, scientists, and artists come to mind instantly, but people who can create useful ideas are highly prized in every field.

A number of pioneers and authorities in the study of creativity are responsible for many of the techniques discussed in this section. For example, Edward de Bono introduced the term **lateral thinking** in 1967. According to Mr. de Bono, "You cannot dig a hole in a different place by digging the same hole deeper." The message is clear—to come up with different results we can't just try harder in the same direction; we have to *change* direction.

Alex Osborn, a pioneer teacher of creativity, devised a number of techniques. His work was later modified by Bob Eberle and further described in Michael Michalko's book, *Thinkertoys*, published by Ten Speed Press. You might also enjoy Roger Von Oech's *A Whack on the Side of the Head* (Warner Books) or *A Kick in the Seat of the Pants* (Harper Collins).

Creativity techniques work by forcing us out of our normal context. They have us twist our problem every which way, look at it from different points of view, stretch it, shrink it, dissect it, and morph it.

All of the techniques included in this section can be used to generate workable ideas that can be applied to websites or multimedia software. Of course, we are most interested in devising new, powerful ways to connect the user to a system's functionality. But in the process of your work, you will likely find yourself creating ideas for new features and capabilities that your client may find valuable. These ideas may be more accurately categorized as marketing ideas than pure interface suggestions, but the two are often closely linked. Sharing such suggestions with clients can help strengthen the working relationship and makes the project much more rewarding.

Although the techniques may seem a bit strange at first, with practice they will become like old friends. If you find that a particular technique does not help you produce useful solutions to your problem, then try others. You will soon begin to learn which technique is likely to work best in a given situation.

To use these techniques, start by defining, as specifically as possible, the problem you want to solve. As philosopher John Dewey said, "A problem well stated is half solved." It is not enough to describe your problem as "I want to make this website better." You have to be able to state *how* you want it to be better. The following are some examples of reasonably well-stated problems:

- "I want to make it incredibly easy for online shoppers to compare similar items so that they can select the one that best satisfies their needs."

- "I need a more intuitive way to allow users to select portion sizes of foods so that they can see the nutritional content."

- "I want each potential client who views our portfolio to see the projects we've worked on that are most like their needs."

- "I need a way to provide context-sensitive information to my users without them having to search through an entire Help file."

- "I need to show students, at a glance, the changes that occur in predator and prey populations in each generation."

Once you have stated clearly the problem you want to solve, it's time to apply the techniques and see what kinds of ideas you can generate.

| TIP |

Creativity techniques work best when your attitude is that *anything* is possible. Use them with the full expectation that you *will* produce ideas that will solve your problem.

The "No Constraints" Technique

The "no constraints" technique is a great technique to use when you want to create powerful new feature ideas. The ideas it produces often can be converted to workable solutions. To use this technique, ask yourself the following question: "How would I solve this problem if there were no constraints to consider?"

If there are no constraints, then your solution does not need to fit within the confines of a computer. You can ignore such pesky physical limitations as time, space, money, and resources. If necessary, you can read minds, conjure up helpful people and objects, and instantly transport yourself to whatever destination you wish.

Now let's try applying this technique to develop ideas for solving a real problem. Since this technique works so well on suggesting new features, we'll say our client's goal is to improve online sales at a website that sells specialty gourmet foods. Our question is "How could we get people to buy more gourmet food items if there were no constraints limiting us?"

As you think about possible answers to this question, remember not to judge any of the ideas yet. Premature judgement can stop the idea generation process cold. Record your answers to the question. When I asked myself the question, I came up with the following unconstrained ways to get people to buy more items:

1. Each time someone bought one item, they also bought all the other items that went along with that item. For example, if someone purchased gourmet crackers, they also bought various cheeses, jellies, and other things to spread on them, plus other appetizers, hors d'oeuvres, etc.

2. Each time a shopper looked at an item, a customer who had already bought that item magically appeared and told the shopper how great the item was.

3. Instead of customers having to access the site, the site would send items to the shopper's home that could be purchased.

4. Every time someone bought an item, every other shopper would be notified.

5. Every time someone bought an item, they would automatically buy 100 of the item instead of just one.

The next step is to examine each of your answers to see if anything useful can be derived. We'll use the list above, and you can use the ideas you generated. Let's start with the first item and go down the list.

1. Each time someone bought one item, they also bought all the other items that went along with that item. For example, if someone purchased gourmet crackers, they also bought various cheeses, jellies, and other things to spread on them, plus other appetizers, hors d'oeuvres, etc.

This idea might lead us to automatically suggest related items when a shopper selects a particular item to examine or purchase on the site. We might also offer a compelling theme, such as a "Spring Lake Picnic," containing several related items, such as crackers, cheese, fruit, and a bottle of wine.

2. Each time a shopper looked at an item, a customer who had already bought that item magically appeared and told the shopper how great the item was.

Although making a happy customer "magically appear" might prove difficult, we could certainly include positive comments from actual customers on item description pages. We could invite buyers to give us feedback about the items they purchase, and ask those who wrote especially enthusiastic reviews to give us permission to use their comments on the site.

3. Instead of customers having to access the site, the site would send items to the shopper's home that could be purchased.

With visitors' consent, we could send out periodic e-mails advertising new products, special discount offers, and other promotions.

4. Every time someone bought an item, every other shopper would be notified.

Although our first impulse might be to reject this idea instantly, perhaps we can just twist it slightly to wring something useful out of it. For example, notifying every other shopper might mean that we publish a list of the best-selling items prominently on the website. This might entice shoppers to purchase items they had never previously thought to try. Taking this a step further, we could provide different top-10 lists for different parts of the country (or world). Shoppers could see what were the most popular items in different areas and be exposed to a larger number of excellent products.

5. Every time someone bought an item, they would automatically buy 100 of the item instead of just one.

This idea might lead us to offer incentives to shoppers to purchase items in higher volumes. For example, we might provide discounts for multiple-item purchases or free shipping on larger orders.

In the space of about 10 or 15 minutes, we have generated five reasonable ideas to help improve sales at the website. You may have come up with different answers that may have led you to ideas that might be even more successful than those listed here. Your client may be impressed enough to ask you and your team to help implement one or more of them. The key was digging a different hole rather than just digging farther in the same one. Let's continue on our journey.

A variation of the no constraints technique is the "constraints" technique. Instead of removing all constraints, you introduce exaggerated constraints to see how they might influence a solution. For example, using the gourmet food scenario, we might ask ourselves how we might sell more products if all of our customers suddenly became vegetarians. This might lead us to a number of ideas:

- Allow users to display just those foods that accommodate a particular diet restriction or preference.

- Include special icons, such as sugar free, wheat free, and meat free to identify those products wherever they are displayed.

- Include full nutrition information for all of our products.

- Provide links to related sites for people who request foods that accommodate a particular diet restriction. For example, those requesting vegetarian foods could be shown a list of links to vegetarian organizations and sites.

The "Break the Rules" Technique

When you apply the **"break the rules" technique**, you ask the question, "What is the last thing on Earth that someone with sense would do to solve this problem?" We are looking for those ideas that defy logic—that run counter to conventional wisdom, rules, or standards of appropriate behavior. In short, we want ideas that break all the rules!

To illustrate how to apply this technique, let's say that you are redesigning a website for a company that manufactures printers for small businesses and consumers. They offer 12 different models ranging from modest ink jet printers all the way to high-speed laser printers. Each printer has a different feature set and price that targets it to a specific audience.

| TIP |

Great ideas can come along at any time of the day or night. Keep a notebook and pencil handy to record your ideas. There is nothing more frustrating than getting a terrific idea but forgetting what it was before you had a chance to write it down.

The current site includes a table that lists the features of each printer, but visitors to the site have complained that they still find it difficult to figure out which printer best suits their needs. How can we redesign this function to make it easier for prospective customers to choose the right printer?

Using the break the rules method, we ask ourselves, "What is the last thing on Earth we'd want to do to help customers select the printer that matches their needs?" Here are some thoughts that come into my mind. Once again, your ideas may be different from these.

1. Try to convince customers that they don't really want a printer and show them some other office equipment instead, such as a paper shredder.

2. Try to convince them that we don't offer a printer that meets their needs.

3. Show customers the printers we offer which *don't* meet their needs.

4. Rave about our competitor's printers and provide a link to *their* site.

5. Mix up all of the printers and their descriptions so customers have no idea which printers offer which features.

Now let's look over these suggestions to see if we can find any wheat among the chaff.

1. Try to convince customers that they don't really want a printer and show them some other office equipment instead, such as a paper shredder.

Although this suggestion might lead us to advise the customer how they can get more life out of their existing printer, I can't think of a way that this will help them choose the right printer.

2. Try to convince them that we don't offer a printer that meets their needs.

Perhaps our approach will let customers know if we do not offer a printer that meets their needs, but this still doesn't help us figure out how to help them choose the right printer.

3. Show customers the printers we offer which *don't* meet their needs.

At first this seems a lot like the second idea. As I was thinking about it, though, an image of lights flashing on and off came to me, and I thought of an idea. The problem with most product feature grids is that you must read every grid cell to determine if the feature it describes matches your needs. By the time you have finished, you often find that no product meets all of your needs, and you may not be sure which product was the closest match.

Why not create a smart, easy-to-use, interactive grid that shows clearly which printers meet and don't meet the user's criteria? Our grid's first column will contain a list of criteria used to select a printer. Each row contains a different criterion, such as initial cost, color or black and white, print speed, envelope feed or other special features, operating costs, etc. Each column after the first one is for each printer model. If a particular printer meets a given requirement, then the cell at the intersection of that requirement row and printer column is highlighted in some fashion—like a light turned on—that makes it stand out clearly. This is our way of indicating that the printer at the top of this column meets this particular requirement.

When the grid is first displayed, none of the cells are highlighted. Let's say the first row is for selecting whether the printer should support black and white or color printing. The first or last choice for each requirement is "No Preference" or something similar. If the user selects this choice, then all of the cells in that row are highlighted. In our case, the user selects "color," so just the cells in that row that are in columns headed by printers with color-printing capabilities become highlighted.

The user continues selecting criteria. When finished, if a printer meets all of the user's criteria, then that printer's icon at the top of the column is highlighted. If no printer meets all of the user's requirements, then the printers with the most cells in their columns highlighted are likely to be the best choices. Of course, if the user has a particular requirement that must be met, then the user can just consider the printers that meet that requirement. Figure 5-1 shows a wireframe diagram of this idea.

When first displaying the grid, we could initially highlight all of the cells instead of highlighting none of them. This entails setting the default value for each requirement to the "No Preference" choice. Then, as the user selects criteria, we remove the highlight for those cells and printers that did not meet the criteria. One possible disadvantage of this approach is that it might be a bit overwhelming to see everything lit up when the grid is first displayed. It also might be more exciting (and better from a marketing perspective) for the user to see choices lighting up rather than dimming as selections are made.

If necessary, the order of the grid can be switched so that the products are listed along the side, and the user makes selections at the top of each column. In that case, rows with the most highlighted cells are the ones that satisfy the greatest number of the user's requirements. Keeping

figure | 5-1 |

This interface idea for a product selector shows at a glance which printer meets the criteria that the user specifies.

Simplified Printer Selector

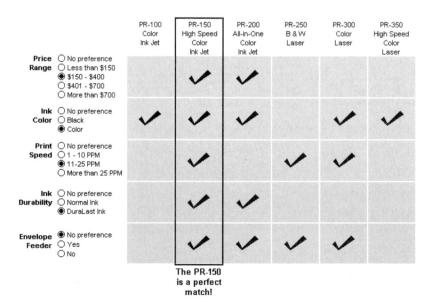

in mind that our goal is to show the entire grid without scrolling if possible, the number of criteria and the number of products will help dictate the best orientation.

Well, we got good mileage from that idea! Actually, we probably should have examined the final two ideas before devoting so much time and effort to this one, but that is easier said than done. When ideas take on a life of their own, sometimes we just have to follow where they lead. Let's finish looking at the rest of the ideas.

4. Rave about our competitor's printers and provide a link to *their* site.

Although this idea is sure to generate good will among our customers, it still won't help them select the right printer for their needs.

5. Mix up all of the printers and their descriptions so customers have no idea which printers offer which features.

This might suggest creating a concentration-style game where the user must match a printer to its features. Although this may be an interesting approach, I know from my own experience that people who are trying to make a buying decision don't want obstacles placed in their path. Although there is a time and place for entertaining games, this is probably not it.

It should be clear from our discussion of this technique that coming up with usable ideas can be a hit-or-miss proposition. Our "hit rate" was only one out of five, and yet this statistic isn't all that important. Thinking of one really good idea will quickly make you forget about all the bad ones!

The "Reversal" Technique

The **reversal technique** is useful in a variety of situations. The beauty of the reversal technique is that it is very easy to apply. To find potential solutions, you simply reverse your problem or situation. For example:

- What if, instead of asking users for their telephone numbers via e-mail, we asked them for their e-mail addresses via telephone?

- What if, instead of asking users to find the functions they need, we found out what functions users needed most and just presented those?

- What if, instead of having users navigate to different screens, we had the users stay on one screen and brought functions to them?

Here is an example of how we used the reversal technique to help solve a problem. Our team was working

on the design of some web-based interactive math tools. The tools were a series of *virtual manipulatives*, or computerized versions of the manipulatives, such as spinners and mats, used in many schools to allow students to experiment with various math concepts. We were thinking of ways to increase the tools' flexibility and ease of use for both students and teachers. Faced with this issue, we applied the reversal technique to the problem.

We asked, "What if, instead of selecting Help from within the math tools, users selected the tools from within Help?" This led to the idea of creating online lessons (the "Help") that contained links to the tools. Students could read the lesson, come to a math problem, and click the link to access the appropriate tool that was needed to solve the problem. This approach emphasizes the lesson rather than the tool, which makes it easier for teachers to understand and ensures that students select the correct tool for each situation.

▶ Driving Home the Message

HOW CREATIVITY TECHNIQUES CAN INSPIRE MEMORABLE TV ADS

As you become familiar with these creativity techniques, you will develop the ability to recognize when they have been used to create concepts for television commercials and print ads. As we've said, advertising is a field that requires a steady diet of creative ideas. And wherever creativity is required, you can bet that creativity techniques aren't far away. For some reason, automobile commercials come quickly to mind as recent and not so recent examples.

A recent Volkswagen campaign shows cars without drivers driving around by themselves and occasionally pausing in front of different people standing along the road. You can picture the brainstorming session with ideas flying around the room. Suddenly, someone offers up, "What if, instead of people shopping for cars, cars shopped for people?" Right. It's a simple reversal that supports Volkswagen's slogan "Drivers wanted."

Back in the early 1960s, Hertz was already starting to make its mark on the auto rental industry. The computer-generated magic so common to today's films, television shows, and commercials was non-existent. So when Hertz took a man and a woman and seemed to literally float them through the air and down into the front seat of a moving convertible, it made for memorable television. Their theme was, "Let Hertz put *you* in the driver's seat." It was a classic "no constraints" answer to the question, "If we had no limits, how could we get more people to rent and drive Hertz cars?" Why, we'd just pluck them out of wherever they happen to be, and drop them right into the front seat of one of our cars!"

Sometimes it's the "break the rules" ads that are the most memorable. In the mid to late 1980s, the corporate spokesman for American Isuzu Motors was Joe Isuzu, a walking stereotype of a sleazy, dishonest car salesman. Joe, played by David Leisure, would make outrageous, obviously false claims about the 4 X 4 Isuzu Trooper. He once said that it could easily carry an entire symphony orchestra, finishing with, "and if I'm lying, may lightning strike my mother." Cut to a sweet-looking, little old lady standing by an Isuzu truck who, with a blinding flash, vanishes in a puff of smoke. Who is the last person an automobile company would ever pick to be its spokesperson? Someone like Joe Isuzu, who single-handedly turned the company's name into a household word.

The "Adopt and Adapt" Technique

Using the **adopt and adapt** technique, you look for problems similar to yours that have been solved in other fields. You then look for ways to adapt these solutions to your problem. For example, let's say that you are working on a website or software program that requires displaying many photographs—too many to appear on one page or screen. Your problem is to figure out how to organize the images. Using the adopt and adapt technique, you think of other ways, outside of computers, that you have seen photographs displayed.

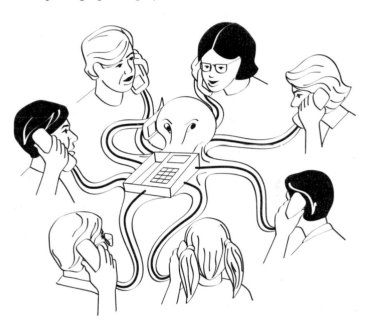

- In a photo album, perhaps displayed chronologically
- In a museum, perhaps with different pages for different "rooms"
- In a magazine, yearbook, newsletter, or newspaper
- On someone's desk or wall
- In an advertising brochure
- In the post office, as a most-wanted list
- On billboards along the highway

Any of these ideas may generate approaches for displaying your photographs, suggesting ways to organize them and possible graphic treatments to develop.

Although this example is quite a literal one, you can use this technique on problems that aren't quite as straightforward. For example, let's say that you are trying to design the toolbar for a website or multimedia application. You realize that the number of options you must present is larger than the space you have available. You might use the adopt and adapt technique to think of other situations that solve the problem of too many items to view all at once.

- A chest of drawers solves the problem by organizing its contents in slide-out units. Perhaps some of the less frequently used functions could slide into view when a particular control is clicked or rolled over with the mouse cursor. In clothing drawers, the most often-worn clothes rise to the top of the drawer. Perhaps this is how a Microsoft designer developed the idea for the dynamic pulldown menus critiqued earlier in this book.
- A file cabinet organizes papers in tabbed folders. Perhaps we could use a series of tabs to organize functions. Clicking on a tab reveals its corresponding controls.
- Some corner kitchen cabinets are fitted with lazy Susans that rotate to reveal their contents. Perhaps we could create a lazy-Susan toolbar that reveals its contents when rotated using the mouse.

- Modern cell phones allow us to "dial" commonly accessed telephone numbers by saying the name of the person we want to call. This type of interface requires no screen real estate whatsoever. Would a voice-activated menu system make sense for this application?

Although this method has us look primarily outside our own field, don't overlook the value of mining ideas from other websites and software. Whatever your problem or situation, chances are that other designers have faced similar problems and have devised workable solutions. Never pass up an opportunity to look at a new website or software program. You will often discover new ways of doing things that you hadn't considered. You might consider screen capturing, annotating, and filing the screens that contain ideas that impress you.

The "Random Word" Technique

What if finding ideas was as easy as pulling them out of a hat? Using the **random word technique** is a very fast way of generating new ideas. You simply apply a random word to your problem or situation and think of ways that the word could apply.

The random word technique requires that you first create a list of words to use as triggers. Some creativity authors recommend opening a dictionary and selecting a word at random. I prefer to use a list of words chosen for their ability to suggest lots of possibilities. The list can include nouns, verbs, adverbs, and adjectives. It can also include words that you can interpret in different ways. For example, the word "block" can be used as a verb to mean to stop or inhibit. It can also be a noun that means either something used to construct or a section of a town enclosed by four streets.

Table 5-1 contains a list of trigger terms to use as a starting point. Feel free to add your own words to the list, especially ones that trigger ideas for you. You can also delete words that you don't find particularly useful or evocative.

Now let's give this technique a try. Let's say we are working on a multimedia software project whose goal is to teach people to play guitar. We choose the word "skip" as our random trigger word. Here are some ideas that this word suggests to me.

- We can arrange the guitar instruction into weekly lessons, allowing users to skip lessons if they are already proficient.
- We can supply audio that contains a rock group's instruments, but skips the guitar part, which is supplied by the student. The student can speed up or slow down the playback of the accompaniment, record his part, then hear the song with his part included.
- Kids like to skip rope as a diversion. We could provide mini-lessons that work on a particularly catchy guitar riff or technique. Students can use these as a break from regular practice.
- We could present difficult songs in stages, allowing students to skip the hardest parts until they have mastered the techniques necessary to play them.

table | **5-1** | Select one of these words at random, then think about what the word represents and how its characteristics might help you solve your current problem.

TERMS TO USE FOR THE RANDOM WORD TECHNIQUE

tree	swing	towel	sun	store	parent
mask	air	watch	x-ray	sense	case
apple	wing	heart	window	cover	bottle
stem	friend	skip	arm	place	wide
roll	wear	block	chest	bank	light
camp	show	tire	file	shoe	child
stream	ball	slice	spin	drink	bite
coat	seed	test	hide	bolt	top
stick	door	spare	band	fan	run
expert	goal	star	root	fence	ring
seal	smile	step	wind	pick	bark
wheel	switch	safe	spoil	pipe	book

Making Creative Connections

The reason that the random word technique works so well is that the mind loves to make connections between things that seem, at first glance, to have nothing in common. For example, combine fish with bicycle, and you can pretty easily come up with new inventions such as:

- A pedal-powered fishing boat
- A two-wheeled vehicle that you propel forward by wiggling your body back and forth like a fish
- Bicycle wheels covered with scales to reduce wind resistance
- Fish-shaped handlebar covers
- A fishing rod holder for your bicycle
- … and so on.

Try this yourself with the two words "mall" and "swim." What new inventions or concepts can you create?

When you select a word, think of all of its possible meanings and contexts. For example, the term "wear" can suggest the act of putting on clothes or protection. It can also mean the thing that is being worn, such as rainwear. Wear can also mean to degrade with use, as in wear away or wear down. Thinking of different contexts for each word will help you generate the most ideas.

The "Incubate" Technique

Sometimes the best approach to developing new ideas is to do nothing. The **incubate technique** is a way to set your mind to the task of developing new ideas or solving a problem while you go on with the rest of your life. When you use the incubate technique, you seed your mind with information regarding the problem you are trying to solve. Then you stop consciously thinking about the problem and allow your subconscious mind to devise its own solutions.

State the Problem

To use the incubate technique, first state your problem or need as clearly as possible. Imagine how great you will feel when you generate that new idea that solves your problem. Visualize how it will improve your project or otherwise enrich your life.

Using what motivates you best, imagine yourself being richly rewarded for coming up with the idea. Feel free to fantasize, magnifying the rewards as much as you'd like. When you are visualizing, try to actually *see* yourself enjoying the rewards of your efforts. Perhaps you see yourself sitting in a convertible, waving to throngs of adoring fans while ticker tape streams down all around you. Maybe you see yourself accepting the Nobel prize for your creative efforts. Or there you are sitting in front of the world's largest chocolate fudge brownie, eating yourself into happy oblivion. It's your fantasy.

Do Your Homework

Next, do your homework. Analyze the problem or need from every possible angle. Research the problem by reading about it in books or magazines, asking instructors, friends, or experts, examining the competition, and doing anything else you can think of to prepare your mind for the challenge that lies ahead. Continue until you are certain that you have prepared yourself as well as possible.

Give the Direction

Once you are finished consciously working on the problem, it's time to give your mind the directions required to do the work. Tell your mind what you expect it to accomplish. Be specific. If you have a time limit, then state it, or ask your mind to alert you as soon as it comes up with a solution. If it seems silly to be directing your brain in this manner, remember that you are constantly making demands on your brain—to remember names and numbers, to speak, to instruct your muscles to move, etc. You've just been doing it so long, that you don't have to consciously think about it any more.

Let It Go

Once you have made your wishes clear to your mind, stop thinking about the problem altogether. Go do something else. Work out, go to a movie, have dinner, go to work on something else, or do anything other than work on your problem. Expect that your problem is on its way to a solution, and that the solution may come at any time.

Wait for Results

At some point over the next hour, day, week, or even month, you will become aware of a thought that demands your attention. It may simply pop into your mind, or it may form at the edge of your consciousness and slowly crystallize. You will know intuitively that this is the idea or solution you have been seeking. The idea may appear in written or verbal form, or as an image or symbol. Sometimes the idea or solution will arrive fully formed, like a gift there for the taking. Other times, it may arrive in a slightly encoded state, and you must peel away its layers to reveal the meaning.

Try this technique a few times, and chances are you will be rewarded with valuable ideas and a new respect for the creative power of your subconscious mind!

GROUP BRAINSTORMING

The creativity techniques we have covered so far in this chapter were designed to stimulate your own thinking by forcing you out of your "normal" context. **Group brainstorming** is a technique used by a group of people to generate spontaneous ideas to solve a particular problem. Group brainstorming relies on participants to suggest ideas. These ideas stimulate the other participants to think of additional ideas.

When done right, brainstorming is a wonderful source of creative ideas. When done poorly, it can alienate its participants and generate few useful ideas. Just follow some simple guidelines, and your group brainstorming sessions will enhance the creativity of all its participants and produce some amazing results.

Most importantly, group brainstorming participants leave their titles and preconceived notions at the door. There is no room for superiors, subordinates, dictators, or slaves. The brainstorming session is not the place to showcase ideas garnered elsewhere. The magic of the brainstorming sessions is that "it all happens here."

What You Will Need

Here is what you will need to get the most from your group brainstorming sessions.

- A group of people (no more than 15 if possible). The more diverse the group, the better variety of ideas you are likely to produce. All participants should check their preconceived notions at the door. The power of brainstorming is its spontaneity.

- A secretary, who writes each idea on the flipchart or board. The secretary need not be excluded from contributing ideas.

- A facilitator, often yourself, who tracks the time and keeps the session moving along smoothly.

- A whiteboard, blackboard, or flipchart. A flipchart is best, since, as sheets of paper are filled with ideas, they can be torn off and displayed around the room.

- Markers or chalk to write down the ideas.

- A large conference table or tables arranged in a "U" shape. If these are not available, then any room where the participants can relax and see the written ideas.

- Notepads and pencils or markers for each participant so they can write their own ideas, notes, or doodles.

Running the Group Brainstorming Session

Begin the group brainstorming session by stating the problem. This often takes more time than people anticipate. As we've previously discussed, take as much time as necessary to state the problem clearly and succinctly, to ensure that the ideas the group generates are directed properly. Write the problem to be solved prominently and display it where everyone can see it.

Some groups like to set a time limit of 20–30 minutes for idea generation. Larger groups need more time to ensure that everyone gets the opportunity to express their ideas. Some groups set a longer time limit, but take breaks whenever the group seems to need or want them.

Encourage the group to come up with both wild and "normal" ideas. Let them know that it is forbidden to criticize or judge any idea. Pick a person to start, and ask that person to contribute one idea. The secretary records the idea on the flipchart or board. If using a board, write just large enough so that everyone can see the ideas.

Go around the room, inviting each person in turn to contribute an idea. Have fun, and don't take the session seriously. Laughter encourages creativity. If a person cannot think of an idea, then skip to the next person. Perhaps the skipped person will think of an idea the next time around. Continue until time is up or until the group is no longer coming up with new ideas.

The Evaluation Phase

Next, it is time to sort the ideas and determine which are best. Start the evaluation phase by crossing out or erasing duplicate ideas and those that are obviously impractical. Note that these impractical ideas have value to the session since they may have been what triggered a truly practical new idea.

Rate each remaining idea as *excellent* (meaning it is practical and easy to implement), *promising* (meaning it may need some further analysis or refinement), and *presently unworkable* (P.U.!). Resolve disagreements by voting—the majority rules. By the end of this session, you will most likely have generated some very workable ideas that you can include in your design or propose to your client.

Use the creativity enhancement techniques and the group brainstorming suggestions covered in this chapter, and you will be on your way to solving even the most daunting challenges that face you and your team.

| **TIP** |

Some brainstorming groups have the participants shout out ideas rather than taking turns. While this does add to the group's enthusiasm and energy level, the louder members may drown out the quieter ones. Try this alternate method with your group to see what you think.

SUMMARY OF KEY POINTS

- Everyone was born creative, and everyone can learn to tap into their creative abilities.

- Creativity techniques help us approach problems from different angles. This change in perspective enables us to think of new ideas.

- The first step in creative problem solving is to define the problem as clearly and specifically as possible.

- With practice, you will learn which creativity techniques to apply in specific situations.

- When you are thinking of new ideas, resist the temptation to judge them too quickly. Just concentrate on compiling as many new ideas as possible.

- Group brainstorming, where participants play off each others' ideas, can be particularly productive in producing new ideas.

THE ART OF CREATIVITY

robin landa

Robin Landa is an accomplished author of books on art and design. A professor at Kean University, Robin gives lectures around the country and has been interviewed extensively on the subjects of design, creativity, and art. She also serves as a creative consultant to major corporations.

Creativity seems mysterious. When I ask illustrious creative directors, art directors, designers, and copywriters how they come up with creative ideas, many claim that they don't know. Some say they don't think about a problem directly, but rather go off to take in a film or museum exhibit and a solution seems to come to them in a state of relaxation. Other creatives are able to articulate something about their thinking process:

"I noticed how…"

"I saw that and thought of this."

"I heard someone say…"

"I thought, What if…"

After years of doing research into creative thinking—observing, teaching, designing, writing, formulating theories, and interviewing hundreds of creative professionals—I noted some fascinating commonalities among creative thinkers. What seems to distinguish a creative mind may seem, at first, unremarkable; however, upon further examination, one can see why the following markers can yield rich creative output.

BEING SHARP-EYED Part of almost any design or art education is learning to be an active viewer/seer. Whether you learn to draw a blind contour or observe the position of forms in space, you learn to be completely attentive to the visual world. Maintaining that state of alertness, of being a sharp-eyed observer, allows one to notice the inherent creative possibilities in any given situation. Being watchful when observing one's surroundings, everyday juxtapositions, allows one to see what others may miss or not even think is of note.

BEING RECEPTIVE If you've ever worked with or lived with a stubborn person, then you know the value of a person who is flexible, open to suggestions, other opinions, constructive criticism, and different schools of thought. Receptivity, as a marker of creativity, means more than being open to ideas. It means embracing the notion of incoming information and new ideas.

Being flexible allows one to let go of dogmatic thinking and to shift when necessary, to bend with the path of a blossoming idea.

COURAGE Having the courage to take risks is part of the creative spirit.

For many, the fear of failure or appearing foolish inhibits risk-taking. Fear squashes that inner voice urging you to go out on a creative limb. Fearlessness coupled with intellectual curiosity, a desire to explore and be an adventurer, an interest in many things (not just one thing), rather than play it safe and comfortable, feeds creativity.

ASSOCIATIVE THINKING The ability to connect the outwardly unconnected feeds creative thinking. Bring two old things together to form a new combination. Merge two objects into a seamless different one. Creative people seem to be able to arrange associative hierarchies in ways that allow them to make connections that might seem remote to or even elude all others.

Creativity is truly a way of thinking, a way of examining the world and interacting with information and ideas. Whether you're designing a book jacket or taking a photograph doesn't matter. What matters is how you think about almost anything. When you are sharp-eyed, stay receptive, have courage, think associatively, and approach life with energy, then your work will be buoyed.

in review

1. What are some of the major obstacles to creativity?

2. How do creativity techniques work?

3. Which creativity technique could generate the suggestion to include a coupon for a toaster in a loaf of bread?

4. The large, spaghetti-shaped cleaning cloths often found in mechanical car washes could have been generated by which creativity technique?

5. Which creativity technique was likely to generate an idea for an ultra high-speed shipping service called "The Transporter"?

6. List three things that can interfere with idea production in a group brainstorming session.

exercises

1. You have been hired to help develop a website for a virtual shopping mall. To help develop concept ideas for the project, you imagine that you have been hired as the architect to design an actual bricks-and-mortar mall using a totally innovative approach. Use some of the creativity methods we have discussed (such as the no constraints, break the rules, reversal, and random word techniques to come up with new concepts for the mall. See if you can adopt one of your ideas for use in the virtual shopping mall website.

2. Using any authoring system or environment, develop an application that displays a random word at the click of a button. Use this application to brainstorm new ideas using the random word technique.

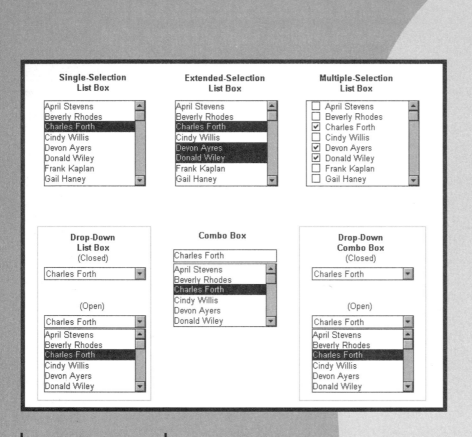

**Single-Selection
List Box**

| April Stevens |
| Beverly Rhodes |
| **Charles Forth** |
| Cindy Willis |
| Devon Ayers |
| Donald Wiley |
| Frank Kaplan |
| Gail Haney |

**Extended-Selection
List Box**

| April Stevens |
| Beverly Rhodes |
| **Charles Forth** |
| Cindy Willis |
| **Devon Ayres** |
| **Donald Wiley** |
| Frank Kaplan |
| Gail Haney |

**Multiple-Selection
List Box**

| ☐ April Stevens |
| ☐ Beverly Rhodes |
| ☑ Charles Forth |
| ☐ Cindy Willis |
| ☑ Devon Ayers |
| ☑ Donald Wiley |
| ☐ Frank Kaplan |
| ☐ Gail Haney |

**Drop-Down
List Box**
(Closed)

Charles Forth

(Open)

Charles Forth

| April Stevens |
| Beverly Rhodes |
| **Charles Forth** |
| Cindy Willis |
| Devon Ayers |
| Donald Wiley |

Combo Box

Charles Forth

| April Stevens |
| Beverly Rhodes |
| **Charles Forth** |
| Cindy Willis |
| Devon Ayers |
| Donald Wiley |

**Drop-Down
Combo Box**
(Closed)

Charles Forth

(Open)

Charles Forth

| April Stevens |
| Beverly Rhodes |
| **Charles Forth** |
| Cindy Willis |
| Devon Ayers |
| Donald Wiley |

menus and controls

objectives

Identify the component parts of menus

Identify the common interface controls

Analyze the capabilities of menus and controls

Select the appropriate control for a given situation

introduction

Menus and controls are the building blocks that perform the work of the interface. Each tool is designed with specific capabilities to handle specialized tasks. Creating an interface that works means selecting the tools that best facilitate and simplify the interactions between the user and system. Although designers and programmers can combine their skills to create a nearly limitless assortment of controls, in this chapter we will concentrate on some of the standard controls and tools that comprise the tool sets of the major operating systems.

Two indispensable references to the user interface controls of the Windows and Macintosh operating systems are *The Microsoft Windows User Experience* (Microsoft Press, 1999) and the *Macintosh Human Interface Guidelines* (Addison-Wesley, 1992). Each of these valuable references may be downloaded for free from the Internet. Anyone who is designing interfaces for either operating system is well advised to read and study these guides. This chapter combines key information about the various controls found in these guides with the experience and observations of the author, other designers, and users.

MENUS AND CONTROLS

There are many similarities between the controls available on Windows and Macintosh systems. This parity of controls is no accident. It would be extremely difficult for developers to create software to run on Macintosh and Windows systems if their user interface controls behaved completely differently. Likewise, today's most popular Web browsers support both operating systems. People who create websites can develop one set of code, and the browsers ensure that the site is accessible to users of either platform.

There are, however, many differences among the various platforms. Some controls that are available to multimedia and applications software on Windows or Macintosh platforms are not available to browsers without significant engineering effort. Some controls that are available to Windows software may have to be custom-developed for the Macintosh. In virtually all cases, however, a control exists to accomplish a given interface task.

MENUS

Menus are an important component of navigation. The Windows and Macintosh operating systems provide developers with tools for the creation of sophisticated drop-down menus. Nearly all applications include drop-down menus. In this section, we will look at the variety of options that these menus offer. Although browsers include these drop-down menus, websites do not. They are often found in multimedia software, however. Figure 6-1 shows a drop-down menu with its component parts labeled.

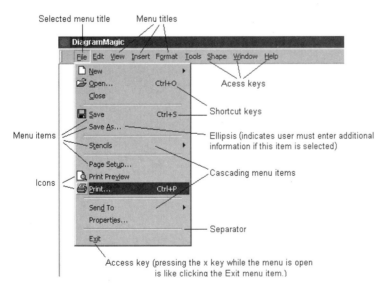

Drop-down menus consist of **menu titles**, which are the top-level names (File, Edit, Help, etc.) that appear on the **menu bar**. In Windows systems, the menu bar appears just below the title bar, which is the top bar of a window. On the Macintosh, the menu bar appears at the top of the screen. Drop-down menus are so named because when you activate them, they drop down starting just below the associated menu title. Menus consist of **menu items**, which can include text and icons.

Users can operate a menu by the mouse or the keyboard. Using the mouse, the user clicks the menu title to drop the menu, then clicks the desired menu item. Using the key-

figure | 6-1 |

The parts of a drop-down menu

board on Windows systems, you type an access key sequence by holding down the Alt key while pressing the key that is underlined in the menu title. For example, pressing Alt-F drops down the File menu in Word. Then you type the key corresponding to the underlined character of the desired menu item (with or without pressing the Alt key). For example, when the File menu is open, the menu item for saving your document is Save. Therefore, you can type the S key while the menu is open to save your document.

Some menu items can be assigned **shortcut keys**. You type a shortcut key without a menu being opened to invoke its function. For example, you can type Ctrl-S while you are editing to save the current document or Ctrl-P to print it. When a menu has a shortcut key assigned, always include the shortcut key on the menu item to alert users to its availability. For example, when you open the File menu in Word, you see that Ctrl-N opens a new document, Ctrl-O opens an existing document, and so on.

Menu Item Types

The most basic type of menu item initiates a process or performs a command when clicked. Some menu items include an ellipsis (…), which indicates that the user must provide more information when selecting this choice. Selecting such a menu item displays a dialog box where the user enters this information.

There are also menu items that can be used to set a particular state or option. Used in this way, the menu items behave independently, like check boxes, or dependently, like radio buttons. Both check boxes and radio buttons are discussed later in this chapter.

Independent Menu Items

When set as independent, selecting one option has no effect on other options. As with check boxes, check marks are used to indicate selected items. Figure 6-2 shows independent menu items used to show selected view options in Windows Paint.

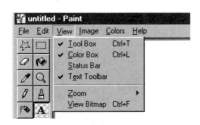

Notice that the independent menu items in Figure 6-2 are grouped and set apart from the Zoom and View Bitmap menu items using a separator.

figure | **6-2** |

Checkmarks are used to show which independent menu items have been selected. Selecting one item has no effect on other menu item selections.

Interdependent Menu Items

When a group of two or more menu items work interdependently, they behave similarly to radio buttons. Only one item in the group may be selected at a time. Selecting an item deselects the previously selected item.

Figure 6-3 shows dependent menu items used to specify line thickness.

figure | 6-3 |

A cascading menu uses interdependent menu items to specify line thickness. Selecting one of these menu items deselects the currently selected item.

Cascading Menus

Many websites and software programs use **cascading menus**, which are also called **nested menus** or **hierarchical menus**. The Windows Start menu contains cascading menu items. When you roll the mouse cursor over the Programs menu item, it displays a secondary menu of all of the installed programs and program folders. Selecting or rolling over a program folder displays yet another menu of the programs stored in that folder.

Some advantages of cascading menus include:

- They provide access to a potentially great amount of content.
- They make efficient use of space—each new menu is displayed in place, without requiring a new page to be displayed.
- They offer users the opportunity to quickly view different menu choices to find the sought-after choice without committing to a choice by clicking it.
- It is generally easy to recover from selecting the wrong menu.

Cascading menus also have some significant disadvantages:

- Many cascading menus require precise fine motor skills, rendering them difficult to use for certain types of users, especially the very young and elderly.
- They are not consistently implemented across applications.
- Their ease of operation depends on how well they are programmed.
- They can be complex and unwieldy, sometimes containing five or more nested menus.

We'll explore cascading menus further in our discussion of navigation in Chapter 7.

Creating Menu Titles and Menu Item Labels

CREATING MENU TITLES Use single words for menu titles, selecting names that clearly indicate each menu's function. Beginning with the leftmost menu title, use the first character of each menu title as its access key. If the first character is already the access key for a prior menu, then use the first unused character.

CREATING MENU ITEM LABELS *The Microsoft Windows User Experience* advises us to use nouns or noun phrases for menu item names if the menu title is a verb. If the menu title is a noun, then use verbs or verb phrases to name your menu items. For example, if the menu title is Insert, used as a verb, then it makes sense to name the menu items nouns, such as Text, Picture, and Document. If the menu title is Table, used as a noun, then menu items such as Insert Table, Delete Row, and Insert Column make sense.

Not all menu items can adhere to this pattern, however. In Microsoft Word, the Edit menu (verb) includes Select All (verb phrase). If the menu title is Reports, you may well want to include the types of reports, such as Summary or Progress, which are adjectives rather than verbs.

COMMON USER INTERFACE CONTROLS

What are the four common states of pushbuttons? What are the differences between a drop-down list box and a drop-down combo box? When should you use radio buttons and when are checkboxes the more appropriate choice? What problems do users have with multiple selection and extended-selection list boxes and how can you make them easier to understand and use? In this section we'll answer these questions by exploring each of the common interface controls.

Pushbuttons

Pushbuttons, sometimes called **command buttons**, are among the easiest controls for users to understand. You click the pushbutton to perform the function described on its label. The pushbuttons provided by the operating system are plain, rectangular or capsule-shaped. As Figure 6-4 shows, however, a pushbutton can be created from nearly any-shaped object.

Nearly all of the graphical programming environments include tools for creating basic pushbuttons. To create more sophisticated-looking pushbuttons, artists create graphics that represent each of the various states that the pushbutton supports.

figure | **6-4** |

Although standard pushbuttons are plain, graphic artists can create pushbuttons from a variety of shapes to help establish the character of the design.

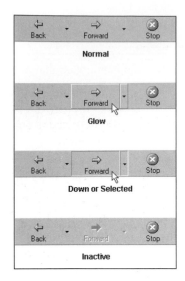

figure | **6-5** |

Here are the common pushbutton states of standard Windows buttons.

When to Use Pushbuttons

Use pushbuttons to begin an action. Common examples of such actions include:

- Navigating to a different page or screen
- Saving or implementing options or settings
- Beginning an operation, such as a search
- Canceling an operation
- Browsing for a file

When used in multimedia software and websites, the four common states of a pushbutton are:

- Normal state
- Glow or highlighted state
- Down state
- Inactive or unavailable state

Figure 6-5 shows the various button states.

Normal Pushbutton State

The **normal state** of a pushbutton is how it appears normally—that is, when it is displayed and available, but not being pointed to or clicked. All pushbuttons need to be displayable in the normal state.

Glow or Highlighted Pushbutton State

Some pushbuttons are programmed so that when the mouse cursor is moved onto their normal state, they are highlighted in some fashion. Sometimes they appear to move out of the screen and toward the user as if magnetically attracted to the mouse cursor. Sometimes the pushbutton label changes color, or the button can appear to glow. This optional pushbutton state is called a **glow** or **highlighted state**. Text and images that are used as links can also have glow states. The website in Figure 6-6a uses small photos as links. Rolling the mouse cursor over the leftmost photo replaces its image with that shown in Figure 6-6b. Rolling the mouse cursor over the first text line (Guggenheim Museum Bilbao) also replaces the photo with the graphic, a somewhat awkward effect. A newer version of this website eliminates the four text lines and simply displays a text label that identifies the rolled-over photo, an improvement.

Figure 6-6c shows simple, effective glow applied to text.

figure | 6-6a and b |

Glow applied to a photographic link. Figure 6-6A shows the normal state, and Figure 6-6B shows the glow state.

 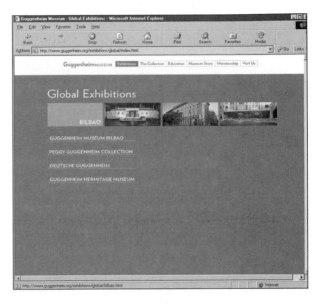

figure | 6-6c |

The rollover glow in this Porsche site conveys its meaning simply and effectively. Notice how well it matches the feel of the site.

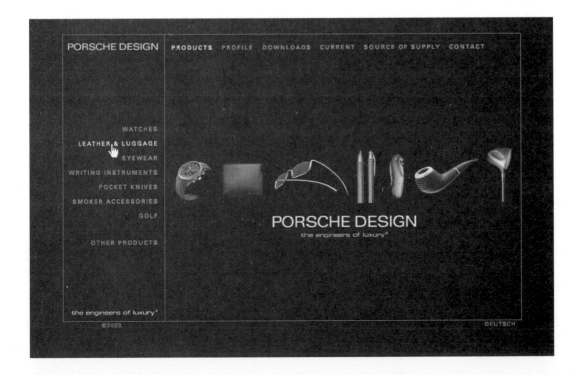

Glow is useful because it provides feedback to the user that the button is active and that an action will result from its being clicked. Figure 6-5 shows a very simple form of glow that is achieved by a couple of simple steps. First, the label is maintained in the same position as the normal state. Second, the appearance of upward movement is achieved by including a light-shaded, single-pixel line on the top and left sides of the pushbutton and a darker-shaded line on the bottom and right sides.

Down Pushbutton State

Most pushbuttons include a state to indicate when the button is in the process of being clicked. Often the button is made to look as if it is sinking down into its background. Such a state is called a **down state**, since the button looks as if it is being pushed down. The Macintosh reverses the button colors to show that a pushbutton is being clicked. If the button normally appears as black text on a white background, the down state shows white letters on a black background.

One of the simplest ways to show a down state is to reverse the light and dark single-pixel lines described above in the section on glow. The effect is accentuated by the fact that the button is in its glow state when it is clicked. This makes the button go directly from a raised to an inset appearance. Figure 6-5 shows this simple down effect.

In most applications, a button click is only processed when the mouse pointer remains positioned on the pushbutton when the mouse is released. This gives users a means to change their mind about clicking a button in mid-click. If the user pushes the mouse button down, then moves the pointer off the pushbutton before releasing the mouse button, then the click is not registered by the software. This can be a valuable failsafe for users.

Some applications program pushbuttons to remain in the down state to indicate that the option controlled by that pushbutton is activated or in effect. For example, when a Microsoft Word user is typing text with bold turned on, the Bold button is displayed in its down state. To cancel the option, the user clicks the Bold button again. In some applications, the user clicks a different button in the same group to cancel the previous option and select a new one. When operating in this manner, the pushbuttons are operating like radio buttons, described below.

Inactive or Unavailable Pushbutton State

The **inactive** or **unavailable pushbutton state** lowers the contrast between the label and the button face color to make it look dim. Such a button is understood to be unavailable for clicking. Figure 6-5 shows the inactive state.

As noted previously, it may not be obvious to users how to make an unavailable button available. For this reason, it is often better to remove an unavailable button rather than showing its inactive state.

Menu Buttons

Notice that the Back and Forward buttons in Figure 6-5 contain a small black triangle. This symbol indicates that these are menu buttons. When the user clicks a menu button, it remains in its down state while the menu is displayed. When the menu is removed, either because the user made a selection or cancelled the menu by clicking outside it, the button returns to its normal state.

Button Labels

Deciding on the label for a pushbutton requires careful thought. The idea is to capture the essence of the pushbutton's function within a word or two. Most usability experts list three as the maximum number of words in a pushbutton label. Although this is a good guideline to follow, avoid sacrificing usability to brevity. For example, it makes no sense to shorten the label "Create Schedule" to "Create" if there are other items besides schedules that could be created in the current context.

If a pushbutton's function cannot be described within a few words, consider adding explanatory text and keeping the pushbutton label short. In the above example, the functions could be grouped and given the title "Schedule Functions." The schedule functions could include buttons labeled "Create," "Modify," and "Delete." Another option when labels must be long to clarify meaning is to switch to a different control, such as a hypertext link.

Whenever possible, use verbs as pushbutton labels. "Create Schedule" is better than "Schedule." Notice the ambiguity in the label "Schedule." It can be construed to mean, "Add something to a schedule," as in "Schedule a meeting for this Friday." It can also be taken as a noun, as in "Show me the current schedule." Such ambiguity often confuses users, yet designers cannot always predict which labels will cause users problems. That is why user testing is so important to the design process.

Capitalize each word of the button label except conjunctions (e.g., *and*), articles (e.g., *the, a, an*) and prepositions of less than three letters (e.g., *in, to*).

Radio Buttons

Radio buttons, sometimes called **option buttons**, are small circular buttons that are displayed in small groups of between two and approximately seven. The selected radio button has a filled-in dot in the middle. They are normally labeled, with the label often positioned to the right of the button. Figure 6-7 shows a group of radio buttons.

If you are curious as to why the name *radio button* was chosen for these controls, chances are you haven't driven a car of the 1950s or 1960s. The

Select a shirt color:
○ Black
○ White
● Red
○ Blue
○ Green
○ Yellow

figure | 6-7 |

Radio buttons show all of the available choices and allow a single selection.

radios in these cars provided access to preset stations via a row of mechanical buttons. When you pushed one of the buttons, it remained in the "pushed in" position, and any button that was already pushed in would be forced back out. In this way, only one button at a time could be pushed in. This makes sense, since only one radio station at a time can be selected.

Radio buttons in software work the same way. They always appear in a group, and there can only be one selected in the group at a time. Clicking a different radio button deselects the currently selected button and selects the one that was clicked. To deselect a radio button, you must select a different button in the group, since radio buttons do not operate as toggles. A group of radio buttons may be displayed without any of them being selected initially. Radio buttons can also be shown in an unavailable state.

When to Use Radio Buttons

Use a group of radio buttons when there are mutually exclusive options or values, of which the user must select one. Some common examples include when users must select one of several:

- Shipping methods (UPS Ground, 2nd Day Air, Next Day)
- Payment options (Visa, MasterCard, American Express)
- Product colors or styles
- Software installation options
- Difficulty levels

When Not to Use Radio Buttons

Don't use radio buttons for navigation. In general, don't use a radio button to initiate an action. To initiate an action, use a control such as a pushbutton. Often radio buttons will appear on a page or screen that includes a pushbutton for submitting or saving the options specified with the radio buttons and other controls.

I believe there are exceptions to this rule, however. For example, if a software program does not include a separate options screen, you may need to include a control for, say, switching between English and Spanish text on an opening screen such as the splash screen. (The splash screen is the opening screen of many multimedia software programs that includes the name of the program, the company that owns it, etc.)

| TIP |

Although you can select a radio button by clicking either its small circle or its larger label, many users don't realize this and aim for the smaller target.

Including these two language options as radio buttons shows the current language selection and allows the user to switch languages. As soon as the user clicks, the text changes to the selected language, so the radio button is initiating an action. I could substitute two pushbuttons instead, but this doesn't do as efficient a job as radio buttons of indicating both the currently selected and optional states.

In general, don't use radio buttons when there are more than about eight choices in a group. It is difficult to scan a large group of radio buttons quickly. In such cases, use a different control such as a listbox, discussed later in this chapter.

Labeling Radio Buttons

Create radio button labels using sentence-style capitalization. Capitalize the first letter of the first word and any proper nouns. Use only as many words as necessary to enable users to understand the choices. Don't use punctuation at the end of a label, except when it leads to another control, as described below.

Avoid repeating words across choices. Instead, pull out the repeated words, and include them once as text above the radio buttons. End this text with a colon. For example, Figure 6-8 shows two different ways to label the same group of radio buttons. Notice how much easier it is to quickly understand the options when the labels do not repeat words.

As mentioned above, a radio button can be used to activate another control, serving as the label for that control. Figure 6-9 shows an example of this.

Sometimes radio buttons are used to enable users to select one of a range of numeric values. For example, a survey might ask users to rate the importance of a given feature, without specifying numbers. Figure 6-10 shows how such a scale can be labeled effectively using a minimum of labels.

Instead of this:

Select a shipping method:
- ○ Ship via ground
- ○ Ship via 2nd-day air
- ● Ship via next-day air

Do this:

Ship via:
- ○ Ground
- ○ 2nd-day air
- ● Next-day air

figure | 6-8 |

Take care to minimize the number of words while keeping the meaning of each choice clear.

Embroider initials on sleeve cuff?
- ○ Yes, embroider these initials: [_____]
- ○ No initials

figure | 6-9 |

A radio button label can be used to label a separate control, such as an editable text box.

How important are these to you?

	Not Important						Very Important	
Product Price:	○	○	○	○	○	○	○	○
Product Quality:	○	○	○	○	○	○	○	○
Product Selection:	○	○	○	○	○	○	○	○
Friendly Return Policy:	○	○	○	○	○	○	○	○
Knowledgeable Staff:	○	○	○	○	○	○	○	○

figure | 6-10 |

Although this design uses a minimum of labels, it is relatively simple to understand and use.

Check Boxes

A **check box** is used to turn a specific option off or on. Check boxes consist of a small square and a label to the right of the square. In its *selected* or *on* state, the square includes a check-mark or X. In its *unselected* or *off* state, the square is empty. You can select or deselect a check box by clicking either the small square or the label, similar to radio buttons.

Which systems will you use to deliver your software?
Select all that apply.

- ☑ Macintosh
- ☐ Windows version 3
- ☑ Windows 95/98/2000
- ☑ Windows NT
- ☑ Windows XP
- ☐ UNIX/Linux

figure | **6-11** |

Adding the instruction, "Select all that apply," helps the user understand that he can select more than one check box.

figure | **6-12** |

Use a check box when the effect of deselecting the box is clear. If the result is ambiguous, as in the example on the left, use radio buttons instead.

When to Use Check Boxes

Use a check box when you have an option or value that must be set on or off independent of any other option or value. Figure 6-11 shows a set of check boxes.

Use check boxes when there are between one and approximately eight options. If the number of check boxes in a group will exceed this number, use another control, such as a multiple-selection list box, discussed later in this chapter.

When Not to Use Check Boxes

Like radio buttons, check boxes should never be used to initiate an action such as navigating to a new page or screen, but to set options or values. Use a different control, such as a pushbutton, for navigation or other actions.

Don't use a check box unless the opposite meaning of the check box label is clear. Figure 6-12 shows an example of a misuse of a check box and an improved design using a different control.

Labeling Check Boxes

Label check boxes similar to radio button labels. Use sentence-style capitalization, and do not include punctuation unless the check box activates a separate control and serves as a label for that control. Whenever possible, try to fit the check box label on a single line. If the label cannot fit on one line, then align the square with the top line of text.

Text Fields

There are several different types of **text fields** that designers can use for either displaying text or receiving text that the user types or pastes. **Text boxes** are for displaying text that the user can select for copying and pasting to another location. They are also used for receiving text that the user provides. **Rich-text boxes** are for receiving user-provided text that can have special emphasis such as bolding, underline, and italics. **Static text fields** are for displaying non-editable, non-selectable text such as that used for titles, labels, and instructions.

On the Web, nearly any text that is not a graphic image can be selected and copied to the clipboard. Static text fields apply to software created for non-Web applications. The Web also sets some of its own rules for displaying text. For example, any text displayed in a scrolling text box is automatically editable. In Windows and Macintosh applications, designers can specify whether or not a scrolling text box should be editable or not. Web designers can simulate a non-editable scrolling text box by creating a frame.

Text Boxes

A text box, also called an **edit control**, has two major modes of operation. It can be configured to enable the user to enter or edit one or more lines of text. It can also be configured to display text that the user can select but not edit. A text box's shape is rectangular. The background color of the text box reflects whether its text can or cannot be edited. Editable text is usually displayed on a light-colored background such as white, and the box itself is given an *inset* appearance, meaning it looks like it is sunken into the background. It can be configured to display or accept a single line of text or multiple lines, as shown in Figure 6-13.

When configured to support multiple-line user input, a text box supports **word wrap**, meaning long lines are automatically broken at word boundaries, and the user can continue to type without pressing the Enter key to break lines.

Text is entered into an editable text box by typing or pasting. When editing text, characters are either inserted in front of the character at the cursor position, or they overwrite existing characters, depending on whether the keyboard is in insert or overwrite mode. Text boxes can include vertical and horizontal scroll bars. In general, avoid horizontally scrolling text, as it is difficult for users to

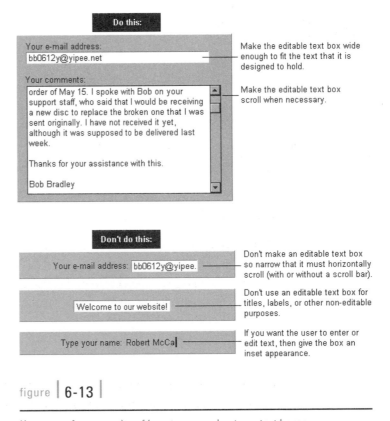

figure | **6-13** |

Here are a few examples of how to use and not use text boxes.

| **TIP** |

Some websites and software programs configure single-line text boxes to store more text than is visible at one time. To scroll the hidden portion of the text into view, the user must use the left and right arrow keys or other cursor-control keys. Try to avoid using a text box in this manner. Either make the text box wide enough to handle the longest possible entry, or increase the vertical size of the box and support more than one line of text.

| **TIP** |

It is better to have users select a choice from a list than to type an entry, since users often make typographical errors when typing. As previously mentioned, a possible exception to this is U.S. state abbreviations, where the user only has two characters to type.

operate the scrollbar controls while trying to read the text. Note that all scrolling text boxes on the Web are editable. Currently, the only way to create a non-editable scrolling text area is by using frames.

WHEN TO USE A TEXT BOX Use a text box when you need the user to supply information for the software to process. Also use it when you have information to display that you would like the user to be able to select for copying to a different location or program.

Examples of when to use text boxes for accepting text entry include when requesting:

- Personal information, such as the user's name or e-mail address
- The name of a new file or other entity that the system saves
- A search word or string
- User comments
- A response box for a short-answer question or essay question

WHEN NOT TO USE A TEXT BOX Don't use an editable text box to display a label or other static text. *Static* text refers to text that is not editable, but is simply displayed for information purposes. When websites or software display labels or other static information in editable text boxes, users get confused because they can change text that is clearly not intended to be editable. It is like being able to change the street name on a corner street sign—even if you could do it, no good would come of it.

Don't use standard text boxes when you want users to be able to include emphasis such as bold, underline, or italics in the text they type. When you want users to be able to use these special text-editing features, use a rich-text box instead.

Rich-Text Boxes

Rich-text boxes include all of the features of standard text boxes, and they support special text attributes such as font, font size, bold, italic, underline, and color. Rich-text boxes also support paragraph formatting options such as indenting, tabs, alignment, and numbering.

Static Text Fields

Use static text fields for displaying non-editable, nonselectable text such as titles and labels in non-Web Windows or Macintosh software. In most cases, using a non-editable text box can be used instead of a static text field, unless you specifically want to prevent users from selecting and copying the text.

Hypertext

Hypertext is a special form of text used to connect the user to documents, Web pages, or other linked content. Words, phrases, or passages can be designated as hypertext and displayed as underlined text. Hypertext is explored further in Chapter 7.

List Boxes

There are a number of variations of **list box** controls, each appropriate to specific situations. Figure 6-14 shows some of the different list box types. We'll start by describing the overall features of the control, then explore the variations.

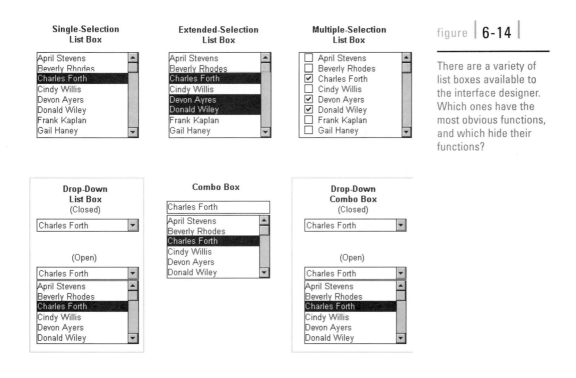

figure | 6-14 |

There are a variety of list boxes available to the interface designer. Which ones have the most obvious functions, and which hide their functions?

List boxes present a list of related options to the user. The user selects one or more choices from the list. List boxes can be configured to display one, some, or all of their choices at a time. If there are more options than can be displayed in the available space, the list box can scroll vertically. If the list is not wide enough to display the longest entries, you can:

- **Truncate** (cut off) the part of entries that are longer than the available width
- Indicate each shortened entry using an ellipsis (…) in place of the missing text, then create tooltips to show the full text
- Enable the list box to horizontally scroll

Of these options, the second one—replacing part of the entry text with ellipses and using tooltips to show the full text—makes the most sense. Truncating entries may eliminate information required to make a choice, and horizontal scrolling should be avoided whenever possible due to usability problems. When using ellipses, show as much of the useful part of the entry name as possible, substituting ellipses for the least important information.

For example, a list of company names could include an ellipsis at the end, since in most cases the beginning part of the company name is sufficient to identify it. A list of path names, such as c:\program files\macromedia\director\director.exe, might include ellipses in the middle of the path, since that portion of the path may not be necessary to identify each entry.

Selecting and deselecting items in a list box depends on which control variation is used and is covered below. List boxes can also support advanced features, such as dragging an entry from one list box to another, or copying and pasting entries. Such advanced operations are relatively rarely implemented.

When list boxes are used for navigation, some designers include a pushbutton labeled "Go" to the right of the box. In effect, the pushbutton enables users to confirm their selection. Otherwise, a user who accidentally clicks the wrong choice will have to return to the current page or screen to reselect the intended choice. In such applications, double-clicking a choice is the same as single-clicking it and clicking the "Go" button.

Labeling List Boxes

Unlike radio buttons and check boxes, list boxes do not display labels of their own. You can include a label, however, by adding a text field above the list box. Use this text field to include a description of the items in the list and instructions for selecting entries in the list. Use the word *select* to describe choosing an item from a list box.

Single-Selection List Box

figure | 6-15 |

The single-selection list box makes it clear that there are a group of options from which to choose. Selecting a choice deselects the currently selected choice. Include a <None> option if you want to enable users to select none of the choices.

Single-Selection List Boxes

As its name suggests, use a **single-selection list box** when you want to present a list of related options of which the user can select just one. This is one of the most valuable controls for showing multiple entries, because users generally have no difficulty understanding that they must choose one of the options presented. Make the box tall enough to show at least three to eight choices. Naturally, the more entries you show at once, the less the user has to scroll to see the remaining choices. Figure 6-15 shows a typical scrolling single-select list box.

Notice in Figure 6-15 that the selected entry is highlighted. To deselect a choice, you must select a different choice. If you want to enable the user to select none of the entries, then you must provide a "None" option, usually as the first entry in the list.

A disadvantage of the single-select list box is that users can scroll the selected (highlighted) entry out of view, making it unclear that a selection has been made. When the control is displayed, always scroll the list so that the selected choice is visible.

List boxes support a number of keyboard commands. The user can type a character and the control will scroll to the first entry containing that character. Pressing the same character key again scrolls the list to the next entry beginning with that character. The keyboard arrow keys and other cursor-control keys can also be used to highlight entries, and pressing the Enter key selects the highlighted entry.

Extended-Selection List Box

If you want users to be able to select more than one entry in a list, then you might use an **extended-selection list box**. This type of list box looks like a single-selection list box, so users may not realize they can make multiple selections or figure out how to make such selections without explicit instructions. Although the exact keys to select multiple entries varies by operating system, the user can select a continuous block of entries or a so-called **disjoint** group of entries—those that may be scattered through the list. To select a continuous block of entries, the user clicks the first entry in the block to select it, then holds down the Shift key while clicking the last entry of the block. All of the entries from the first to the last are selected.

To select disjoint entries, the user holds down a different key (Ctrl on Windows, Command on Mac) while clicking each desired entry. Figure 6-16 shows disjointed selections in an extended-selection list box. Using either of these methods to select entries, clicking a selected entry deselects that entry.

Because of the complex key and mouse sequences needed to make multiple selections, consider using a control such as the multiple-selection list box as an alternative to the extended-selection list box.

Multiple-Selection List Box

A **multiple-selection list box** is actually a group of check boxes in a list box. Figure 6-17 shows an example of a multiple-selection list box.

The multiple-selection list box is an alternative easier to use than the extended-selection list box. The familiarity of the check box controls means the extensive instructions are usually not required to use this control. Creating a multiple-selection list box may require the work of a programmer, as it may not be available as part of the controls of some Web- or multimedia-authoring systems.

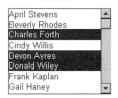

figure | **6-16** |

Depending on the audience, the extended-selection list box may require fairly extensive instructional text to inform users how to make multiple selections.

figure | **6-17** |

Although it requires more programming to create, the multiple-selection list box accomplishes a similar result to the extended-selection list box, but requires fewer instructions.

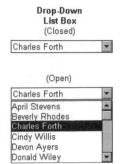

figure | **6-18** |

Users sometimes ignore drop-down list boxes, not recognizing that they contain hidden options. This is especially true on busy pages or screens, where the list boxes can get lost in the clutter.

Drop-Down List Box

The **drop-down list box** works similarly to the single-selection list box, except that it only displays the currently selected entry until "opened" by the user. Figure 6-18 shows both the closed and open states of the drop-down list box.

The main advantage of this control is that it requires very little vertical space, since it normally shows just the selected entry. Its main disadvantage is that users don't always realize that it contains additional choices. If you use a wheel mouse, you have probably come across another disadvantage of drop-down menus. Sometimes you roll the mouse wheel downward intending to scroll towards the bottom of a Web page, only to discover that the focus was on a drop-down list and that you are scrolling different values into that control instead.

One solution to this problem is for designers to call for this control only when it is obvious from its context that additional choices exist. An example that may come quickly to mind is to use it for displaying the abbreviations of the fifty U.S. states, but usability studies have shown that people can type a two-character abbreviation into a text box much faster than they can select it from a list. If the user types the abbreviation, the software must still check the value to determine if it is a valid state abbreviation. It may be difficult to detect whether or not the user has typed in a valid but unintended abbreviation, such as AK instead of AR for Arkansas without verifying it against the zip code entered (assuming the user types the correct zip code!).

A better example of when a drop-down list might be appropriate might be for displaying a list of courtesy titles, such as Mr., Mrs., Miss, Ms., and Dr., that a user enters when filling in a form. With increased use and familiarity, perhaps we can call for this control in more situations. Until then, the single-select list box, which reveals some or all of its entries, is the preferred choice.

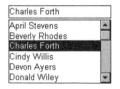

figure | **6-19** |

Users often don't realize they can type text in the combo box's text box.

Combo Box

A **combo box** contains both a text box and a single-selection list box. The user can either select an entry from the list box or type the name of an entry into the text box. As characters are typed, the list box scrolls to the nearest matching entry. Selecting an entry copies its name to the text box. Figure 6-19 shows a combo box with the currently selected entry.

When to Use a Combo Box

One advantage of a combo box is that it clearly displays the currently selected entry. The link between the text box and the list means that users can type characters to make a selection without removing their hands from the keyboard to use the mouse. Without instructions to this effect, though, users may not realize that this capability exists and will select from the list instead.

Drop-Down Combo Box

A variation of the combo box is the **drop-down combo box**, shown in Figure 6-20.

This control looks like a drop-down list. The user must click the menu button to display the list. Once displayed, the control operates like the standard combo box. Users can select from the list or type characters to position the list to a particular entry.

The drop-down combo box saves space by only displaying the currently selected entry. Like the drop-down list, users may not realize that the list contains entries that are hidden from view until the user clicks the menu button.

Table 6-1 compares the features of the various list controls.

figure | **6-20** |

A drop-down combo box has the same liabilities as the drop-down list box, with even more hidden functionality.

table | **6-1** | Here is a summary of the capabilities of the various list boxes.

List Control	Contents Visible Without Clicking?	Can User Select More Than One Entry?	User Selects Entry By:	Shows Selection By:
Single-Selection List Box	Yes	No	Clicking	Highlight
Extended-Selection List Box	Yes	Yes	Clicking (use key sequence and click for extending selection)	Highlight
Multiple-Selection List Box	Yes	Yes	Clicking its check box	Mark in check box
Drop-Down List Box	No; must click menu button	No	Clicking	Displaying as only visible entry
Combo Box	Yes	No	Clicking or typing	Displaying in text field
Drop-Down Combo Box	No; must click menu button or type	No	Clicking or typing visible entry	Displaying as only

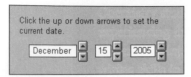

Click the up or down arrows to set the current date.

December 15 2005

figure | 6-21 |

Spinners make this date control relatively easy to figure out. Note that drop-down lists for each of the three fields may allow quicker entry. The up and down arrow buttons may be too small to be easily clicked by some users.

| TIP |

The Microsoft Windows User Experience recommends wrapping the values at either end of the spin box. This means that if the range of values is 0 to 9, then clicking the up button when 9 is displayed rolls the display to 0. Likewise, clicking the down arrow when 0 is displayed rolls the display to 9. I prefer to disable the up button when the highest value is displayed and the down button when the lowest value is displayed. This allows a user who wants to display a 9 to simply click and hold the up button until 9 is reached and the up button is disabled. Of course, if the values wrap, then a user can click the down button once from 0 to display 9, but most users would not guess that such capability exists.

Spin Boxes

A **spin box** is used to allow users to select one of a range of continuous values. The spin box control usually consists of an editable text box and a set of buttons known as an *up-down* control. The value in the box increases as the user clicks the up button and decreases as she clicks the down button. Alternatively, the user can type a value directly into the box. Figure 6-21 shows three spin boxes used to enter the month, day, and year of a date.

The spin control can be configured with an uneditable text box. When so configured, the user must use the up and down buttons to enter the desired value. If the range of possible values is large, it can be annoying to wait until the desired value is displayed. It is generally better to use the editable text box, then check that a user-entered value is valid and within the correct range.

Sliders

A **slider**, shown in Figure 6-22, allows users to select one of a range of values by dragging an indicator along a horizontal or vertical line.

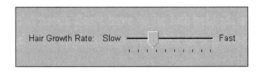

Hair Growth Rate: Slow ———— Fast

figure | 6-22 |

Use the slider control when you want users to be able to access a continuous range of values.

The slider control fits best when you want users to be able to access a continuous range of values. For example, you could use a group of six radio buttons, labeled 0 to 5, to control volume. With so few selectable values, however, it is unlikely that the user would find the exact desired level. You could add more radio buttons representing finer volume gradations, but at too high a screen real estate cost. The slider control ensures that users can select just the setting they want.

Tab Controls

Tabs are a useful means of organizing content in a website or software program. They work just like their real-life counterparts—serving as an easily accessible means of categorizing and storing controls or content. Figure 6-23 shows a **tab control** typical of many applications.

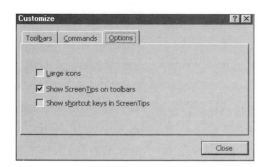

figure | 6-23 |

The tab control effectively organizes content into discrete groups.

Do not use a slider to provide access to a multipage document or for other navigation purposes. The slider does not offer the precision needed for such navigation.

Tabs are grouped in one or more rows, although we've mentioned earlier that multiple rows of tabs are to be avoided. A label—almost always a text label—identifies each tab. Clicking a tab makes it the frontmost tab and displays its contents.

Use the word *click* to describe to a user how to select a tab. For example, "If you want to change your account settings, click the Accounts tab."

The use of tabs is explored further in Chapter 7.

Tree Controls

A **tree control**, also known as an **outline control**, is an efficient, specialized type of menu system that organizes items using an outline format. Because it organizes hierarchies (such as users/groups/departments/company) so well, a tree control is especially useful in administrative applications. The administrator in charge of such an application is often an experienced user who is familiar with this type of control.

Typically the user selects the desired item by clicking it, which displays choices appropriate to that item's level. Each level of the outline can be collapsed to hide its subitems or expanded to show them by clicking a small icon adjacent to the item. Figure 6-24 shows an outline control used to organize a school hierarchy.

If not for the tree control, then accessing all of Figure 6-24's levels could require a series of drop-down list boxes or similar controls. The user would first select a school from a list, which would display a list of the classes in that school. After selecting a class, the user would see a list of students in that class. Selecting a student would display her assignment lists, which would, in turn, display the assignments in that list.

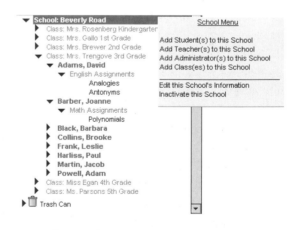

figure | 6-24 |

The tree control organizes large hierarchies of information. The menu that is displayed when the user clicks an option contains only the choices that make sense for that level of the hierarchy.

The tree control displays the whole structure at once. It reduces the number of clicks and presentation of new lists. Instead of repeatedly scrolling, selecting, then waiting for the resulting list to be displayed, the user simply opens an item to see its contents. Because new lists don't have to be generated, this can significantly reduce the delays experienced by Web users, especially those connected via dial-up. Those who are interested can find commercially available tree controls for many operating systems and authoring environments.

Tree controls can confuse inexperienced users for several reasons. First, although most people are familiar with an outline format, users who aren't familiar with the tree control may not realize that there can be hidden subitems within an item. Second, the functions associated with each item are often accessible only by a right mouse click on Windows systems. Once users are taught how the control works, they can take advantage of its power, but they may require training to do so.

Creating an effective user interface means combining the tools we have explored in this chapter in efficient, easy-to-understand ways. With practice and experience, you will gain confidence in your ability to select the correct combination tools for any design challenge you face. In Chapter 7, we will investigate the role that controls such as these play in the design and creation of effective navigation.

SUMMARY OF KEY POINTS

- Cascading menus can provide access to a large number of items, but their design can make them difficult to use.

- When creating pushbutton labels, choose labels that are brief, yet self-explanatory.

- Use radio buttons when users can only select one of a group of choices. Use check boxes if users can select more than one choice in a group.

- Avoid requiring users to horizontally scroll text, as it makes reading the text very difficult.

- There are many varieties of list boxes. Selecting which type to use depends on such factors as the number of items in the list, the number of items to display at once, whether users can select one or multiple items, and whether users can type the name of an entry.

- Tab controls are useful for organizing categories of content and controls. Be sure that the categories are peers of one another.

- Tree controls can manage large numbers of items in an outline format. They work best with experienced users.

in review

1. What is the difference between an access key and a shortcut key?

2. What type of menu item is dependent on the settings of surrounding menu items?

3. Under what conditions is it acceptable to include a radio button without a label?

4. What are the names of the four common button states, and what is each one's purpose?

5. Which two types of list boxes can look identical in both their closed and open states? What is it about their operation that distinguishes one from the other?

6. What is the major advantage and disadvantage of a tree control?

exercise

1. You are working on a website for a store that sells musical instruments. Your client offers five types of instruments (brass, woodwinds, percussion, strings, and electronics). Each of these types includes between five and 10 instruments. Sketch at least two different versions of a menu structure that allows users to select instruments of each type. Describe the advantages and disadvantages of each menu type.

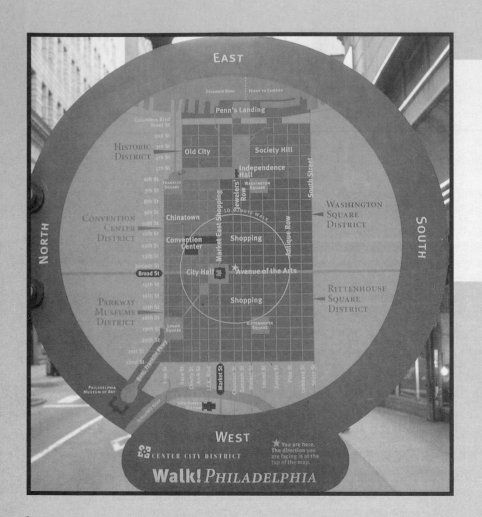

designing usable navigation

7

objectives

Examine the elements of navigation

Analyze various types of navigational systems, including menus, tabs, site maps, categories, and search

Compare good and bad menu and tab designs

Analyze navigational elements such as menus, breadcrumb trails, links, and image maps

Examine advanced search systems

Examine specialized navigation design

introduction

Navigation is the means by which a website or multimedia software program provides access to its content—the features, functions, and information that are its reason for being. As we've noted, the ease with which a user can navigate a software program or website can be as important to its success as the quality of its content. The best navigation systems are nearly invisible, freeing users to focus on the content rather than its means of access. This chapter will help you design navigation systems that meet this standard.

The British architect Christopher Wren (1632–1723) was one of the best known designers of college campuses of his day. When the campus buildings were completed, Sir Christopher would delay the construction of formal walkways for a year. He let the students create their own natural paths in the dirt as they moved from one building to another. Although this plan was likely to cause muddy floors, it succeeded in showing exactly where the walkways needed to be constructed. The most heavily traveled paths were built wider than the less-traveled ones. Wren's approach is a fine example of designing to your users' needs.

ELEMENTS OF NAVIGATION

Discussions of software navigation systems often use the metaphor of a city's street system, since they confront many of the same issues. We travel on streets to arrive at specific destinations, or we ride with no specific end in mind, just to enjoy the adventure. Likewise, sometimes we seek specific information on a website, and other times we just want to browse and take in the sights. In unfamiliar cities, we depend on signs to tell us where we are and how to get to where we want to go. In software, button labels, links, and other interface elements are the signs that help us find our destination.

Like software and websites, when there is only one road, it is easy to find your way, but the trip may take a long time and take you out of your way. Crossroads and shortcuts offer choices that can make it easier to get from place to place, but as the number of available paths increases, so does the possibility of getting lost. We depend on signs to help us find our way, but, as Figure 7-1 shows, too many signs can be as confusing as no signs at all. Similarly, too many choices presented without careful thought may render a website or software product impassable.

figure | 7-1 |

Too many signs can be more confusing than too few signs. Photo by the author.

Rethinking Navigation

In the 1700s, smart city planners, such as Benjamin Franklin, began laying out cities in a predictable grid pattern for ease of use. This was in contrast to cities such as Paris, whose streets are a maze of seemingly random angles, multistreet intersections, and dead ends. Although many would argue that the complexity of Paris's streets adds significantly to its interest and appeal, few would argue that it is an easy city for visitors to navigate.

Naming parallel streets with consecutive numbers and cross streets with consecutive letters further enhances the ease of use of the grid, making it simple to get from any corner to any other corner without extensive signs or directions. As website and software designers, we want to give our users a similar advantage—to access any part of the site or software from any other point with a minimum of signs or directions and in the fewest number of clicks or keystrokes possible.

Keep in mind that city streets are not the only metaphor used to describe navigation. Other metaphors include:

- Turning pages in a book
- Shopping in the aisles of a store
- Instantly teletransporting to any destination
- Being brought goodies by a servant or granted wishes by a genie
- Switching channels on a television set
- Dropping breadcrumbs like Hansel and Gretel did to find their way home
- Traveling in an elevator to different floors in an infinitely high building
- Selecting items from a menu in a restaurant
- Traveling in a time machine
- Searching for gold in river gravel

Regardless of the metaphor used to describe it, navigation can be boiled down to:

- Signs that identify where we are
- Signs that tell us what is available
- Controls that initiate actions

figure | 7-2 |

Use titles to identify pages or screens and help orient users.

Signs That Identify Where We Are

Users depend on signs to identify the current screen or function in software or a website. Figure 7-2 shows examples of these signs, which include screen or page titles and title bars. They help orient users, confirming that they have reached the proper destination or made the intended selection. Include these titles whenever possible, and position them prominently (normally near the top of the screen or page), so that users can see them easily.

A Step in the Right Direction

When searching for a store in an unfamiliar mall, many of us head directly for the mall directory. With just two pieces of information—our current location and the location of our target store—we can relatively easily find our way to any store. As a convenience, the map displays our current location, usually marked, "You are here."

If we are lost on an unfamiliar road or highway and are trying to find our way using a map, we need to look for the name of the road we are on and the names of two cross streets in the order that we crossed them. These two sequential crossroads enable us to locate our present location and the direction we are heading. The mall directory does not require us to know which direction we are heading because it is oriented to match the direction we are facing in relationship to the layout of the mall. Orienting the directory map according to the user's point of view is a significant usability enhancement. The mall is not the only place you can find such smart maps.

In 1996 and 1997, the city of Philadelphia installed dozens of disk-shaped maps mounted on poles throughout the downtown area. The maps, known collectively as Walk!Philadelphia, help visitors easily find the city's many historical sites and tourist attractions. The key to the system's success is that, like the mall directory, each map is oriented to match the viewpoint of the pedestrian. Whichever direction you are facing appears at the top of the map. Figure 7-3 shows one of the Walk!Philadelphia maps, designed by Joel Katz Design Associates.

figure | 7-3 |

Orienting these city maps in the direction the reader is facing greatly increases their effectiveness. Photo by the author.

Signs That Tell Us What Is Available

Signs that tell us what is available include pushbutton labels, the text of hyperlinks, and other labels that give clues about what will happen when we activate a control. These signs are like the destination signs on the front of buses that help passengers identify the correct bus.

We depend on the wording of labels and other signs to help us make correct choices, but some labels, such as those on pushbuttons, have very few words with which to get their message across. Devices such as **tooltips**, the small text boxes that are displayed when we roll over specific controls or images, enable designers to give users more information about the effects of activating a control. When tooltips are used appropriately, they enhance usability. Some websites, however, either don't use them to full advantage or allow them to detract from usability. Figure 7-4 shows an example of a tooltip that partially obscures the same text that is already displayed on the page. This tooltip simply adds visual clutter to the screen.

In some Web pages and software programs, labels are "dimmed" by reducing the contrast between the text and its background to indicate that the associated control cannot currently be selected. Since it is not always apparent why the control has been inactivated, this can cause frustration among users. In general, it is better to completely remove a control that cannot be accessed rather than display it in a dimmed state. An exception to this is application software dialog boxes, where unavailable controls are usually included in their unavailable state by convention.

Controls That Initiate Actions

Controls are the pushbuttons, links, list boxes, and other elements that we explored in the previous chapter. As we learned, each has its own characteristics, strengths, and weaknesses, and each can be an effective component of navigation when used appropriately. When used incorrectly, they confound and annoy users.

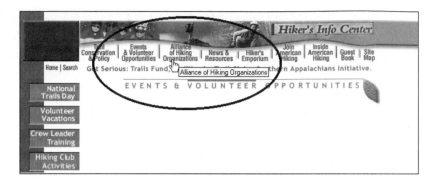

figure | **7-4** |

This tooltip repeats information already provided and obstructs useful information. Tooltips, when used, should provide additional information.

| **TIP** |

Whenever possible, try to match the screen or page title with the label on the control that takes you there. For example, if a pushbutton label says "Today's Specials," then try to include this title in the page that is displayed when this control is activated.

| **TIP** |

Never allow a user to make a selection, click a button, or otherwise activate a control if it doesn't make sense for the user to do it. Nothing is more frustrating than a system that allows you to activate a control, then displays a message telling you that you can't do that here.

COMMON NAVIGATIONAL SYSTEMS AND ELEMENTS

The purpose of navigation is to allow us to access what we want in as few clicks or steps as possible. Some designers live by the rule that a user must be able to reach the desired destination in three clicks or less. Although recent studies dispute that users will abandon a site or software that violates this rule, efforts by designers to reduce clicks or steps are nonetheless worthwhile and essential.

Methods of Organization

There are many different ways to organize the content on a website or multimedia software program. Applications such as e-commerce sites must organize many individual items, yet allow very quick access to those items using a variety of criteria.

Two common means of providing access to lots of content is by organizing that content into categories and by providing a search function. Studies of online shoppers performed by groups such as User Interface Engineering show that most site visitors intending to make purchases prefer using categories rather than search to find items. Some shoppers ignore the search function entirely or only resort to using search when they can't find the desired item by navigating the categories.

Categories

The categories used to organize items must be well thought out and consider both the items and the audience. If our e-commerce site offers clothing, for example, obvious major categories might include Women's, Men's, Girls', and Boys'. When a user selects a major category, the subcategory items for that category are displayed. Women's clothing could include subcategories for blouses, dresses, jeans, shorts, swimwear, lingerie, t-shirts, etc. Selecting a subcategory displays the appropriate items in the center of the page in what is often referred to as a **product gallery**.

We must also anticipate other means by which shoppers might search for items. Using our example, other possible clothing subcategories may include:

• Clothes by a particular designer or label

• Clothing for a particular body type

• Clothing for petite, tall, or other hard-to-fit sizes

• Sale or close-out items

• Best sellers

• Clothing especially suited as gifts

• New arrivals

Providing different categories to access content provides better service to users. If I know I want to find a shirt by Ralph Lauren, why make me look through shirts by many other designers? On the other hand, vendors don't want to miss the opportunity to sell related items. If I like a particular shirt, maybe I'll also purchase some khaki pants to go along with it.

I prefer making both the major categories (Women's, Men's, Girls' and Boys' in our example) and subcategories (blouses, dresses, jeans, shorts, etc.) persist throughout the site. This means that these menus are displayed in the same location on every page. When a new major category is selected, then the subcategories for that category replace those of the previously displayed category. This consistent placement and universal access allows users to instantly select a different major category or subcategory without having to search for the appropriate menu.

Sometimes one of the subcategories requires further classification. For example, the client may want to break down jeans into loose fit, classic fit, slim fit, and lo-rise. If so, then consider indenting this menu under the jeans item, like the menu shown in Figure 7-5. Don't replace the subcategory menu containing blouses, dresses, jeans, etc., with this third-level menu, though, or your users will have to hunt for the subcategories.

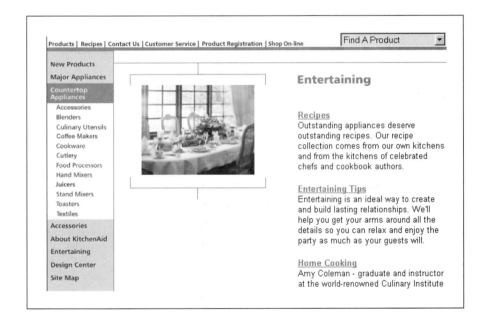

figure | **7-5** |

Here is a good alternative to the horizontal cascading menu system. It is useful when there are too many menu items to organize horizontally, and there is only one submenu per top-level menu item.

Search

Search engines such as Google are one of users' primary means of finding content on the Web. Within a particular website or multimedia software program, some users find it helpful to use a search feature to find particular content. Many users view search as a means of bypassing the site or software's navigation to get right to the sought-after content. Others use search as a last recourse—only resorting to it if they can't find what they are looking for by using the site's main navigation.

Most Web search sites allow users to conduct a precise search by including in the search field symbols such as quotation marks and plus (+) and minus (-) signs. Often logical operators such as "and" and "or" can also be included to narrow the search results. Such features are valuable to those who understand their use, but they are beyond the understanding of many users. Many sites and software can benefit from a carefully designed search system that anticipates the type of searches the users will conduct. For example, Figure 7-6 shows the search screen for a floral design software application. It allows florists to search for flowers and other plant material that meet certain criteria, such as blooming season, usage type (focal point, filler, etc.), color, and vase life.

figure | 7-6 |

Florists and floral design students can use this search function to find plant materials that meet specific criteria. The numbers next to the words flower, focal, and pink show how many entries exist for each criterion. Software copyright Delmar Learning and Dolphin Inc. Graphic design by Derek Richards.

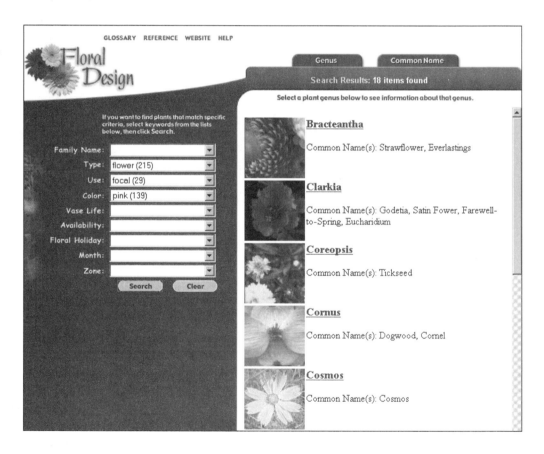

Navigational Elements

Websites and multimedia software offer a number of different common navigation systems and elements to allow users to access content. These include menus, tabs, hyperlinked text or graphics, the browser's Back and Forward buttons with their associated lists, breadcrumb trails, and image maps. This list is by no means exhaustive, as designers can invent navigational devices to fit the needs of the software or sites they create.

Arranging a complex search like a sentence increases its usability.

Menus

Nearly all websites and multimedia software use **menus** of choices to enable users to access functions and content. Besides the system-supplied menus discussed in Chapter 6, designers and developers often create their own menus, represented as a series of text items, pushbuttons, icons, hyperlinked text items, or as an image map.

MAIN MENUS Many multimedia software programs provide a top-level menu that organizes the software's content. Such a menu is commonly called the *main menu*. The means to access this menu is provided on every screen of the software. This is accomplished by repeating the menu on each screen by providing a pushbutton that, when clicked, navigates to the menu, or by displaying the menu as an overlay on the current page.

If a multimedia software menu's items contain submenus, then display each submenu on the same screen as the main menu choices. This is especially key when a pushbutton is used to access the menu. If you design the software so that selecting an item from the main menu causes a new menu to be displayed on a different screen, then you will have to provide separate buttons to access each level of the menu. The only other option in this case is to change the meaning of the menu button depending on which screen is currently displayed, which causes confusion and is never recommended.

WEBSITE NAVIGATION LAYOUT Website designers are more and more frequently adhering to conventions regarding the positioning of the main navigation menus. For example, many websites arrange the main content menu horizontally across the upper part of the page and the menu items

| TIP |

You can make a complex search function more understandable if you set it up like a sentence. For example, let's say you have been asked to design a search function that can look in different sections of a site or software program for single words, combinations of words, or exact phrases. Users must also be able to exclude certain words or phrases from consideration. Figure 7-7 shows how you might set up such a complex search.

| TIP |

One of the best ways to increase the usability of a website is to position the menus consistently on each page of the site. Because the menus persist, this gives the effect of bringing content to the user rather than making the user "go" to find the content. It's like having a pizza delivered to your house instead of having to go pick it up. The result is that users quickly gain confidence in their ability to navigate the site. They can't get lost because they never leave.

| TIP |

Whenever possible, use a label that reflects the contents of the menu, rather than the generic label "Menu." For example, if your menu contains the name of exciting sites in a city, then label the button that accesses this menu, "Places to Visit."

| TIP |

To help reorient a user who returns to a main menu screen, indicate which menu the user last selected. This is easily accomplished when there are submenus—simply display the submenu for the last selected menu item.

figure | 7-8 |

This design provides easy access to multiple categories of items, yet is easy to understand and is cleanly laid out.

for the currently selected category vertically along the left side. Such an arrangement is called an **inverted L**. Note that for languages that read right-to-left, this convention is reversed, with a category's menu arranged along the right side of the page.

Figure 7-8 shows a well-designed navigation system.

Although this particular site is an online grocer, the site's clean layout and simple structure is applicable to other applications. Notice that the site handles three levels of categories. The main categories, arranged horizontally across the top, are Fruit, Vegetables, Meat, etc. We selected Seafood, and the site indicates this by changing the label's color. Directly below the main categories are Seafood's subcategories—Fish Fillets, Fish Steaks, Whole Fish, and so on. We selected Fish Fillets, then Fillet of Sole.

Notice that we can quickly navigate to another type of fish fillet by selecting from the left, choose a different type of seafood, such as Clams or Lobster from the seafood categories, or select a different major category entirely. If only real grocery stores were laid out as cleanly!

LEFT OR RIGHT SIDE MENUS? Interestingly, one recent research study suggested that locating menus vertically along the right side of page was more usable than on the left. The rationale is that the right side of the page is also the location of the vertical scrollbar, an often-used element, so positioning the menu close to it should require users to move the mouse less.

I believe there are more arguments against orienting menus on the right side. A newly emerging reason is that many websites have begun using the right side of the page for short banner advertisements. Figure 7-9 shows an example of advertisements oriented down the right side of the screen. In response, I have begun to "tune out" this part of the page. If others behave similarly, we might mistake menus for advertisements and ignore them completely.

figure | 7-9 |

More sites are placing advertisements along the right side of the page. As users become accustomed to this convention, they might overlook menus placed near this location. Use the left side of the page instead.

There is a more important reason to consider keeping menus away from the right side of the page. Look at the menu shown in Figure 7-10a.

The menu is accessible when the user's browser is sufficiently wide. Unfortunately, users do not always maximize their browser windows. This can result in this page being displayed as shown in Figure 7-10b.

figure | 7-10a |

This right-side menu looks fine when the browser is sufficiently wide...

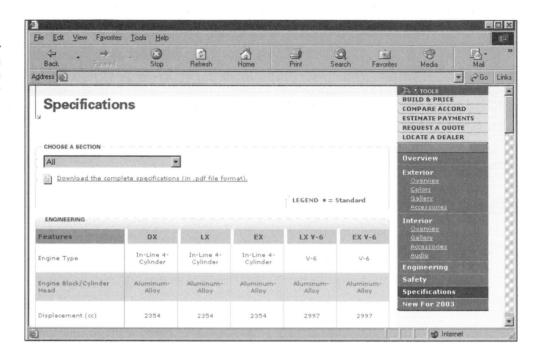

figure | 7-10b |

...but if the user's browser window is narrower, the menu is completely hidden. The horizontal scrollbar is the only indication that there is more information on this page.

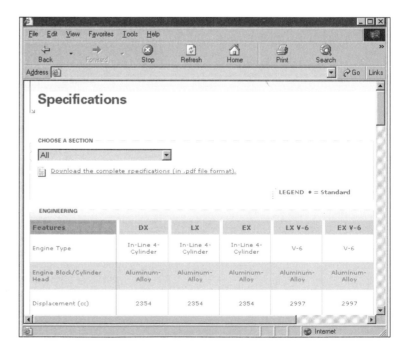

Notice that with the browser window narrowed, the menu is not visible at all. Specifying a fixed width for the page exacerbates this problem, but even if the page width adjusts with the width of the window, parts of the menu can still be cut off. For these reasons, I prefer using the left side of the page for vertically oriented menus.

For the record, here are some points supporting both points of view. Some of these points are discussed in research performed by James Kalbach and Tim Bosenick. Arguments supporting right-side menus include:

- Right-side menus are closer to the scroll bar, meaning less mouse movement.
- Most users are right handed and tend to move the cursor towards the right when idle.
- Some studies of well-designed sites show that users can use both left- and right-oriented menus equally well.
- When printing pages containing right-side menus, if the right part of the page gets cut off, it will be the menu rather than content.

Arguments supporting left side menus include:

- Left-side menus are familiar to users and have become something of a standard.
- Left-side menus are closer to the Back button, which is used very often.
- Left-side menus never get truncated if the browser window is narrowed.
- More and more users have wheel mice, which scroll the page using a wheel. This allows users to scroll from anywhere on the page, without having to access the scroll bar, negating some of the benefit of right-side menus.

CASCADING MENUS As we discussed in Chapter 6, cascading menus can be difficult to use. The menu system shown in Figure 7-11 is especially difficult for several reasons. First, because the menu items are displayed using a small font, the resulting height of each menu item is very low. Therefore, the user must carefully position the mouse on a choice, such as Motorcycles, to display the Motorcycles menu.

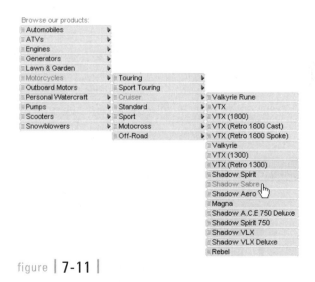

figure | **7-11** |

Using this cascading menu system requires a precision of mouse movement beyond the capabilities of many users. The small graphic to the left of each menu item adds needless clutter.

To make a choice on the Motorcycles menu, the user must *very precisely* move the mouse cursor along the Motorcycles choice, past the triangle at the end of this choice, and onto the Touring choice. If your mouse movement is anything but nearly perfectly horizontal, you will display the wrong menu. Moreover, if you accidentally move off a menu and onto the page for a fraction of a second, all menus except the first one disappear and you are back to square one.

This particular menu system could be improved somewhat by implementing two changes. First, increase the height of each menu choice to give users a larger target area. Second, if the user moves the mouse cursor off a menu, keep it displayed for several seconds before hiding it or keep it displayed until the user clicks elsewhere on the page. This will allow a user who accidentally moves the mouse cursor off the menus to simply move the mouse cursor back over the choices. Although these two suggestions will improve this menu system, it may still be difficult for some users to slide the mouse cursor horizontally to land on the next menu of choices.

Figure 7-12 shows a cascading menu that requires much less mouse precision.

This design is easier to use because the pathway to the second-level menu is the full width of the menu, rather than just its height. Note that this design requires that the top-level menu

figure | **7-12** |

Orienting the main menu items horizontally allows their submenus to be displayed directly beneath them. This is a much easier menu system to use than that shown in Figure 7-9 on page 149.

items be few enough to be arranged horizontally without scrolling. It only supports two-level menus. If a third-level menu is required, then it can be placed on the page that is displayed when the user selects from the second-level menu.

Figure 7-5 shows another type of cascading menu that works well when there is just one submenu, but when there are too many choices to arrange horizontally. This menu design eliminates the need for precise cursor movement, and there is no question which menu the submenu belongs to. The designer increased the contrast of the submenu by whitening the background to call attention to it. A bright color was chosen for the selected menu to highlight it.

As we've illustrated, some cascading menu designs are easier to use than others. In general, though, avoid the use of all cascading menus if possible. Instead, use category menus or other strategies that don't hide choices from users.

Tabs

Tabs can be a very effective means of organizing the content of a website or multimedia software program. To maximize the effectiveness of tabs, follow these guidelines:

- Use tabs to organize related items at the same peer level
- Apply the tab metaphor thoroughly and consistently
- Confine each group of tabs to one row only

USE TABS TO ORGANIZE RELATED ITEMS AT THE SAME PEER LEVEL First and foremost, tabs must adhere to the same conventions as real-life tabbed folders. This means that the items organized using tabs must be peers or siblings. If the relationship of the elements is parents and children or some other hierarchy, then choose a different control.

For example, you wouldn't have four tabbed folders in the same file labeled Cars, Boats, Buick, and Chrysler. Buick and Chrysler are siblings, and Cars and Boats are siblings, but Buick and Chrysler are children of (subsidiary to) Cars. Such a filing system is sure to cause confusion. It does make sense to have tabs labeled Cars, Boats, Trucks, and Airplanes, or Pontiac, Buick, and Oldsmobile.

APPLY THE TAB METAPHOR THOROUGHLY AND CONSISTENTLY If you are going to use the tab metaphor, then *use it*. This shows clearly that the information and controls belong to the selected tab. Figure 7-13 shows a well-executed tab system. Notice that the selected tab appears clearly in front of the others. Also notice how the background color of the tab label has been extended down into the information area. This makes it clear that this information belongs with the selected tab.

figure | 7-13 |

A well-executed tab system makes clear which tab has been selected and which content goes with that tab.

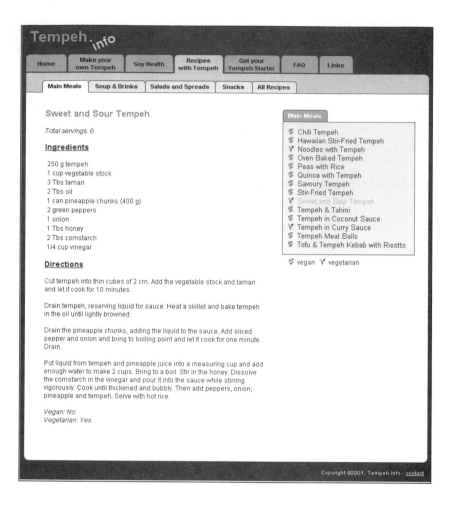

Many sites, such as the one shown in Figure 7-14, simply use graphics that look like tabs on standard pushbuttons. The visual separation caused by the line below the buttons spoils the illusion of a tabbed folder. Therefore, the potential benefit of using a tab metaphor is lost.

There are many examples of poorly designed tabs on the web. Most of the problems are caused by misusing the tab metaphor or by inconsistently implementing the tabs.

Figure 7-15, a and b, shows an example of tabs implemented inconsistently.

figure | 7-14 |

This site uses button graphics that look like tabs, but it doesn't carry the tab metaphor through the design. Users must roll the mouse cursor over each "tab" to see its label, another disadvantage.

Figure 7-15a shows what looks like a well-designed tab system. Since we are on the Home page, the Home tab is darkened and is easily distinguishable from the other tabs. The area below the Home tab is the same color as the tab, showing that its contents are part of Home. Clicking the other tabs produces a similarly satisfactory result, as each tab in turn appears to jump to the forefront and darkens to match the color beneath—until we get to the Financial tab. As Figure 7-15b shows, clicking the Financial tab displays an entirely new set of tabs. This is disorienting and reduces a user's confidence in the site.

| TIP |

If you are going to use tabs for navigation or to organize content on a website, make sure that the metaphor can be applied consistently to all of the tabs. If most of the tabs behave properly, but one or two behave differently—perhaps displaying their pages using a different style—then do not display these as tabs, but as buttons or links instead.

figure | **7-15a** |

This looks like a well-designed tab system. In most cases, clicking a tab appears to bring it to the front, and there is little doubt that the page's content belongs to that tab. Clicking the Financial tab brings an unexpected result, however, which is shown in 7-15b.

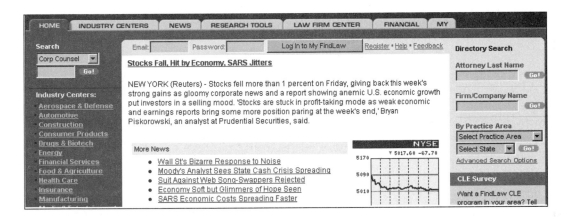

figure | **7-15b** |

Clicking the Financial tab displays an entirely new set of tabs, breaking the flow of the navigation.

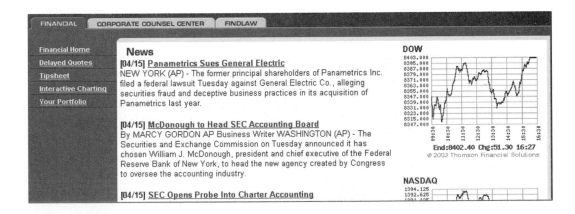

| TIP |

When providing a link to another website, it used to be common practice to display the new site in a separate browser window. This allowed the user to view the new site, then close the window to resume viewing the original site and thus maintain context. There are a couple of problems with this logic. First, it assumes that your site is the primary site, which is often not the case. Second, the opening of new browser windows may be suppressed by utility software that hinders the display of pop-up ads.

| TIP |

When a link will take the user to a different website, some usability specialists recommend including the address of the link's destination directly beneath the link itself. However, since a link may fall within the text of a paragraph, it may not be acceptable to include an address within this text. Instead, consider including the address as a tooltip that is displayed when the user rolls the mouse cursor over the link.

CONFINE TABS TO ONE ROW ONLY As we illustrated in Chapter 2, tabs only make sense when they can fit in a single row. To implement multiple rows of tabs, the selected tab's row must move down to the front so that its contents can be displayed. Users quickly lose confidence in the control when they can't depend on each tab maintaining its horizontal and vertical position.

Hypertext and Hyperlinks

Hypertext, a term coined by Ted Nelson, is one of the underlying concepts behind the Web itself. Nelson's original concept for hypertext was a much more ambitious, two-way linking system. Today, hypertext supports the fundamental idea that documents can be linked or cross-referenced to each other. We have expanded the term hypertext to hyperlink, which also encompasses images used for the purposes of connecting documents or other information.

You click on a hyperlink to explore a particular piece of information. For example, "Thomas Jefferson spent many years in Monticello, the family home he built." We have learned that clicking on Monticello is going to provide us with more information about Monticello, although the passage doesn't necessarily give us a clue to what sort of additional information we will see or hear. It could be additional text, a photograph or drawing, or a video or audio file. A new Web page or an entirely new website may be displayed, or we may remain on the current page and information may pop up on this page.

Breadcrumb Trails

In the Grimm fairy tale, as Hansel and Gretel were being led deep into the forest, Hansel left a trail of white pebbles that helped the two children later find their way home. When they were led a second time into the woods, this time with no pebbles, Hansel tried the same trick with a crumbled piece of bread. The birds ate the breadcrumbs, foiling the plan, but an important navigational aid was born.

A **breadcrumb trail** is a horizontally oriented list of text links that represents the path taken through the pages of a website to get to the currently displayed page. Each text link represents one page visited, and the text links are usually separated by a right angle bracket (>). Breadcrumb trails are usually found near the top of the page, although sites with sufficient content to require vertical scrolling sometimes include the bread-

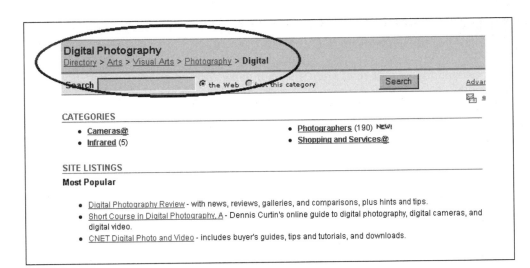

figure | 7-16 |

Breadcrumb trails
such as this one can
help users efficiently
navigate a site with
lots of levels or hier-
archies.

crumb trail at the bottom of the page as well. Figure 7-16 shows a typical breadcrumb trail.

Breadcrumb trails are most often used on hierarchically organized
sites—ones that enable users to drill down to access increasingly specific categories or levels of information. In Figure 7-16, the user first
accessed a Directory, then selected Arts, then Visual Arts, then Photography, and finally Digital Photography. Unfortunately, they are also
sometimes used on sites with poor navigation to help users find their
way "home." Never use a breadcrumb trail as a substitute for well-
designed navigation.

The power of breadcrumb trails is that they allow the user to instantly
skip to a previously accessed level. From the Digital Photography page,
I could jump directly back to the Directory, Arts, Visual Arts, or Photography page. Note that the breadcrumb trail does not just string along
the pages the user accesses, but maintains the hierarchy of the pages. For
example, if I clicked the Visual Arts link, the breadcrumb trail would
include Directory, Arts, and Visual Arts. The Photography and Digital
Photography items would be removed from the list because they are farther down the hierarchy than the currently displayed page.

A powerful, although slightly cryptic variation of the standard breadcrumb trail is to use drop-down list boxes instead of text links for one or
more steps of the trail. Figure 7-17 shows an example of this variation.

| TIP |

Although the last item in a breadcrumb trail is often bolded or otherwise highlighted to indicate
that it is the currently displayed
page, include a separate title on
the page. Don't depend on the
highlighted item of the breadcrumb trail to serve as the only
page identifier.

figure | 7-17 |

An innovative twist on a breadcrumb
trail design gives users access to all
choices at all levels of a hierarchy.
Making a selection hides all levels to
the right of the selected level.
Inexperienced users may have difficulty understanding this design.

| TIP |

Test the operation of the Back and Forward buttons from every page of the websites you design and develop to ensure that you allow visitors to return to previously viewed pages.

Each drop-down list shows all of the choices that exist at that level of the hierarchy. This is a definite advantage, since you can truly access virtually any page from any page in the site. For example, the list that contains Visual Arts might also include the items Art History, Museums, Performing Arts, and other Arts topics. Selecting one of the items in a drop-down list displays that page and deletes the items to the right of that level in the breadcrumb trail. The user is then free to select a choice at that level to continue.

Keep breadcrumb trails, including the drop-down list variation, in mind when you are creating navigation for a site that is organized by levels. We will discuss drop-down lists and other interface elements in the next chapter.

Back and Forward Buttons

When users explore hypertext links that display new pages, they rely on the browser's Back button to return them to a previously visited page. The use of this button is so common, well understood, and expected, that interface designers are including it in more and more CD-ROM software that doesn't even use a browser.

Some Web developers program this button to redisplay the current page, trapping the user. Although this trick may keep visitors at your site a little longer than they would be inclined to stay, chances are they won't knowingly return to your site.

| TIP |

If you are designing a multimedia software program that requires Previous and Next buttons to move from screen to screen of content, position these controls near the bottom right of each screen that requires them. Position them precisely in the same spot from screen to screen to allow a user to click either button repeatedly through screens without having to adjust the mouse position to find the button.

If you use the Back button to display previously visited pages, you use the Forward button to step through pages to return to the original page you were viewing when you first clicked the Back button. The operation of these buttons is more complex than their labels indicate. Move around enough through different pages and sites, and users can begin to confuse the basic concepts of back and forward using these buttons.

Part of the problem stems from the fact that the Forward button on most browsers includes a right-arrow icon. This is the same symbol that users click in many applications to proceed to the next, as yet unviewed screen. In a browser, the Forward button never displays a page you haven't already visited, but "walks you back" toward the page that was displayed when you clicked the Back button.

On most current browsers, the Back and Forward buttons also include a small arrow button that contains a sequential list of the pages you've visited. Using this feature requires that Web developers be specific in naming the various pages of a website. Sometimes the Back or Forward lists contain two or more entries in a row with exactly the same name, even though they represent different pages. This makes it difficult for users to select the specific page they want to revisit.

Site Maps

A site map is a set of links that describes a large, complex website's architecture. A site map presents the organization of the site and allows users to directly access nearly any page of the site. Although many users don't know that site maps exist for many sites, others use them as the primary means of navigating a site. Site maps are needed when the structure of the site is not easily understood using the site's primary navigation.

To be successful, a site map must be laid out simply and clearly. It should not require any special interface other than simple links. It is best if the site map is confined to the equivalent of one or two pages rather than requiring the user to scroll through page after page of links. If the site you are designing is large or complex enough to warrant a site map, consider providing links to it throughout the pages of the site.

Recently, more websites have begun formatting their site maps as alphabetic indexes, similar to those found in the back of a book. Figure 7-18 shows an example of an indexed site map.

Organizing the site map as an index may provide excellent access to the site's content, but it may require considerable effort to create the index and keep it current as the site is updated.

Site Map

A | B | C | D | E | F | G | H | I | J | K | L | M | N | O | P | Q
| R | S | T | U | V | W | X | Y | Z

A

Arts
Ask the Experts
AutoLIVE

B

Back Issues
Betsy Hiel's Middle East Reports
Monroeville News
Betting -- Sports
Blairsville Dispatch
Business Headlines
    Real Estate Headines
    Business Calendar
    Gallery
    Trib 30
Business Listings

C

Calendar, Business
Calendar, Entertainment
Calendar, Public
Calendar, Social
Chat
Chalk Talk Fan Forum
Circulation/Subscriptions
Classifieds
Club Listings
Columnists
Computer News
Cranberry News
Crossword Puzzle

figure | 7-18 |

An indexed site map may be impractical to maintain for sites whose content changes frequently.

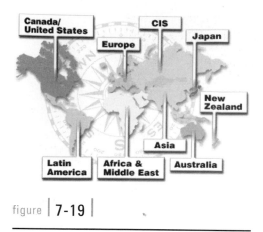

figure | **7-19** |

Use image maps to define irregularly shaped areas that can initiate actions such as displaying a new page.

Image Maps

An image map is a graphic that has a number of active areas that the user can click individually. Each of these active areas can be programmed to link to a separate page, display information, or play an audio or video file or animation. Figure 7-19 shows an example of an image map that is literally a map.

To distinguish an image map from a plain graphic, the cursor should change when it is rolled over the map. It is especially helpful to use glow or highlighting to make the part of the image under the mouse cursor stand out from the rest of the image. This gives users positive feedback that this is the part of the image that will be selected if they click. Some sites add tooltips to each section of an image map to give further information.

Specialized Navigation

Multimedia software often requires specialized navigation to handle content-specific situations. Designers must understand the audience requirements in such situations and design navigation that satisfies these needs. For example, educational software and computer-based training programs often provide tests or quizzes containing multiple-choice or short-answer questions. This requires a navigation system that allows users to:

• Move from the current question to the next question

• Move to the previous question

• Tell at a glance which questions were skipped

• Navigate directly to a skipped question or any other question

Figure 7-20 shows a proposed navigational control for a series of multiple-choice questions that attempts to satisfy the above requirements.

The questions are displayed one question per screen. The navigation control consists of a left and right arrow for moving to the previous and next question. Between these arrow icons is a series of numbers, with each number corresponding to a question. The user can click the left or right arrow to display the previous or next question, or click any of the numbers to directly display the associated question. This navigation system allows direct mapping between the controls and the associated content.

The control shown in Figure 7-20 also shows, at a glance, which questions have been answered and which remain unanswered. The unanswered questions are displayed in reverse—white numbers on a dark background. This gives the skipped question numbers more visual "weight," to call the user's attention to them.

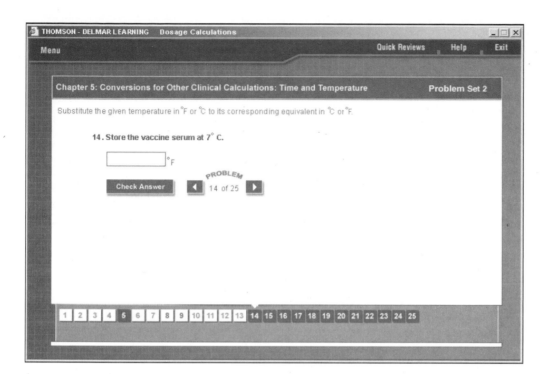

figure | **7-20** |

In this prototype screen, a question navigator is provided that shows students which questions are unanswered and allows direct access to any question. Software copyright Delmar Learning and Dolphin Inc. Graphic design by Derek Richards.

A Question of Color

Although it may not be apparent in the illustration, the designer has attempted to also convey which questions the user answered correctly (green numbers) and incorrectly (red numbers). Note that a usability principle is that color should not be used *by itself* to convey meaning. This is important because as many as 10% of adults have difficulty differentiating colors.

The designer felt that using these colors in the design was acceptable because the software also provides an easily accessible report that indicates which questions have been answered correctly and incorrectly without using color for meaning. In the designer's mind, offering color-sighted users the chance to see at a glance which questions were answered correctly and incorrectly outweighed the complexity that multiple-colored numbers imposed on the design.

Do you agree with the designer? Do you think that users will be able to easily figure out the meaning of the green and red color? Those who are tempted to answer, "It doesn't matter—just explain it in the Help file" might want to reconsider such a response. Except in rare situations, good designers do not require the user to read a Help file to understand the user interface.

There may be other factors to consider when judging the usability of this design. For example, if the product is intended for use in countries outside the United States, do all of these countries use the same convention of red for incorrect that is familiar in the United States? Conducting usability tests using the target audience is the only true way to determine the likely success or failure of this and all designs.

Wizards

A **wizard** is an interactive aid that guides a user through the completion of a complex task, such as installing software, creating a specific type of document, or configuring system options. The wizard presents the steps of the task one at a time, and the user must complete each step successfully before moving on to the next step.

Wizards generally confine the user's navigation to returning to the previous step or advancing to the next step. This lockstep approach emphasizes ease of understanding over speed, which may frustrate advanced users. Some wizards provide additional navigation features to allow users to display any step in the process, an improvement. Figure 7-21 shows such a wizard, which allows Microsoft Word users to create résumés.

Most designers prefer to limit their use of wizards to complex tasks that users access infrequently.

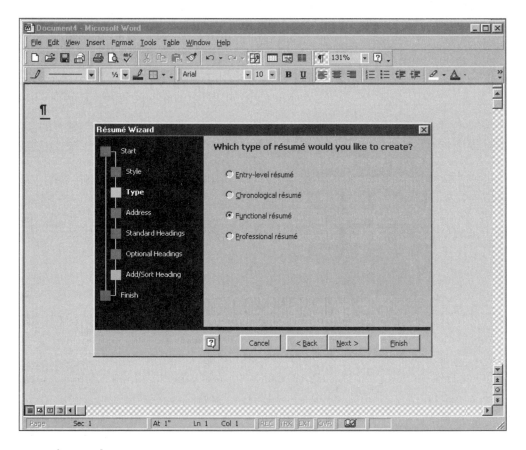

figure | 7-21 |

A wizard guides the user through a complex procedure one step at a time. This résumé creation wizard from Microsoft Word also displays a list of all the steps in the procedure. This enables users to jump directly to any step, an improvement over the lock-step design of most wizards.

Creative Navigation

Navigation systems can creatively match the style of the site or software they navigate. For example, Figure 7-22 shows a menu that appears on an architectural/interior design firm's website. Although the boxes don't give a clue as to their meaning until you drag them to different positions along the diagonal line, the site makes up for this failing with its sense of humor and playfulness. The fun of the site is the sense of discovery you get when you click on one of the boxes and a related item pops out of the hole in the floor. Design firms take risks with navigation design that some "standard" sites cannot.

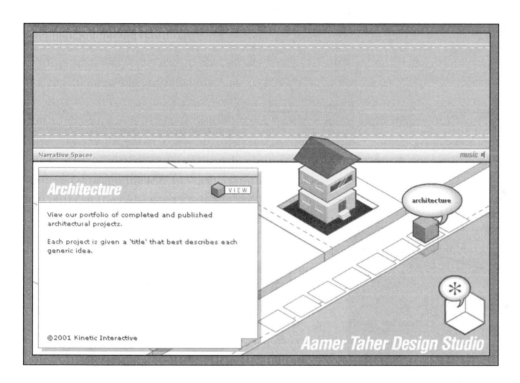

figure | **7-22** |

Design firms create unique navigation schemes. This one offers a sense of mystery, discovery, and fun.

The early 1990s were a boom time for the production of consumer CD-ROM titles spanning a wide variety of subjects. Some of these products were proving grounds for new concepts in navigation design, many of them creative and wildly unsuccessful. One of my "favorites" of the era was a virtual reality menu system that had you move through space in three dimensions searching in vain for your destination. Menu items would be displayed in tiny, unreadable fonts until you drifted sufficiently close to them. Making a selection was a tricky maneuver that required you to line up choices on two separate axes. By the time you successfully made your choice, you often forgot why you made the selection in the first place.

Don't let your creative tendencies overcome your common sense. As always, let users try your design at an early stage, and observe their reaction.

As we've seen, navigation is one of the most important components of a usable website or software program. Like other facets of software design, the navigation you design must anticipate the needs of the audience as it meets the functional objectives of the site or software. Creative approaches to navigation are welcome provided they are fit for their intended purpose and meet the high standard of usability.

SUMMARY OF KEY POINTS

When designing navigation, remember these few simple rules:

- Make it easy for users to figure out where they are.

- Make it clear what the options are and how to select them.

- Deliver the content you promise when the user makes a selection—don't promise one thing and deliver another.

- Always provide an easy means for users to change their mind.

- Try to anticipate and follow your audience's mental model—their concept of how the site or software is organized based on their experience in real-life situations or similar software.

- Test the navigation on real users.

in review

1. How can different navigational metaphors affect the navigational design?

2. What are the three components of navigation?

3. What are two reasons for *not* positioning a category menu down the right side of a Web page?

4. What are two things that are wrong with horizontally oriented cascading menus and how can you improve them?

5. How can you improve the usability of a complex search by formatting?

6. What types of websites are most likely to benefit from breadcrumb trails?

7. Name one advantage and one disadvantage of an indexed site map.

exercise

1. For the following groups of items, specify whether a tab control would be appropriate for organizing the items in each group:

   • Clothing, Sporting Goods, Hardware, Cosmetics, School Supplies

   • Baseball, Football, Basketball, Hockey, Soccer, Standings, Player Statistics

   • Cars, Trucks, Boats, Airplanes

   • Maples, Firs, Pines, Beeches, Walnuts, Oaks, Aspens, Cedars, Spruces, Firs, Lindens, Sycamores, Hickories

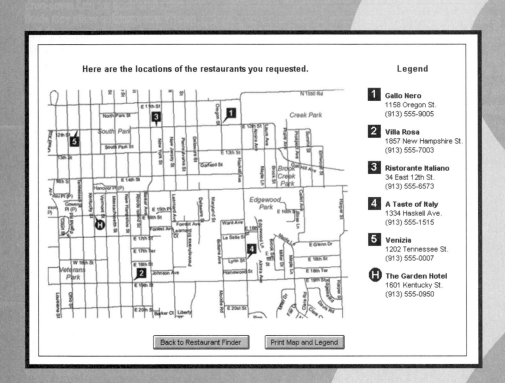

Here are the locations of the restaurants you requested.

Legend

1 **Gallo Nero**
1158 Oregon St.
(913) 555-9005

2 **Villa Rosa**
1857 New Hampshire St.
(913) 555-7003

3 **Ristorante Italiano**
34 East 12th St.
(913) 555-6573

4 **A Taste of Italy**
1334 Haskell Ave.
(913) 555-1515

5 **Venizia**
1202 Tennessee St.
(913) 555-0007

H **The Garden Hotel**
1601 Kentucky St.
(913) 555-0950

[Back to Restaurant Finder] [Print Map and Legend]

solving design problems

CHAPTER 8

SOLVING DESIGN PROBLEMS

objectives

Examine a number of design challenges

Analyze possible solutions to each challenge

Compare advantages and disadvantages of various approaches to each challenge

Evaluate each design solution to determine how well it suits its intended purpose

introduction

Each new interface design project presents its own unique set of challenges and opportunities. Even seemingly simple jobs offer hidden complexity and opportunity for innovative problem solving. No matter how talented or experienced the designer, there is always some new lesson to be learned.

Naturally, we can't anticipate all of the types of interface design problems that you may be called upon to solve. Instead, in this chapter we will present several design challenges. For each challenge, we will work through the process of designing a solution. We will record our thought processes as we go. This will help illustrate how designers propose approaches, sketch them, analyze them, refine them, and repeat this process as necessary to arrive at a workable solution. The solution we propose will be just one of many, and you may come up with more elegant approaches than the ones we propose.

DESIGN CHALLENGE 1: ASSIGN STUDENTS TO CLASS

Our first challenge is to improve the usability of a dialog box that assigns students to a homeroom class. When you look at Figure 8-1, try to figure out how to select students for inclusion in Mrs. Pierce's homeroom and how to remove students from the list once they are selected.

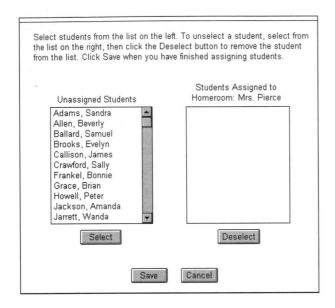

figure | 8-1 |

This is the screen that we have been asked to improve. See if you can figure out its operation without reading the instruction text.

First, we can assume that the user intends to assign students to Mrs. Pierce's homeroom, and that the selection of Mrs. Pierce's homeroom as the target class was made in a previous dialog box or screen. Were you able to figure out how to operate the controls to get the job done? What has the designer done to help you understand how to assign students, and what obstacles stand in the way of your understanding?

First, what did the designer do right? The titles, "Unassigned Students" and "Students Assigned to Homeroom: Mrs. Pierce" do a reasonably good job of explaining the reasons for the two lists. The fact that the list of students assigned to the homeroom is initially empty indicates clearly that there have not yet been any assignments made. The designer arranged the pushbuttons so that one is under each list. Users are likely to infer from this that the Select button applies to the list of unassigned students, and the Deselect button applies to the assigned-students list.

We'll talk about the positioning of these two pushbuttons in a moment, but first let's discuss the pushbutton labels. The left pushbutton contains the caption "Select," and the right button is captioned "Deselect." How well do these two captions represent their functions? Select is what you do when you click a name in a list, not what you do to act on that selection. Instead, the caption should describe the action that the pushbutton initiates—which is to assign students. Our first improvement will be to change the left button caption to Assign.

Likewise, the action that the right pushbutton initiates is to remove the selected name from the list of students in Mrs. Pierce's homeroom. The designer selected the caption Deselect, which most users associate with removing the "selected" indication (highlight, check mark, etc.) from a previously selected item.

At first, Unassign may seem like a better caption choice, but a quick check of the dictionary indicates that unassign is not actually a word. Remove is the better choice, especially since it accurately represents the action that we are initiating—removing a student from the list. This pushbutton will be displayed in its inactivated state if there are no students assigned to the class.

Should we consider renaming the Assign pushbutton Add, since it makes a better opposite to Remove? This is not an easy decision, but Assign seems to better represent the action that the user is here to perform. We'll keep Assign and Remove as our pushbutton captions.

Figure 8-2 shows our progress so far.

Notice that when you first look at the screen, there is nothing that immediately suggests that a relationship exists between the two list boxes, except that they are displayed side by side. The pushbuttons apply to the movement of names between the two lists in either direction, yet their location suggests that their action is confined to the list itself.

What if we positioned both the Assign and Remove buttons between the two lists? This might make it clearer that they control the movement of names from one list to another. We could enhance this suggestion by including small arrow icons that indicate the direction that the selected name(s) will move. Figure 8-3 shows such an arrangement.

| TIP |

This caption discussion illustrates that a design solution is often a compromise among many conflicting needs. There are points that support a particular decision and points that oppose it. A designer must develop the ability to create alternatives, then quickly evaluate the advantages and disadvantages of each approach to determine which one works best (or offends the least).

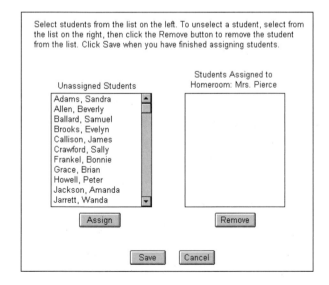

figure | 8-2 |

Changing the pushbutton labels below the list boxes helps clarify their function.

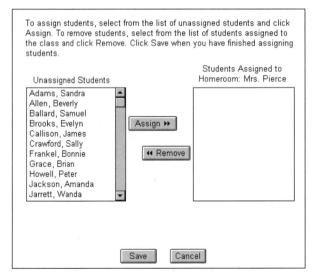

figure | 8-3 |

Repositioning the Assign and Remove pushbuttons between the two lists helps suggest the relationships between the two lists and between the pushbuttons and the lists.

In Figure 8-3 we revised the instructions to reflect the new captions. We also positioned the Assign button slightly closer to the list of unassigned students as a cue. When the user selects a name, as they move the cursor to the right, the Assign button is the one they will come to first. The same logic applies to positioning the Remove button closer to the list of assigned students. User testing will determine whether our redesign has been successful or if further tweaks to the design are necessary.

If this application is delivered on a Windows PC and is not a browser-based application, we would probably recommend using a multiple-selection list box instead of the extended-selection list box shown. The check boxes inside such a list box would make it clear that the user could select multiple students, then click the Assign button once to move them all to the "assigned" list. Such a control would have to be custom built for the Macintosh environments and is not supported by today's browsers unless custom created using an environment such as Shockwave or Flash.

There is another option that we should consider. We could eliminate the Assign and Remove buttons altogether by enabling users to drag and drop entries between the two lists. To add a student to Mrs. Pierce's homeroom, you drag a name from the list on the left to the one on the right. To remove a student from the homeroom, you drag a name in the opposite direction. Figure 8-4 shows this design, with updated instruction text.

Dragging and dropping a lot of names from one list to another can become tedious. Enabling users to extend their selection to multiple entries, then drag them all at once to the other list is probably a good idea. Keep in mind, however, that some users will not know that selection can be extended in this manner. Part of the user testing for this function could include both the Assign/Remove pushbuttons and drag-and-drop methods of including students in the class to determine if users favor one method over the other.

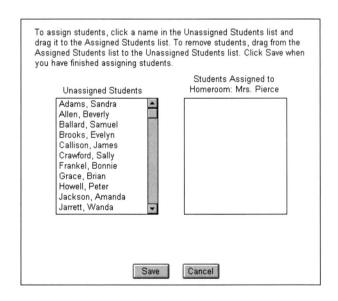

figure | **8-4** |

Using a drag and drop interface between the two lists is appealing because the elimination of the Assign and Remove pushbuttons simplifies the screen layout. It may come at a usability cost, however.

DESIGN CHALLENGE 2: ONLINE GLOSSARY

You have been hired to redesign a glossary of medical terms for a consumer-oriented medical information site. The sponsors of the site are unhappy with the performance and usability of the present glossary's design. Figure 8-5 shows storyboards of the present site.

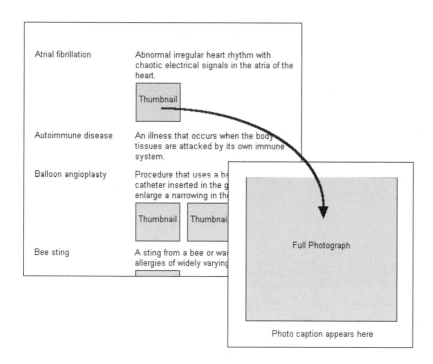

figure | **8-5** |

The existing glossary loads all of the terms, definitions, and thumbnails onto a single page. Users click a thumbnail to see the large version of the image.

Here are the glossary's specifications:

- The glossary includes about 300 terms.
- All of the terms are included in a single scrolling page.
- The definition for each term is displayed along with the term.
- Over half of the terms also include at least one photograph. A thumbnail (reduced-size image) is displayed for each photograph associated with a term in the list. Clicking a thumbnail displays the full-sized version of the image in its own browser window. Terms may include up to three images.

The problems your client is experiencing and their goals for the site include:

1. Users must wait an extremely long time for the full page of terms, definitions, and thumbnails to load. Many of the site's visitors use a dial-up service, and these visitors experience especially long delays waiting for the glossary to load.

2. The site's sponsors intend to expand the total number of glossary terms to 350.

3. The sponsors are considering adding an audio pronunciation for each term in the glossary.

They have asked that the design be flexible enough to accommodate this feature in the future.

Your client suggested that dividing the glossary into separate pages—one page for each letter—might improve the glossary's load times. They are interested in pursuing this approach, but they are not sure it will solve their problem. They want the glossary to be easy for users to navigate and be fast loading. To redesign the glossary so that it solves the current problems and allows for the expected growth, we will proceed as follows:

1. Analyze the site so that we understand the cause of its problems.

2. Propose approaches that might solve the problems.

3. Examine each possible approach, listing its advantages and disadvantages.

4. Modify or combine approaches to overcome shortcomings in suggested approaches.

5. Select the approach that seems to have the greatest advantages and least significant disadvantages

Analyze the Situation

In this case, getting to the root cause of the problem is relatively easy. Remember that the glossary contains around 300 terms, and that over half of them include thumbnails. Loading all that content, including over 150 thumbnail images, to a single page is bound to be slow, especially for dial-up users. The current design might work well if there were many fewer entries, but the client expects to increase rather than decrease the number of terms.

Propose Possible Approaches

Here are some possible approaches to improve the performance and design of the site:

1. Display a list of all terms on a single page with no definitions or photographs. The user clicks a term to see its definitions and any associated thumbnails.

2. Display all of the terms on a single page with their definitions. If a term has one or more associated thumbnails, do not display it, but provide a link to the thumbnails or full images.

3. Spread the terms across multiple pages, organized by alphabetic character. Display each term, its definition, and any associated thumbnails.

Examine Each Approach

Let's examine the key advantages and disadvantages of each proposed approach. Our goal here is to identify the best approach.

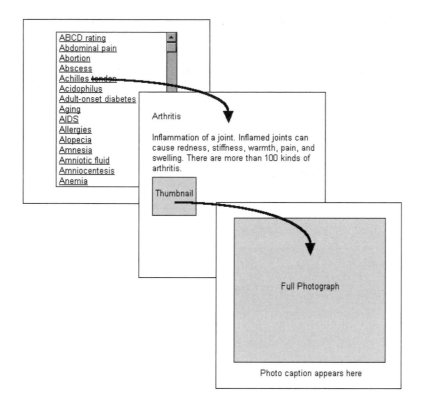

figure | 8-6 |

This approach loads only the terms to the page. Users click a term to see its definition and thumbnails, then click a thumbnail to see the larger image.

All Terms on Single Page, Link to Definition and Image

This approach is to display a list of all the terms on a single page with no definitions or photographs. The user clicks a term to see its definitions and any associated thumbnails. Figure 8-6 shows storyboards for this approach.

ADVANTAGES OF THIS APPROACH

1. The site should load more quickly than the present site, since no content is loaded until the user selects a particular term.

2. All terms will be accessible from the same page. This means the user will not have to first pick an alphabetic character to access its associated terms.

DISADVANTAGES OF THIS APPROACH

1. Users cannot see a term's definition without clicking it, a potentially serious drawback.

2. Users must scroll through a long list of terms to find the sought-after term.

All Terms with Definitions on Single Page, Link to Image

In this approach, we display all of the terms on a single page with their definitions. If a term has one or more associated thumbnails, do not display them, but provide a link to them. Figure 8-7 shows storyboards for this approach.

ADVANTAGES OF THIS APPROACH

1. The site should load more quickly than the present site, since no thumbnails are being loaded except when the user selects a particular term. Then only the thumbnails for the selected term will be loaded.

2. All terms and their definitions will be accessible from the same page. This means the user will not have to first pick an alphabetic character to access its associated terms.

DISADVANTAGES OF THIS APPROACH

1. The user must scroll through a lot of information to find a particular term and definition, a potentially serious shortcoming.

2. Although not loading all the thumbnails will definitely shorten load times, loading all 350 definitions may still cause a delay for dial-up users.

figure | **8-7** |

This approach loads all terms and definitions onto the page. Users click to see thumbnails, then click a thumbnail to see the larger version of the image.

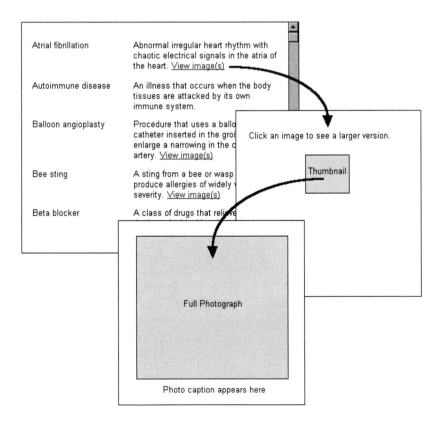

Page for Each Alphabetic Character, Display Content

In this approach, we spread the terms across multiple pages, organized by alphabetic character. Each of these pages contains each term that begins with the character, its definition, and any associated thumbnails. Figure 8-8 shows the storyboards for this approach.

ADVANTAGES OF THIS APPROACH

1. The site will load more quickly than the present site, since only the terms, definitions, and thumbnails for terms beginning with a specific alphabetic character are loaded.

2. This option can readily accommodate future expansion, since the load imposed by adding new terms is divided among the various character pages.

DISADVANTAGE OF THIS APPROACH

1. The user must select a character to see the terms that begin with that character. If this approach is chosen, we may consider adding a term search capability to enable users to type a few characters, then click Search to navigate to the term that most closely matches the typed term.

The third option, shown in Figure 8-8, seems to offer the best combination of reasonable load times, ease of use, and expandability. Although users must click a character to see the terms that start with that character, such a mechanism is easily understood. The search capability will likely reduce the time it takes to find a particular term, an added benefit. Figure 8-9 shows a sample wireframe of this approach.

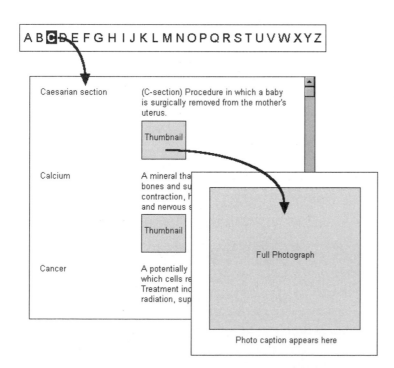

figure | 8-8 |

This approach organizes terms by alphabetic character, displaying the terms, definitions, and thumbnails for the selected character. Click a thumbnail to display the larger version of the image.

figure | 8-9 |

A sample wireframe diagram of the glossary design, including alphabetic character selector and search text box.

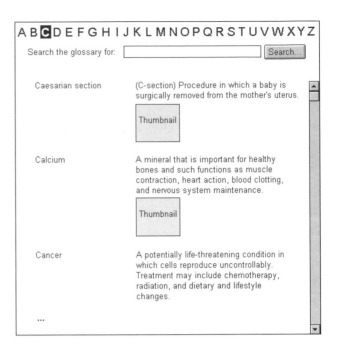

Note that when a user enters a search term and clicks the Search button, we have several options. If there is an exact match in the glossary, we can display the page containing the found term and scroll the page so that the found term is at the top of the screen. If load times are still an issue, we could display just the found term and its thumbnails in a separate browser window. The user could read the definition, then click a thumbnail to see the larger version of the image, also in a separate window.

If the term the user enters is not found, we can display a message to that effect. Perhaps better yet, we can display the page containing entries that start with the same character as the search term, and scroll the page so that the term displayed at the top is the one just before where the search term would have appeared if it were in the glossary. If so, we will still display a message to the user that the term entered did not match any in the glossary.

DESIGN CHALLENGE 3: CITY RESTAURANT FINDER

A medium-sized city's tourism bureau has asked you to submit some preliminary concept screens for a new application they want to develop. The concept screens need not be graphically rendered, but they must show your ideas clearly and persuasively. Note that the project itself, restaurant names, addresses, and telephone numbers are all fictitious.

The purpose of the application is for city visitors to be able to find restaurants meeting various criteria during their stay. For example, a user should be able to search for informal Italian restaurants that offer moderately priced dinners. The tourism bureau is not sure whether the application should be delivered to hotels via CD-ROM or made available as a website. They would like you to help them decide this.

Your clients have also asked that the software display a map showing the location of restaurants that meet a user's criteria. The map will show the location of the restaurants as well as the location of the user's hotel. This will allow users to see which restaurants are within walking distance of the hotel and which require transportation. The map will be printable, so visitors can take a copy with them. To save paper, users should not have to print maps for each restaurant selected. Instead, the map should include several of the restaurant locations.

For the moment, we will postpone any decision about whether to develop the application for CD-ROM or the Web until we have explored some of the design issues further. Here are some initial thoughts that will probably influence the design of this application.

| TIP |

You may find it useful to begin your design work with one of the most important elements of the application. It may help get you started and keep you focused on the reason you were hired in the first place.

Beginning at the End: The Map

In this case, a very important element of the application is what the visitor takes away—the printed map showing the locations of restaurants that meet the criteria the visitor specified. The map must be printable on one page and clearly show street names, the hotel location, and the location of each restaurant.

Printing the names of the restaurants on the map itself will probably interfere with its readability, since the restaurant names may obscure street names. Therefore, we may represent each restaurant on the map by a number or letter. On a separate legend or key, we'll include, for each restaurant, the reference number or letter and the name of the restaurant. For good measure, we'll add the restaurant's telephone number, in case the visitor needs to contact it. This legend may be printed on the same page as the map or on a second page to allow the map to be as large as a full page.

Our client has specified that the map will include the location of the visitor's hotel, and this application will be made available to all of the city's major hotels. Somehow we have to accommodate users from any of the hotels served by the application. We could show the location of every hotel on the map, but this will make a very busy map! In addition, the application will gain wider acceptance by hotel managers if the application is somehow individualized for each hotel it serves. In other words, users should feel as if their hotel is the only one represented. Figure 8-10 shows a rough design of the map that includes the location of the visitor's hotel and five restaurants that met the selection criteria. Figure 8-11 shows the legend that explains what each of the symbols on the map represents.

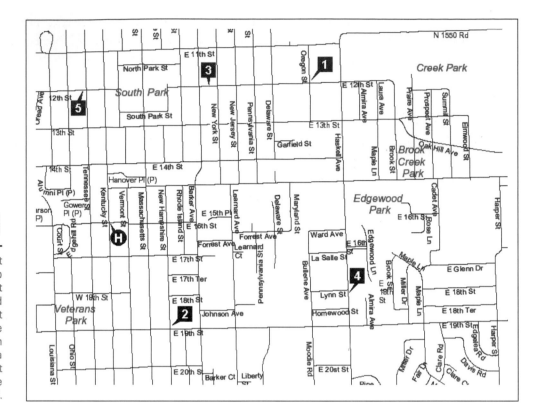

figure | 8-10 |

Here is what the printed map might look like. It includes numbered rectangular call-out boxes to identify the location of each restaurant and a round call-out to locate the user's hotel.

figure | 8-11 |

The map's legend displays the name, street address, and telephone number of each selected restaurant and the user's hotel.

1 **Gallo Nero**
1158 Oregon St.
(913) 555-9005

2 **Villa Rosa**
1857 New Hampshire St.
(913) 555-7003

3 **Ristorante Italiano**
34 East 12th St.
(913) 555-6573

4 **A Taste of Italy**
1334 Haskell Ave.
(913) 555-1515

5 **Venizia**
1202 Tennessee St.
(913) 555-0007

H **The Garden Hotel**
1601 Kentucky St.
(913) 555-0950

The application will need some means of knowing from which hotel it is being run. There are several ways to accomplish this. The hotel can select the name of their hotel at installation, or the user can select the hotel each time the application is run.

Select the Hotel During Installation

If this is a CD-ROM application, we could ask the person installing the application to select the hotel. The software will have been programmed to know the map locations of each hotel it serves. When the installer selects a hotel, this information is stored in a file on the delivery system's hard disk. The software application will look in a known location for this file to determine which hotel it serves. This will prevent users from having to enter the name of the hotel each time they use the application.

Selecting the hotel at installation also means that users will not be able to select a different hotel and show its location on the map. The hotel managers may not mind this limitation at all, since they may not necessarily be interested in publicizing hotels other than their own.

Ask User to Select the Hotel

If this is a Web application, we can store the identification of this hotel in a cookie, but there is no guarantee that the cookie will be present beyond this session. In fact, there is no guarantee that the system that runs the application will even have cookies enabled. To be safe, if this application is to be delivered via the Web, we will probably need to ask each user who runs the application to select her hotel from a list. The server that stores the application will include the full list of hotels and the coordinates of each hotel's location on the map.

Setting the Maximum Number of Restaurants

How many restaurants should we allow to be plotted on the map? Since our user is probably only going to visit one restaurant for a given meal, it might be sufficient to just allow her to select one restaurant for printing. Allowing users to view and print a map with several restaurants plotted offers some true advantages, however, namely that the user can compare the locations of several restaurants.

Our illustration showed five restaurants plus the hotel location. This seems like a reasonable limit, as it prevents the map from becoming too crowded. When we work on the design of the search portion of our application, we will have to figure out how to limit the number of restaurants plotted if more than five are retrieved.

We will also have to be careful that the black rectangles representing two or more restaurants, or restaurants and a hotel, don't plot on top of each other, making them difficult or impossible to read. One way to avoid this is to create a test graphic. Although this process is a bit tedious, it will ensure that none of the restaurant rectangles and hotel circles will interfere with each other. Start with the graphic of the map, then place rectangles close to the locations of all of the restaurants. Create them on a separate layer so you can move them around. Place circles close to the locations of each hotel.

Remember that you will be drawing lead lines from the rectangle or circle to the actual location of the restaurant or hotel, so be sure to locate each shape close to, but not directly at, its building's location. Then draw the lead lines for all of the restaurants and hotels, making sure that none cross other shapes and that none cover street names. We do this process because we can't be sure which five restaurants will be selected for plotting. Figure 8-12 shows a portion of the map with rectangles drawn.

figure | 8-12 |

This portion of the test map shows the locations of all of the restaurant and hotel call-outs. The program will position call-outs in these locations. This is one way to ensure that call-outs do not plot on top of each other or obscure street names unnecessarily.

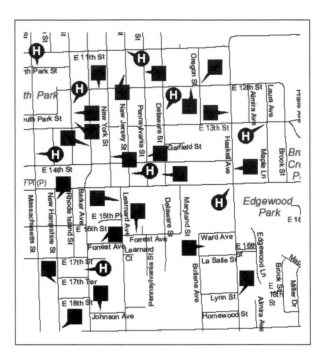

Although our test map in Figure 8-12 looks very busy, remember that our users will see only six symbols or less. At some point before development of the software begins, you will need to record the coordinates of each symbol in relation to the map, so that each can be placed accurately. The program will place the graphics for the numbers 1 through 5 in the center of each rectangle. We included the letter H in the hotel circles, since this information is not dynamically created. Our hotels will always be marked with an H. (Let's hope that test users don't mistake our hotel H for the standard Hospital symbol—if so, we'll create a more stylized H.)

Notice that our map legend in Figure 8-11 does not include walking or driving directions from the hotel. Printing such directions for up to five restaurants may make it difficult for the legend to fit on one page. It may also cause odd formatting, since the sets of directions will be of varying lengths. Our goal is to make the map sufficiently clear that visitors will have no difficulty locating each restaurant. Perhaps we can use the extra space on the legend sheet to print a coupon or special offer from the restaurants that are represented on the map.

The Search Function

The search function is the heart of our application. It is here that our users will specify what type of restaurant they are interested in visiting. The search must be simple to use, yet it must provide meaningful selection criteria to allow the user to make a proper choice. One important design goal is that, if possible, we should include the search results on the same screen as the search criteria. This will enable a user to evaluate the results and narrow or widen the search without having to navigate to a different page. Figure 8-13 shows two approaches to organizing the search and results areas.

We will also need to make it clear to users whether the criteria they specify are being combined or treated separately. For example, if we allow a user to select both Chinese and French cuisine, should we display restaurants that serve either Chinese or French cuisine, or should we display only restaurants that offer both Chinese and French? Perhaps we should restrain users from selecting more than one item in a category.

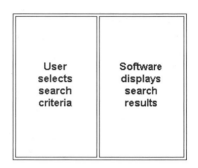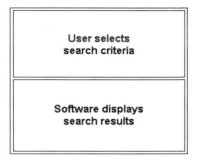

figure | **8-13** |

Here are two logical ways to arrange search items and search results on the same screen or page.

I prefer allowing multiple selections in each category and retrieving restaurants that meet any of the criteria in that category. In our example above, we would return restaurants that served either Chinese or French cuisine. We will combine the criteria in different categories when determining which restaurants to retrieve. For example, if we select both Chinese and French as our cuisine, then select casual dress and moderate prices, we will display only Chinese and French restaurants that allow casual dress and offer moderate prices.

In each category, users will have the option of selecting "no preference." This will qualify any restaurant for retrieval in this category. Of course, these will still be combined with the selections in other categories to determine which restaurants are retrieved. For example, if we specify Italian cuisine, but select "no preference" in all of the other categories, we will retrieve all of the Italian restaurants stored in the system.

We'll work on laying out the search criteria first. The following list includes the items of information that our client has requested we include for each restaurant. This list may grow in the future, depending on the application's success.

Information Stored for Each Restaurant

- Restaurant name
- Address
- Telephone number
- Description (can include specialties such as pizza or seafood as well as general information)

- Cuisine (Italian, Chinese, Greek, etc.)
- Hours
- Meals served (breakfast, lunch, dinner)
- Price range for entrees
- Dress code (informal, jacket required, etc.)
- Standardized restaurant quality rating, if available
- Additional information
- Location on a city map
- Link to a sample menu, if available
- Link to the restaurant's own website
- Optional photo

Although our database will include all of the above items, not every item need be a search item. Let's go down the list of items and try to determine which items we must include as search items, which would be nice to include, and which, if any, we can eliminate. Remember that the purpose of our application is to allow visitors to select restaurants that meet certain criteria. The first set of items will be those that one would need to make an informed decision.

Must-Have Search Items

- Cuisine (check boxes or a list box representing all of the types of cuisine represented by our restaurants)
- Meals served (check boxes)
- Price range for entrees (check boxes)
- Dress code (check boxes)
- Standardized restaurant quality rating, if available (check boxes) (Note that we may want to discuss this possibly controversial item further.)

The next list contains items that it would be useful to include. Each item includes its rationale for including it.

Nice-to-Have Search Items

- Restaurant name (text box that will allow visitors to search the database for the name or partial name of a restaurant they may have heard or seen)
- Address (text box used for, say, a visitor who heard of a great restaurant on East Sixteenth Street but cannot remember its name)
- Description (text box that enables visitors to enter a word or phrase, and software that will retrieve restaurants whose description contains that word or phrase)

figure | **8-14** |

Positioning search items on the left consumes half the available screen space. The controls seem reasonably well laid out.

We'll start by including our must-have items, then add the nice-to-haves if possible. Figure 8-14 shows the search items arranged on the left side of the screen. This arrangement calls for the list of restaurants meeting the selection criteria to be displayed on the right half of the screen.

Notice in Figure 8-14 that "No preference" appears as the first check box option in each category. This will enable users with no preference to check the first box and ignore all of the rest of the selections in that category. Since we have used checkboxes for selections in nearly all of the categories, users can select more than one item in each category. This allows the illogical condition where the user sets the "No preference" check box and also sets one or more other check boxes in the same category.

Since eliminating this possibility would require an awkward combination of controls, we will allow the condition to exist, but we will follow the rule that if the user sets the "No preference" check box, we will ignore any other set check box in that category.

Also notice how the Rating category differs from the others. This is the only category that uses radio buttons instead of check boxes. It would have seemed logical to set up this category with check boxes representing no preference, one star, two stars, three stars, four stars, and five stars.

Think of how this category will be used. First of all, are many users going to specifically request restaurants rated at only one star? It is doubtful that our client would include restaurants of such low quality (unless perhaps forced to by a judge). Most users will want to see restaurants of good or better quality. Using the check box arrangement described, users will almost always have to check more than one box to get the desired results. By including the words "or more" after each set of stars except the maximum, five stars, we allow users to set a minimum quality rating without explicitly having to select all of the possible choices. The radio buttons ensure that the user only selects one ratings choice in the category.

Figure 8-15 shows a top-bottom arrangement that displays the search area in the top part of the screen and restaurants that meet the selected criteria in the bottom part. We include both layouts so that we can evaluate which of the two layouts seems to work better. Look at both layouts and form an opinion about which seems to do a better job of arranging the two functions. Be sure to be able to cite examples from the two layouts that support your opinion. Also keep in mind that this opinion is preliminary. We won't be able to truly evaluate both layouts until we complete the screens by including the restaurant list.

figure | 8-15 |

Positioning search items on top consumes more than half the available screen space. It looks like it may crowd the search results.

My preference is for the first layout, the one shown in Figure 8-14. It offers some key advantages over the arrangement shown in Figure 8-15, including the following:

- The side-by-side arrangement shown in Figure 8-14 enables users to quickly scan the categories to find a particular category.

- The top-bottom arrangement shown in Figure 8-15 takes up more screen real estate and will crowd the list of qualifying restaurants into a space smaller than that used for the selection items.

- The top-bottom arrangement will require an awkward display of the list of restaurants that meet the selection criteria. The short vertical area will force restaurants to be arranged in several short columns.

Based on the amount of space required just to list the must-have selection criteria, at this point I suggest not adding the nice-to-have criteria from our list. If we later think of a way to simplify the search criteria area, we can consider adding one or more items from this list. Of these items, the ability to search for a particular restaurant's name is probably the most desirable item of the nice-to-haves.

Displaying Restaurants That Match Search Criteria

The user selects various criteria and clicks the Find Restaurants pushbutton to search for restaurants that meet those criteria. The application searches the database and displays a list of restaurants that qualify. But what exactly should we include in the restaurant display?

As is often the case, there are several possible approaches we can take. They are:

1. Display just the names of all of the qualifying restaurants. The user clicks on a restaurant to see its full information.
2. Display the names of the qualifying restaurants along with limited information, such as its address and telephone number and a brief text summary description of the restaurant. The user clicks on the restaurant name to see its full information.
3. Display all of the information for each qualifying restaurant in a long scrolling list.

Let's quickly evaluate these approaches. The first option will enable us to display the most restaurants without scrolling or displaying the list across two pages. Its major disadvantage is that users who are unfamiliar with the city (a large part of the target audience, in other words), won't have any information other than the restaurant's name to determine whether or not they want to explore that restaurant further.

The second option, displaying the restaurant with limited information may be a viable choice. Users can see the written location of the restaurant and read a brief description. If they are interested based on the information they read, users can explore the restaurant further by clicking its linked name. A disadvantage of this approach is that some users may not realize that additional information exists. They may ignore one of the key features of our application—the ability to plot restaurants on a map.

The third option, displaying the full information for each qualifying restaurant, eliminates the possibility that users will ignore a particularly useful part of our application. It may be daunting to users, however, to have to read or scan so much information, especially if many restaurants meet the selection criteria.

We'll eliminate the first option and begin laying out the screen to see if it gives us a better idea whether choice 2 or 3 makes more sense. Figure 8-16 shows our first attempt to lay out the basic search results area, with each qualifying restaurant's information shown. Notice that we

figure | 8-16 |

Our first attempt to lay out the search results shows that there is insufficient space to display more than three restaurants' information.

have included text at the top of this area that indicates how many restaurants met the user's search criteria.

One positive part of the design so far is that users can view their search criteria and the results of those criteria on the same screen. This trial layout shows that the entries will definitely need to scroll or link to additional pages to show all of the restaurants found. We also need to provide some means for users to indicate which restaurants they want to plot on the map.

Remember that we decided to limit the number of restaurants that could be plotted on a map to five. How will we determine which five restaurants to plot if our search retrieves more than five? One possibility is to choose five restaurants at random. This is not a very satisfying method, however, since the user is likely to wonder why these particular restaurants were chosen over the others that were retrieved. Such a decision will hurt the integrity of the application.

Another possibility is to choose the first five restaurants that are retrieved. The problem with this alternative is that the restaurants may be stored and displayed alphabetically. This means that restaurants whose names are near the beginning of the alphabet will get plotted more often than their alphabetically challenged counterparts.

One equitable, workable solution is to provide the means for users to select as many as five retrieved restaurants for plotting. This means that a restaurant's description and supporting data will determine whether or not it is selected. Since the restaurants themselves will be responsible for contributing their own description copy, this seems like an equitable, non-arbitrary solution. We will still have to determine whether we can design this selection feature to be easy for users to figure out and use.

Next we'll refine our design. We'll start by adding a scrollbar to the restaurant information area and include check boxes next to each restaurant name to enable users to indicate which restaurants they want to map. Once a user has clicked five check boxes, we will deactivate the remaining check boxes if possible. If this is impossible, then we will display a message to a user who attempts to select a sixth restaurant. We'll also add a pushbutton at the bottom of the screen, below the scrolling list of restaurants, to enable users to view or print the map containing the restaurants they've selected.

Remember that we want to be sure users realize that more information exists for each restaurant that is displayed in the list. Originally, the plan was to make each restaurant name a link to the additional information. The instruction text would reinforce this. However, since many users won't read the instructions, we will add a more explicit link to each restaurant's information. We can include information about the mapping feature in the instruction text ahead. Figure 8-17 shows our refinements.

figure | 8-17 |

Refinements, such as adding necessary scroll bars and additional space between the telephone number and description, further reduce the amount of information that can be displayed before scrolling. There doesn't seem to be any way to prevent this.

Note that we are still working with wireframes of the design. If we win this project, we will try to reduce the size of the text areas somewhat to allow room for the graphic treatment.

Next, we will create a wireframe to show the screen that is displayed when the user clicks the find out more link for a restaurant. It is on this screen that the full information for each restaurant is shown. Figure 8-18 shows a possible layout for this information screen.

figure | 8-18 |

The additional information screen will benefit from a graphic treatment that helps organize the various elements.

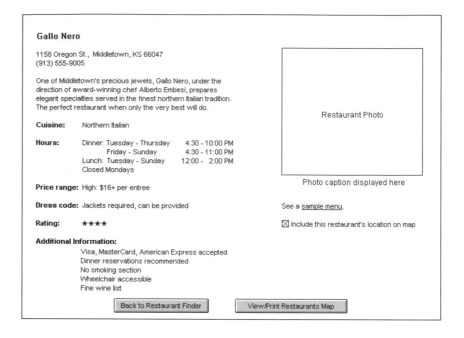

By including both a check box to include the displayed restaurant's location on the map and a pushbutton to view or print the map, we may be circumventing our client's request to save paper by including multiple selections on a single map. Of course, if the user has selected any other restaurants on the restaurant finder screen, these locations will also be plotted. If the client objects, we can remove the View/Print Restaurants Map pushbutton from this screen and only include it on the finder screen.

A selection made for this restaurant on either the finder screen or the additional information screen will be reflected in the other screen. So if we select the check box on the additional information screen, it will be displayed accordingly on the finder screen.

There is just one more screen to show for this application. It shows the results of clicking the View/Print Restaurants Map pushbutton. Remember that we have to display both the map and a legend that shows the meaning of the numbered boxes in the map. Figure 8-19 shows a possible layout of this screen.

As we have worked through this design, you no doubt realized that this assignment required a great deal more thought than the first two presented in this chapter. As we progressed through the design, you probably thought of a number of enhancements to our restaurant finder application. If this were an actual project, we would include the best of these ideas in our proposal as optional enhancements to the project.

Remember that we said that we would recommend whether this application should be delivered on a CD-ROM to be installed on a PC or Macintosh system or as a Web-based application. Based on our design, this application will probably best be delivered on CD-ROM. Here are some valid reasons for this decision:

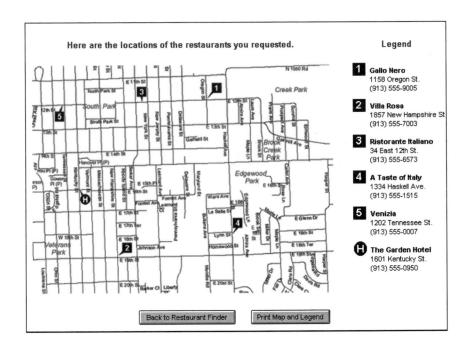

figure | 8-19 |

This shows how the map and its legend will be displayed on screen. Although the map shown looks a bit blurry, the production version should be clear enough to read easily.

1. If this application is delivered via the Internet, we will have to ensure that users cannot access other websites while using this system. We are not developing this application to give hotel visitors free Internet access. Developing the application as a CD-ROM application will allow us to control the environment so that the restaurant finder is the only application that users can access from this computer.

2. There is a cost associated with maintaining a connection to the Internet. Since this application in its current form does not require this connection for it to operate, we can save the cost of the connection by delivering it as a standalone application that is installed on a PC or Macintosh.

3. If, for some reason, the hotel's Internet provider was to have some sort of trouble that resulted in the loss of the connection, then the application will be inaccessible. If developed as a standalone application, it will always be available as long as the power is on.

4. When you print from a browser, you are printing the same image you see on screen. You don't have the same flexibility in formatting the printout as you do in a CD-ROM application. If we deliver in CD-ROM, the printout can be formatted differently from the screen image.

There may be other, equally compelling reasons for developing this application as a CD-ROM application.

Hopefully, working through solutions to the three design challenges presented in this chapter has given you insight into a designer's attempts to minimize user frustrations with the software. Experience can help the designer make the right decisions, but, as always, user testing is the only ruler that accurately measures success.

In the next chapter, we will turn our attention to how the visual nature of our work affects its usability.

SUMMARY OF KEY POINTS

- Because design solutions are often a compromise among conflicting needs, designers must be able to create alternatives, then quickly evaluate the advantages and disadvantages of each approach to determine which works best.

- Whenever possible, position interface elements such as pushbuttons close to the functions they control or represent to strongly suggest their relationship.

- Try designing an application "backwards," starting from the desired outcome or user's experience, then putting the screens or pages in place to make that outcome possible.

- Whenever possible, include search results on the same page as the search criteria. This will enable users to easily modify the search criteria rather than having to go back to a different page.

- It may be worthwhile to delay decisions about how to deliver an application until more is known about the application's design.

in review

1. What purpose does positioning controls such as pushbuttons between two lists serve?

2. When proposing potential solutions to the slow loading of the glossary in the second design challenge, why did we include ideas that didn't seem all that workable?

3. Why did we go to the trouble of creating the test map with all of the restaurants and hotel locations shown, even though this map would never be viewed or printed?

4. What is the main advantage to displaying both the search items and the results of the search on the same screen or page?

5. Why didn't we use the same check box controls in all of the search items?

6. Why didn't we leave plenty of room for the graphic treatment of the screen when we created the wireframes?

exercise

1. There are 20 students available for assigning to five different classes. Using a minimum number of controls, design a Web page that allows the user to assign these students to any of the five classes. The user can unassign students from each class as well as assign them.

visual considerations

objectives

Describe how grids can help you organize a site's content

Examine how the technique of unfocused attention can help you review a screen or page design

Align screen controls, labels, and other elements

Describe what elements to include above and below a Web page's "fold"

Increase the readability of text

Examine how to select graphics for a website

introduction

For the vast majority of users, websites and multimedia software are primarily visual experiences. In website design, the goal is to convey your message to visitors as quickly and strongly as possible. The site or software's visual organization predicts the experience users are likely to have. When information is visually well organized, users quickly gain confidence and are free to focus on the content. If users cannot quickly make sense of the visual structure, they soon lose confidence in the site or software's ability to provide what they are seeking.

The various parts of the visual puzzle are the colors, fonts, and images that heighten and enliven the user's experience. When these elements are carefully thought out and executed, they work together to produce a whole that is greater than the sum of its parts. The end result is design that strongly supports the goals of the site or software.

VISUAL CONSIDERATIONS

figure **9-1**

Use a grid to help lay out the content on a Web page. The grid helps ensure that the various elements are well organized and pleasing to the eye.

STRUCTURING INFORMATION

A site or software's content provides the basis for its visual structure. Like an outline organizes its content, arrange the various content areas into a hierarchy that reflects the importance of each area to the screen or page. Without a strong visual organization, a site or software looks haphazard, and users must expend significant effort to find particular pieces of information.

Anchoring Visual Elements

Although the Web is a relatively modern medium, designers can learn much about usable visual design from book publishers, who have been perfecting this art for years. One important technique that publishers use is to anchor visual elements horizontally and vertically on the page.

Think of a Web page or software screen that you are about to lay out as a grid rather than as a blank piece of paper. This will help you structure the content so that is well organized and pleasing to the eye. Some sites, like the newspaper site shown in Figure 9-1, adhere strictly to the grid, even using it as a design element, while others more loosely interpret the grid.

Figure 9-2 shows a schematic representation of a Web page. It highlights the forms and masses that make up the page without providing details such as actual text or image content. Such a representation is useful in examining the visual structure of the page. See the sidebar to learn a technique for seeing websites and screen designs in this fashion.

figure **9-2**

This schematic diagram of an actual Web page is a useful tool for analyzing the visual organization of the page. The shaded blocks approximate the visual weight of the various elements of the page.

Even from the sketchy diagram shown in Figure 9-2, it is clear that the Web page it represents is clearly and logically composed. Figure 9-3 shows the website that was the source of the representation shown in Figure 9-2. Its strong, simple organizational structure helps visitors understand, at a glance, what content it contains and what options exist.

figure | 9-3 |

This is the Web page that the diagram in Figure 9-2 represents. Notice how effectively the page's elements are organized and presented.

Look At It This Way...

There is a method of looking at things that can be of great use to a designer or anyone whose job it is to evaluate visual designs. The technique goes by a number of different names, including **unfocused attention** or **splatter vision**. Art students are often taught this technique to explore paintings or other works of art.

To practice the technique, look at a painting or image "all at once," without focusing on any one part of it. One way to do this is to widen your vision so that you become aware of objects at the limits of your visual field. With just a little practice, this technique will attune you to the balance and contrast of a composition. Some parts of the painting will seem to draw you into them, while others recede.

Unfocused attention is a valuable technique for evaluating the visual organization and graphic design of websites and multimedia software. Looking without focusing allows us to concentrate on the composition of the screen elements instead of jumping to interpret the content. When we look at a website page or multimedia screen in this fashion, the text areas soften into masses, and we can evaluate the design based on the forms that result. This becomes a valuable tool for the designer who wants to improve a website or multimedia software's organizational structure.

For example, you can use it to determine if a design uses areas of light and dark to focus our attention appropriately. Using this technique, you may notice that Web pages and software products often focus our attention inappropriately. A graphic element with a minor role sometimes commands too much attention, diverting us from more important areas of the screen.

Native Americans used splatter vision to spot movement in the natural landscape. By alternating between splatter vision and focused attention, they could scan large portions of land in search of animals to hunt. Splatter vision was also useful in locating animal tracks and trails. The faraway look that is evident in photographs of native Americans is characteristic of splatter vision.

Now look at the diagram shown in Figure 9-4.

In this diagram, representing another Web page, there is no clear hierarchy or differentiation among the various components of the page. The uninterrupted blocks of gray represent large, continuous text blocks. Only the right side of the page contains headings that visitors can skim to determine if they want to read further. To derive the rest of this page's content, visitors are going to have to do an awful lot of reading.

Figure 9-5 shows most of the Web page that Figure 9-4 diagrams.

Figure 9-5 bears out our predictions about the readability of the site. First the good news. The menu buttons on the upper left part of the screen are readable and their meaning is clear. The text on the right side of the page contains headings that offer clues as to the content.

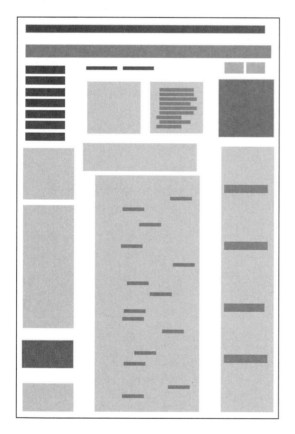

figure | 9-4 |

This diagram of another Web page predicts a much more chaotic visual experience for the user than the previous example.

The choices below the menu items on the left and the major text section down the middle of the page offer serious challenges to visitors. The choices on the left under the heading "Popular Sections" would have been easier to read if they did not contain the icon. The icon is being used as a bullet in this case, but is repeated too many times to be an effective attention getter. The icon also prevents the text from being perceived as indented below the heading, causing users to perceive the entire area as one large text block. Finally, if the text extends to a second line, it should be formatted as a *hanging indent*—with the second line starting directly below the first line of text, and not below the icon.

The items preceded by the logo are all links, as are the bolded words and phrases in the center text section and the headings on the right side of the page. One must move the mouse cursor over the items to discover this fact, however. The page would be improved if the designer used a standard underline for linked text. On the right side of the page, the CLICK HERE NOW links beneath each text section would be unnecessary if the headings appeared underlined as standard links.

The page would be easier to read if there was more white space. Skipping a line between each item on the left would help. So would skipping a line after each bulleted point in the center text section. The center section text should be organized in several categories such as Keep in Touch, Member Benefits, and Lobbying Efforts.

figure | 9-5 |

The large blocks of uninterrupted text that characterize this page will make it difficult for users to quickly find a particular piece of information.

AIR CONDITIONING CONTRACTORS OF AMERICA

SITE MAP   FEEDBACK   LEGAL NOTICES   CONTACT

The contractor's competitive edge!

52 Ways contractors save money &

- All About ACCA
- Join ACCA
- Info for Contractors
- Info for Consumers
- HVAC Career Center
- ACCA MemberTools
- Events & Training
- THE ACCA STORE

ACCAlert
Free newsletter!
Tips, news, and know-how for HVACR contractors.

Email Address:

Go

We **never** share email addresses. Period.
Read the Current Issue

Popular Sections
- ACCA Chapters
- ACCA Staff
- Government Affairs
- Technical Services
- Health Fairness Action Center
- ACCA Conference & Indoor Air Expo
- Thermal Energy Storage
- **Find a Contractor**
- **Find a HVAC Vocational Program**
- **HVACR Industry Buyer's Guide**
- **Members: Update Your Contact Info!**
- Download ACCA Logos for Your Website!

IMAGINE AMERICA without air conditioning.

Upcoming Events
- Manual J Instructor Certification
- ACCA Quality College
- 2004 ACCA Conference & Indoor Air Expo
- National Calendar of Events

Home → About ACCA

ACCA's mission is to help the best HVACR contractors in the country acquire, serve, and satisfy customers. We're a non-profit association whose only goal is the success of the HVACR contracting industry we've served for over thirty years.

- ACCA Member Benefits
- ACCA Awards
- ACCA Board of Directors
- ACCA Staff
- ACCA Affiliates
- Member Profiles
- ACCA Educational Institute
- ACCA Constitution and By-laws
- Government Affairs
- ACCA Code of Ethics
- Join ACCA

ACCA members gain access to resources and tools unmatched anywhere else. These resources help our members grow their businesses and expand their profits. If you were a member of ACCA, you could:

- Know what's going on with **ACCA InfoTools™**, including ACCA's weekly **INSIDER**; our magazine, *Contractor Excellence*, full of tips from America's most successful contractors; and full access to our website.
- Learn from your peers in a small-group setting through ACCA's exclusive **MIX® Group** program, which brings non-competing contractors together for advice and guidance.
- Educate consumers (and support sales efforts) with **ComforTools™**, a series of brochures that explain the value of indoor comfort products and services;
- Check out our full range of **member benefits**, from financing and insurance programs to fleet leasing and pre-employment screening. Save money with ACCA's buying power!
- Gain more customers through ACCA's online **Contractor Locator**, the leading online consumer source for HVACR contracting businesses;
- Support the HVACR contracting industry's efforts to lower taxes and promote responsible, efficient indoor comfort systems through ACCA's aggressive **government affairs program**;
- Get exclusive member discounts on the **leading business and technical publications** in the HVACR industry;
- Get deep discounts on the industry's **best education programs** to keep your business ahead of the curve;
- **And so much more!** (Keep your eyes peeled, we're announcing new benefits and programs all the time.)

Search

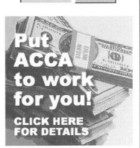
Put ACCA to work for you!
CLICK HERE FOR DETAILS

Find a Contractor Near You!
Homeowners and building operators, find a qualified HVACR professional by searching ACCA's membership of more than 4,000 contractors. Search by zip, city or state.
CLICK HERE NOW!

ACCA Books, Software & Resources
ACCA is the leading developer and provider of HVACR technical, business and management books. From our industry-standard design manuals to low-cost software and management tools, you can find what you need direct at the ACCA Online Store!
CLICK HERE NOW!

Contractors, Get More Sales Leads Now!
Click here to get a completely free subscription to *Sales & Marketing Insider* published by Hudson, Ink, ACCA's premiere member-marketing partner. You'll discover what's hot and what's not in HVAC Marketing, plus simple strategies, real results and little-known tips that work. They'll work for you too!
CLICK HERE NOW!

Contractors, Find a Supplier!
Search the ACCA Buyer's Guide for the suppliers or service providers you need. From AC equipment to vehicles and ventilation, browse ACCA's listing of associate members and support the companies who support your industry!
CLICK HERE NOW!

Arranging Labels with Controls

When designing data entry forms, a designer must decide how to align the labels and the text boxes, list boxes, or other elements that they identify. Figure 9-6 shows three different alternatives to laying out the labels and other elements. Usability research supports the bottom alternative as the best alignment.

LEFT-ALIGNING LABELS AND MINIMIZING SPACE BETWEEN LABELS AND TEXT BOXES The top option in Figure 9-6 tries to keep the text boxes and drop-down list box as close to the labels as possible. The labels are left aligned and the top four text boxes are right aligned. No attempt has been made to align the State drop-down list with the Zip code text box.

It is relatively easy to see why this first choice is not the best arrangement. It appears disorganized and haphazard. The viewer's eye cannot quickly make sense of the organization. It is clear that the text boxes need to be left aligned to create a more pleasing line.

RIGHT-ALIGNING LABELS AND LEFT-ALIGNING TEXT BOXES The middle option in Figure 9-6 left aligns the labels and right aligns the text boxes. The top four text boxes are right aligned.

Some readers may prefer this arrangement since it eliminates the small gaps between the labels and the text boxes or drop-down list. The ragged left edge of the labels will make it harder for users to orient to each new label, however. This problem is not severe in this example, but is exaggerated when the text labels are longer.

LEFT-ALIGNING LABELS AND TEXT BOXES The bottom option in Figure 9-6 left aligns both the labels and the text boxes. The top four text boxes are right aligned.

This alternative's left alignment of both labels and controls creates two pleasing lines. The clean line of the labels makes it very easy to quickly identify each label. The left alignment of the text boxes is equally important to help users make quick visual sense of the arrangement. Also contributing to this arrangement's clean lines, although to a lesser degree, is the line created by aligning the right edges of the four long text boxes. This is the preferred arrangement. If the text labels are of widely varying lengths, then wrap the long labels and left-justify them to maintain the clean left edges.

Arranging Controls for Clarity

When laying out multiple sets of controls such as radio buttons, it is important to arrange the elements in a way that clearly shows which controls are grouped. Figure 9-7 shows two different ways of laying out three sets of three radio buttons.

The top example in Figure 9-7 shows an arrangement that makes it difficult to determine which radio buttons belong to each group. Are the controls grouped horizontally or vertically? This layout is confusing because the spacing between each radio button is about the same.

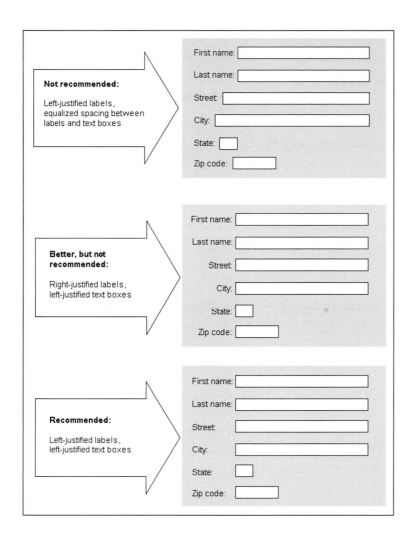

figure | **9-6** |

Here are three different ways to align labels and text boxes. The bottom option, with both the labels and text boxes left justified, is the preferred alignment.

figure | **9-7** |

Notice how minimizing the space between the grouped radio buttons gives important clues about which choices go together. Adding titles further clarifies the choices.

Without actually reading the choices, there is no clear way to determine which radio buttons belong to each group.

The bottom example in Figure 9-7 shows how the arrangement of the same set of radio buttons can be improved. The distance between each radio button in a group has been decreased, while the distance between each group has been increased. The addition of a label at the top of each group further clarifies the relationship among the buttons and groups.

Above and Below the "Fold"

Newspapers displayed for sale are folded and stacked on the stand. The area above the newspaper fold is the part that is visible to passersby. Newspaper editors, aware of the need to sell their product, arrange the front page such that the most important stories appear above the fold. Articles considered of lesser importance are located below the fold.

The Web's version of the fold is the bottom of the browser window. The area that is **above the fold** is the visible area of the page—the part that is in view without having to vertically scroll the page. The area **below the fold** is the remainder of the page that is initially hidden when the page is displayed and must be scrolled into view. Figure 9-8 shows a sample Web page with the areas above and below the fold labeled.

Place the most important information, including key text, navigation buttons, links, and images, in the area above the fold. This increases the chances that your audience will see the most important content on each page. Your clients will be able to tell you which information they consider most important.

figure | 9-8 |

The area above the fold normally contains more important images, navigation, and links.

| TIP |

As Patrick Lynch and Sarah Horton point out in the excellent *Web Style Guide* (Yale University Press/ 1999), the area above the fold should contain the highest priority items, the most graphics, and the highest density of links. The area below the fold contains lesser priority items and fewer graphics, and the density of links is less critical.

Note that a Web page's fold is not quite as absolute as a newspaper's. The fold will differ depending on each user's screen resolution and the size of the browser window. The top left part of a Web page is sometimes considered the most valuable real estate because it is visible regardless of the user's screen resolution or browser window size. Perhaps it is no accident that companies usually choose this area for their logo or identifier.

Avoid Using the Area Above the Logo

We don't expect to find much important information above the company logo. One reason for this may be that this area of the page is very close to the browser's toolbar area. Experienced Web users are accustomed to tuning out this toolbar area unless they need to access one of its functions, such as the Back button. Websites that challenge this convention by locating controls near this area risk usability problems. For example, look at the website shown in Figure 9-9.

This is a relatively simple, clean page. The white space and photograph draw your eye nicely into the page. Above the company logo, however, the choices (Reservations, Schedules, etc.) are almost unnoticeable. The problem is partly due to their position and partly to their lack of a graphical treatment. Making these choices graphic buttons would improve their visibility. Moving them below the logo would be even more effective in helping visitors easily locate these important controls.

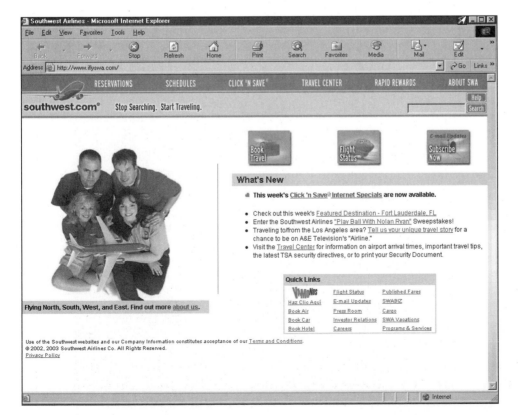

figure | 9-9 |

Positioning controls above the logo may cause users to overlook them. This may have led the designers of this site to create undesirable duplicate controls.

In fact, the Reservations option at the top of the page and the more noticeable Book Travel button below display identical pages (as does the Book Air option in the Quick Links list). Providing multiple access points to the same function, perhaps necessitated by the obscurity of the top row of options, unnecessarily complicates the page. An improvement to this site would be to devise a single set of well-positioned, visible controls. This would simplify the display by reducing the number of elements and eliminate confusion about which of multiple similar options the user should select.

TYPEFACES AND THE DISPLAY OF TEXT

Because of its relatively low resolution, a computer monitor cannot display text nearly as well as a printed sheet of paper. Reading large quantities of on-screen text can be a profoundly tiring experience. Yet the Web makes more and more text content available to us every day. There are a number of steps that designers can take to increase the readability of a website or software's text.

Select Readable Typefaces

Start by selecting a typeface that is easy to read in its intended medium. Newspapers and books often use a **serif typeface** such as Times New Roman as their primary typeface, as it is easily read on paper. Serif typefaces include the tiny lines at the bases and tops of characters such as A, I, and M. Although serif typefaces look good in print, they are generally less readable on a computer screen. The lower resolution tends to blur the serifs' fine detail. Consider using them in websites or multimedia software when you expect your audience to print the text for reading on paper.

According to Lynch and Horton, the height of characters such as the lower-case "x" (the x-height) and the overall size of the typeface determine the legibility of screen text. The serif typeface Georgia was designed with an exaggerated x-height and a large overall size when compared to other typefaces of the same point size. Unlike Times New Roman, Georgia looks great on screen, but appears large and awkward on paper.

| TIP |

Websites and software that include too many different typefaces, typeface sizes, and styles have an amateurish look. Select very few typefaces, sizes, and styles and use them consistently throughout the site or software.

A **sans serif typeface**—one without serifs, such as the commonly used Arial, Helvetica, and Verdana typefaces—is more readable on screen than a serif typeface. If your website or software has a lot of text, and you expect most of it to be read on screen rather than printed, then use a sans serif typeface.

Figure 9-10 shows examples of both serif and sans serif typefaces.

If the typeface you specify is not installed on a user's system, then you must provide it or the browser or software will substitute one of the

Serif Fonts	**Sans Serif Fonts**
Times New Roman	Arial
Georgia	**Verdana**
Bookman Old Style	Futura
Souvenir	**Lucida**
Courier	Tahoma

figure | 9-10 |

Some typefaces were designed for legibility on screen, while others are more easily read when printed on paper.

installed typefaces. Often this substitution yields less than satisfactory results. Products such as Macromedia Flash and Director allow you to include typefaces with your applications, but these must be downloaded with the Flash application, increasing the download time. For this reason, designers often confine their choices to the most common typefaces on each platform. Choosing Verdana, Arial, Times New Roman, and Georgia are usually safe bets.

Maximize Contrast between Text and Background

Text requires contrast for readability. As Figure 9-11 shows, text becomes more and more unreadable as the contrast between the typeface and the background is decreased.

| **TIP** |

A **watermark** is a faint graphic image used as a background for other elements such as text. When using an image as a watermark, lighten it enough that you can just see the image without distracting the user's attention from its overlaid text. Simply lightening a graphic to use it as a watermark does not change its file size. You can, however, reduce the file size by reducing the number of colors in the image. This can enable web designers to realize the visual benefits of watermark graphics, while keeping file sizes relatively small.

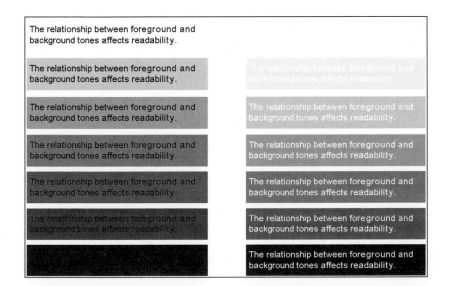

figure | 9-11 |

Text is most legible when the contrast—the difference between the foreground and background—is greatest. For large amounts of text, black text on very light backgrounds is recommended.

Dark text on a light background is easier to read than light text on a dark background. Whenever possible, use dark text on the lightest shades for blocks of text such as sentences, paragraphs, and bulleted points. Confine your use of light-colored text on dark backgrounds to titles or headings or to bring attention to a particular text segment.

Figure 9-12 shows the effects of darkening a watermarked image on the readability of the text.

figure | 9-12 |

When overlaying text over a graphic image, reduce the contrast of the image and increase the brightness until the image is just discernable. This will maximize the text's legibility. Photo by the author.

Use Left Justification for Multiple-Line Text

The type of justification you choose for blocks of text can significantly affect its readability. In general, left-justify text when it extends beyond a single line. Figure 9-13 shows samples of text that has been left justified, center-justified, and right-justified for comparison.

Notice that it requires effort for your eye to locate the beginning of each line of center- and right-justified text. It requires much less searching for your eye to find the beginning of each left-justified line. This is not to say that multiple-line text should never be right justified, but be aware of the usability cost.

Figure 9-14, a portion of a Web page, illustrates several problems with text. The designer of this page decided to alter the size of the typeface to fit the space. The unintended result is that some questions seem more important simply due to the size of text. The size of the question text should be consistent throughout. The text of each button is consistent except for the one that reads, "What are my ordering options?" This text uses two different sizes. For some reason, this is the only button without the single-line box, an apparent oversight.

Notice how the center justification of the text makes the questions harder to read and breaks each first line unnaturally. Left-justifying the text would give it a clean left edge and make it more readable. These options might be better represented as links instead of rectangular buttons. The background of the buttons alternates between light blue and light yellow. This only adds to the visual confusion. A single background color would serve the page better. Finally, the Products and Prices and the Client Photo Gallery should be given a different graphic treatment, since they are not questions like the others.

figure | **9-13** |

Left-justified text is easiest to read because the user doesn't have to search for the beginning of the next line.

Left-justified Text	When text extends to multiple lines, it is easiest to read when left justified. Center-justified and right-justified text leave a ragged left edge that requires more effort to locate the beginning of each text line.
Center-justified Text	When text extends to multiple lines, it is easiest to read when left justified. Center-justified and right-justified text leave a ragged left edge that requires more effort to locate the beginning of each text line.
Right-justified Text	When text extends to multiple lines, it is easiest to read when left justified. Center-justified and right-justified text leave a ragged left edge that requires more effort to locate the beginning of each text line.

figure | **9-14** |

This web page illustrates several common text problems. Multiple lines of text should be left justified rather than centered, and the text size should be kept consistent.

Welcome to Great Northern Sand & Gravel Company
Washed & sieved scale size sand, gravel, crushed stone and scenery materials.

Who is Great Northern Sand & Gravel Company?	How will my order be shipped?
How are these products processed and packaged?	Who can I contact?
What are my Ordering Options?	What about Privacy?
Products and Prices	Client Photo Gallery

Building Kit Offer

Arrange Lists Vertically

It is generally easier to find a particular item in a list arranged vertically than horizontally. Figure 9-15 contains a list of fictitious team names. Try to find the Harrisburg Ramblers in each list.

Bar Harbor Marimbas, Oakland Braves, Columbus Steeds, Raleigh Blue Lightning, Harrisburg Ramblers, Rochester Blazers, Eugene Hornets, St. Thomas Wildfire, New Britain Cougars, Wildwood Wildcats, Cheyenne Broncos, Provo Coyotes, Oklahoma City Sun Devils, Scottsdale Cardinals, Princeton Hawks, Frankfurt Lions

Eugene Hornets
Columbus Steeds
New Britain Cougars
Scottsdale Cardinals
Harrisburg Ramblers
Oakland Braves
Princeton Hawks
Rochester Blazers
Cheyenne Broncos
Oklahoma City Sun Devils
Provo Coyotes
Bar Harbor Marimbas
Frankfurt Lions
Raleigh Blue Lightning
Wildwood Wildcats
St. Thomas Wildfire

figure | 9-15 |

It is easier to locate an item in a vertically oriented list than in one that is horizontally oriented. This is especially true when each item can contain more than one word.

Most people can find the team name faster in the vertically oriented list. The vertical list is especially helpful when some or all of the entries in the list contain two or more words. The vertical orientation, with one entry per line, helps us by showing us the length of each entry. In the horizontal list, we have to do the work of searching for commas to determine where each entry ends and the next begins.

We purposely chose unfamiliar team names to keep you from using any previous sports knowledge to help you locate the target team. We also arranged things so that the Harrisburg Ramblers were the fifth entry in both lists. This was done to make the test as fair as possible, since it might take more time to find a term near the end of a list than the beginning.

An informal or formal test to determine the speed of finding items in horizontal or vertical lists could be designed on a computer. In each trial, the subject would be asked to find an entry in a list. The list would vary in each trial, as would the search term. Sometimes the entries in the list would be horizontally arranged and sometimes vertically. The computer would keep track of the time it took the subject to find the search term. The computer could compile and compare the time to search for items in horizontal versus vertical lists.

USING GRAPHICS TO SUPPORT USABILITY

Graphic images offer many important benefits to websites and multimedia software, including:

- They help create the mood of the website or software.
- They help establish an emotional connection with our audience.
- They add life to websites and software, creating an interesting departure from text.
- They can motivate users to make a buying decision or explore further.
- They give users important clues about the nature and priorities of a website or software program.
- They can provide detailed product views, enabling users to make informed decisions about products they may be considering buying.

These benefits come at the expense of potentially large file sizes that require long load times on narrow-bandwidth systems. For this reason, designers must ensure that the site's graphics are chosen carefully and truly support the site's goals. Each image selected must carry its own weight.

Images Create a First Impression

Many home pages include a relatively large image in the prominent position below the organization's name. Such an image can be very effective in attracting the user's attention.

Figure 9-16 shows the area above the fold of an automobile museum's home page.

| TIP |

When selecting or evaluating a photograph or image for a website, ask what value it provides to the site's visitors. If visitors had the choice, would they choose to keep or eliminate the image? If you believe visitors would eliminate this image, then what type of image might they be likely to keep?

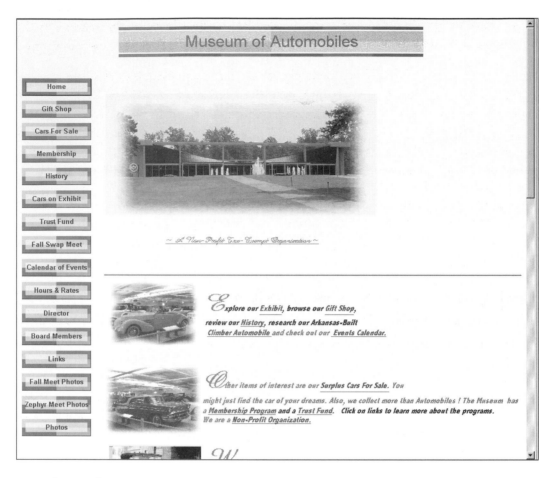

figure | 9-16 |

Strive to select images that do justice to the subject of your website. The photo of the museum does not create an emotional connection with the site visitor.

Notice that the most prominent image on the page is the long shot of the exterior of the museum itself. How strongly or weakly do you think this image likely connects with the site's visitors? Does this image deserve such a prominent position on the homepage?

If the building itself were of significant architectural significance—such as the Guggenheim Museum in New York—then featuring it prominently might be a good idea. This building, although attractive with its fountains and wide expanse of lawn, looks reasonably similar to thousands of other commercial structures. Perhaps there are automobiles displayed behind the glass windows of the entry, but we are too far away to know.

The value of the museum is not the building itself but the collection of vintage automobiles that it houses. A professionally shot photograph of part of the exhibit area or a close-up of the fins or other details of a single automobile would likely create a stronger connection with the site's audience. At present the automobile photos on the page are given much less prominence.

While we are looking at this site, perhaps we can make some additional suggestions to improve it. The italicized text on the page is difficult to read and would be improved by changing its style to normal. There are three different colors used for the text (four if you count visited links). This should be reduced to one or, at most, two colors. The italicized script typeface that says, "A Non-Profit Tax-Exempt Organization" is particularly difficult to read and should be changed to a more readable typeface.

Some of the menu options on the left could be combined to reduce the visual clutter of the site. For example, the last three photo options could be combined into a single Photos item. The Director and Board Members could be part of an About Us item. Many of the text links next to the auto photos simply duplicate the menu choices on the left without giving additional information. This area could be used to further the goals of the organization, such as highlighting the benefits of museum membership. There is currently no easy-to-find link to driving directions or a map of the museum.

The graphic look of the site could be enhanced to highlight its subject matter. For example, the site's graphical elements could suggest the interior of a vintage automobile's dashboard. A talented graphic artist could strengthen the connection between the site's look and its subject matter.

Next, look at Figure 9-17.

In this example from an interior page of a popular theater's website, the image chosen is a photo of the actual box office. Although this is a relatively small photo, what purpose does it serve? If people were having difficulty locating the box office once inside the theater, perhaps one could make an argument for featuring it prominently. To suggest

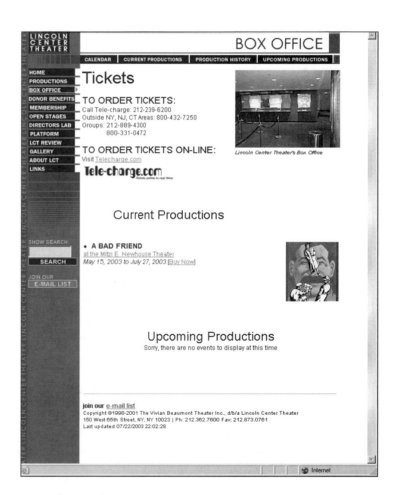

figure | **9-17** |

Although this image is small, how does it serve the site's audience?

a replacement, we might ask what type of image would be useful or motivating to someone who had chosen to visit a Box Office link to a major theater.

Perhaps showing a crowd of happy, attractive theater attendees on an opening night would be an effective image. Another option might be to display a photograph depicting a dramatically visual scene from a production. The idea is to use this important bit of Web page real estate to make an important point or create an emotional link with the audience.

Notice that this theater offers ticket sales through a third party, represented by a link. Selecting this link from the box office page displays the third party organization's home page. Users must then search for the theater's current productions. Perhaps it would be better if clicking this link displayed a page that featured ticket sales for just this theater's current productions. Visitors could select the desired production to purchase tickets for it. If the theater's current productions were not of interest to the visitor, there could be links to other entertainment options as well.

figure | 9-18 |

The top photo shows the existing menu. We altered the bottom version to simplify the menu visually and call attention to the selected menu choice.

The graphic style of the menu on the left side of this page detracts from its readability. Figure 9-18 shows the present design on top and a suggested alternative below.

The designer of the original page chose to shorten the black background of each menu item. This adds a lot of unnecessary visual clutter to the page. The redesigned version includes this effect only on the selected option, giving it emphasis and improving the readability of the page. We also increased the space between the menu items and the ticket ordering information, thereby making it easier to read.

Some companies understand very well how to use images to convey a powerful message. Figure 9-19 shows a chocolate company's home page. The strong imagery, simple layout, and classic look of the page can lead a hungry reviewer to overlook the harder-to-process horizontal arrangement of the menu items. Of course, not all companies are lucky enough to have such photogenic products to include!

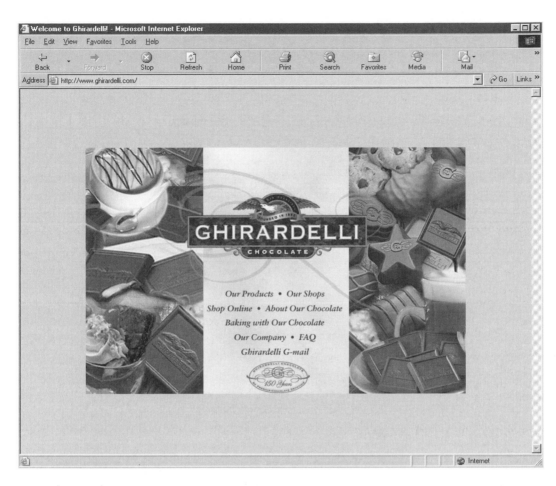

Some companies are lucky enough to have visually compelling products and smart enough to feature them prominently.

Images for Functional Purposes

Although images often help create the important first impression of a site, they also can serve a more functional role. Figures 9-20 and 9-21 were captured from very similar websites. The purpose of these sites is to allow those who are purchasing ice hockey tickets to see the view from any part of the arena. The application itself is excellent because it uses the power of the Web to add real value to the user's experience. It would be difficult, if not impossible, to duplicate this capability in any other medium.

Now let's examine the way the two different sites handle this application. We'll focus on how each site uses visual information to convey its message, starting with Figure 9-20.

As we roll the mouse over a section in the diagram, it displays a photograph of the view from that section. For this example, we rolled over section 125. The view from section 125 is displayed in the upper right part of our screen. We'll refer to this page as the Gorillas' page.

Next, take a look at Figure 9-21, a similar seat selector for the Grand Rapids Griffins.

To use this application, we click on a section and its view is shown in a new browser window. In this example, we've clicked on section 118. We'll call this page the Griffins' page.

Let's start with the seating section view. The Gorillas' page has users mouse over a section to see the view, while visitors to the Griffins' site must click the section. The Gorillas' page will

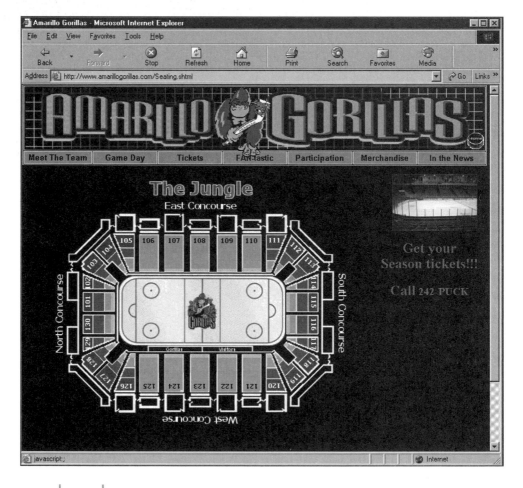

figure | 9-20 |

The Amarillo Gorillas seat locator

allow users to compare views more easily, but the Griffins' page wins because of the size and clarity of the view itself.

A key difference between the two sites' photographs is certainly the size of the images. Although the small size of the Gorillas' images allows them to load very quickly—fast enough to be displayed on mouse roll over—the images are too small to convey useful information about the view.

Even more important, the Griffins' photograph shows players on the ice during an actual game. This provides the sense of scale that is essential to evaluating the view. The photographs

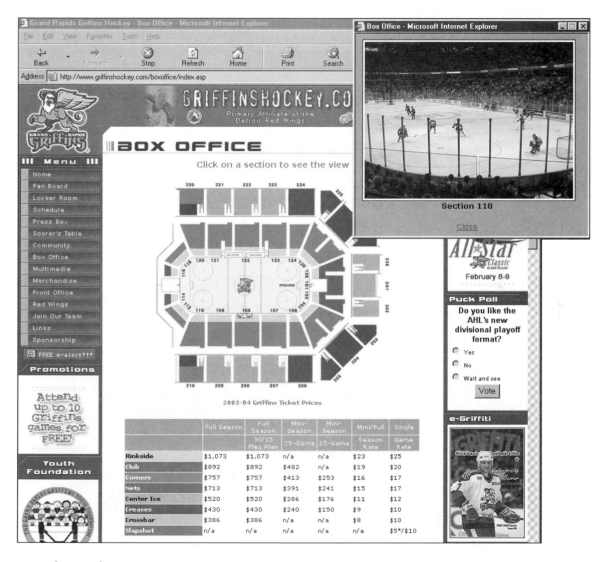

figure | 9-21 |

The Grand Rapids Griffins seat locator

of the Gorillas' arena were taken when the building was empty of spectators and players. This must have made it very convenient for the photographer to shoot the images. The result, however, is barren and lifeless. It fails to communicate the excitement of watching a live, lightning-fast sporting event.

Now consider the plight of the Griffins' photographer, attempting to photograph the arena during a live game. It must have been difficult to dodge the crowds, squeeze into each section, wait for the action, then squeeze off a few shots before moving on to the next section and repeating the whole process. The results certainly justify the effort, however.

There are a number of other observations we can make in evaluating the two sites. While the Griffins' page attracts the eye with its use of white space, the Gorillas' site is predominantly dark, echoing the lifelessness of the arena images. It feels almost as if we were visiting the site during its off hours.

Neither site does a particularly good job of labeling the arena sections in the diagrams. The Gorillas' site is readable in the top half of the arena, but sections 118 through 128 should be labeled normally instead of upside-down. The Griffins' site gets the orientation right, but would be more effective if the sections themselves were numbered instead of the ice and surrounding area. This would make it more obvious which sections the numbers refer to.

The Griffins' site designer was most likely concerned about the contrast problem that would result from overlaying the section numbers on the colored sections. This could have been overcome by including a small rectangle of white background along with the numbers. The white provides the necessary contrast for the black numbers, as shown in rough form in Figure 9-22.

In reviewing these two sites, it was striking how strong a visual

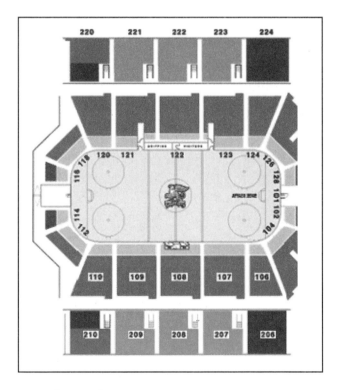

figure | 9-22 |

We have redrawn the section numbers on the lower part of the arena to more clearly identify each section.

impression the Griffin's site made. Within the first few seconds, the visitor's confidence in the site grows. There is an attention to detail, such as the angling of the corners near the top of the page and the expanse of white to suggest an ice rink. The page is bright and well organized.

The ticket pricing information on the Griffins' site adds significant information directly related to the visitor's purpose—to see arena seating views and purchase tickets. On a single page, visitors can both compare views from different sections and see the difference in pricing among the various choices. (Better still if the site could show which sections had seats still available for specific upcoming games!)

The Gorillas' site only shows the seating chart. The pricing information is buried deep in another page that includes a smaller, non-interactive version of the seating diagram. Moving this information onto the same page as the interactive seating view would encourage ticket sales by making the process of selecting seats and purchasing tickets as easy as possible.

In reviewing the Gorillas' site, there was another problem that was revealed. The photos appear very close to the menus labeled Merchandise and In the News. Normally this is not a problem, since the photos are revealed only when the mouse rolls over a section. The HTML doesn't execute quickly enough, however, to prevent the photo from remaining on screen if the mouse is moved very quickly off a section.

If you then move the mouse cursor over the Merchandise or In the News menus, the menu is displayed in back of the photo, as shown in Figure 9-23.

This is an example of unanticipated events causing things to work unexpectedly. The person who coded this site wasn't concerned that the photos were displayed on a layer closer to the viewer than the menu. It seemed impossible for this condition to occur—if the photo was displayed, then the mouse cursor must be positioned over a section and not over a menu.

The particular behavior that caused the problem, namely the failure of the processing to keep up with the user's mouse movement, may not have occurred on the developer's system. This emphasizes the need to continually test the code on a variety of different systems.

Using the techniques discussed in this chapter, you will improve the readability, usability, and overall appeal of the websites and software you design. By combining your creative ideas with good visual design techniques, you will ensure the best experience possible for your audience. In the next chapter, we will discuss how to write for the Web and multimedia software.

figure | **9-23** |

This unwanted effect emphasizes the need to have all your work carefully checked by an independent quality tester.

SUMMARY OF KEY POINTS

- When designing a Web page or software screen, thinking of it as a grid may help you create an organizing structure for the content.

- Use the unfocused attention technique to quickly evaluate the balance and contrast of a composition and to observe where the user's eye is drawn.

- Place the most important content of a website above the fold, where it is easiest to see.

- Enhance the readability of text by choosing fonts designed for screen display and by increasing the contrast between foreground and background.

- In general, left justify text that is greater than one line long to increase its readability.

- Vertically oriented lists are easier for users to scan than horizontally oriented lists.

- Choose graphics that add real value to Web pages. Avoid using images that merely provide decoration, as they are not worth the time it takes to download them.

in review

1. What is gained by looking at a screen or page design with unfocused eyes?

2. What purpose does creating a visual hierarchy serve on a website or in software?

3. What is the best way to align a page of labels and text entry boxes? Why?

4. Name a typeface that was created especially for display on a computer monitor rather than for printing on paper. What is it about this typeface that lends itself to viewing on screen?

5. Why is center- and right-justified text more difficult to read than left-justified text?

6. What are some important goals for a large graphic used on the home page of a website?

exercise

1. Find a website that is not well organized and appears visually complex. Create a schematic diagram of the site like the ones shown in Figures 9-2 and 9-4, using blocks of tones to approximate the visual weight of the elements. Try to redesign the information on the site by reorganizing it, repositioning elements, or other means to make it simpler visually. Show the "before" and "after" versions of the site to your fellow students.

writing for usability

objectives

Analyze how Web visitors are different from most other types of readers

Examine how the inverted pyramid structure helps users read content efficiently

Examine how carefully worded titles and headings can help users scan your page's content

Analyze techniques to reduce the amount of text on your pages

Describe when and why to add personality to your Web writing

Describe how to help keep users from prematurely leaving your site

Examine why ambiguity is detrimental to instructional writing and how to avoid it

Examine the importance of voice, pace, and sequence in instructional writing

introduction

Most users of websites and multimedia software are goal-driven. They have a specific task to accomplish and want to complete that task as efficiently as possible. Well-structured, well-written text is the key to satisfying these users' needs. This chapter will give you specific strategies for improving the quality of your Web writing.

User interface designers are often called upon to write instructional text. In its simplest form, this means crafting brief operational instructions for software or websites. If you are a skilled writer, you may be asked to write detailed training material or Help text for a multimedia program or website. We will explore techniques for writing instructional materials that minimize obstacles to learning.

Get ready to improve your writing skills!

WRITING FOR USABILITY

WRITING FOR THE WEB

Hand someone an advertising brochure, and they can see your complete message in whatever context you choose to present it. Create a television or radio ad, and viewers are likely to see or hear it in its entirety.

Although a website is a powerful means of delivering visitors to you, it doesn't allow you to control how each visitor will experience your message. Many visitors will reach your site through a search engine, which is likely to drop them somewhere in the middle of your site. These visitors will miss any written introduction you may have provided on a different page unless they choose to navigate there.

To anticipate the many paths that visitors might take to a page of your website, you must provide the means for users to quickly orient themselves to the site's identification and purpose. Include the name of the company or organization and the main navigation controls on every page of the site where possible.

To entice users to spend more of their valuable time at your site, you must find a way to quickly establish a connection with them. Writing is one way to establish such a connection, but you must first know what motivates Web users. Let's explore how a Web user's behavior differs from that of other types of readers and how we can use this information to improve our Web writing.

Website Visitors Scan More Than Read

Because the Web gives us access to so much content about so many topics for such little effort, Web users have become information foragers, quick to spot a promising morsel and equally quick to turn away if their needs are not immediately met. How can a writer convince such visitors to pause long enough to digest the site's content?

The answer is to communicate your site's messages as clearly, simply, and concisely as possible. Website visitors are extremely self-oriented. As such, they are only interested in your message as it affects them or their goals. To appeal to today's Web users, follow these guidelines:

| TIP |

When writing for the Web, assume that each visitor has navigated to the current page without seeing any other page of the site.

- Write concisely using as few words as possible.
- Write using an inverted pyramid structure, starting with the most important information and following with supporting details.
- Use page titles and headings to organize the page's content and help direct users to the information they seek.
- Use lists and bullets rather than paragraphs when possible to make it easy for users to scan information.
- Include a meaningful tag line.

- Let some personality show.
- Don't call attention to the Web medium.
- Use links to support your site, not detract from it.

Each of these guidelines is explored below.

Write Concisely

The simple fact is that many websites are overloaded with text. Attempting to scan large volumes of information on a variety of different sites can be exhausting and frustrating for users. Many sites can be vastly improved simply by eliminating all but the most essential information on each page.

To write concisely, start by creating an outline before writing the text for each page of a site. The outline will ensure that your thoughts are well organized and your message carefully constructed. It requires far fewer words to connect well-organized thoughts than it does to link haphazardly created ones.

Once your text is written, review it carefully, eliminating all unnecessary words and distilling your message as much as possible. Ask someone else to review and edit your text. If at all possible, use an experienced editor. They are adept at catching and fixing things that even great writers miss.

Write Using an Inverted Pyramid Structure

In some forms of writing, the author strings together statements, building toward a conclusion or main idea. This is known as a **pyramid structure**, since the foundation is lain and the supporting structure built row by row until the top (the conclusion or most important idea) is reached.

Writing for the Web works best when you use an **inverted pyramid** structure, a term borrowed from journalism. You start by stating the most important idea first, then add supporting information beneath in order from most important to least important. Visitors will know by scanning the first sentence whether the information contained in the paragraph is of value to them. If the information is not of interest, they can simply skip to the next paragraph. Those who are interested can continue reading the paragraph for the supporting details and additional information.

Figure 10-1 shows a diagram of the pyramid and inverted pyramid structures.

Example 1 uses a pyramid structure, which is not recommended for Web writing. Notice how the most important information is not revealed until the end of the passage.

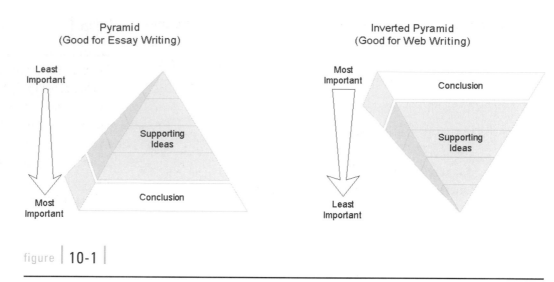

figure | 10-1 |

These diagrams illustrate the difference between the pyramid and inverted pyramid writing styles.

EXAMPLE 1: PYRAMID STRUCTURE Earlier this year, we at Coulter Design successfully completed a project for Allied Power Company. Allied was looking for a firm that could redesign their website to make it more usable. They had received many complaints from customers who found it difficult to find account balances, pay their bills online, and transfer service to a new address. Using our proven analysis and design methodologies, we reduced the number of complaints at Allied by 93 percent!

Example 2 uses the inverted pyramid structure that is best for writing on the Web. The reader gets the most important information first, then can read on for supporting information and additional details.

EXAMPLE 2: INVERTED PYRAMID STRUCTURE RECOMMENDED FOR WEB WRITING Coulter Design helped reduce usability complaints at Allied Power by 93 percent! Allied's customers were having difficulty finding account balances, paying their bills online, and transferring service to a new address. Allied asked Coulter Design to redesign their website to make it more usable. We successfully completed the project earlier this year.

Notice that readers of the pyramid-structured text in Example 1 will miss the main point unless they read to the end of the paragraph. Readers of the inverted pyramid text in Example 2 only have to read the first sentence to get the most important message.

Write using simple sentence structure, breaking long sentences into smaller ones to keep them short. Include just one thought per paragraph, since visitors who scan the text may skip a paragraph after reading the lead sentence. If another thought is buried within the paragraph, the reader is likely to miss it.

If you include descriptions of product or service features in your writing, be sure to include the benefits that each feature offers to the customer. Try to avoid using meaningless marketing names, such as "super-strong 1200D material" that mean nothing to the reader.

Use Page Titles and Headings

Include a page title that summarizes the main purpose of the page. Page titles are important for several reasons. Search engines use them to help locate pages that meet the user's search criteria. The page title is what appears in the title bar of the browser window and in the Favorites list when you store a page in Favorites. You should also include the page title in a large, prominent font style near the top of the page.

Headings are subtitles that introduce the various content areas of the page. Use headings to introduce each new topic on the page. Figure 10-2 shows a good example of headings used to introduce new topics.

The headings make it easy to scan the page, providing a summary of this page's content. Visitors can read just those sections of interest or read the entire page. The text within each heading is kept brief and to the point, so visitors can quickly get the facts they need.

| TIP |

It's okay to create clever titles and headings to try to entice visitors to read more. Beware of including obscure or local references or tricky metaphors, though. If the titles or headings are too difficult to understand, visitors may not take the time to try to figure them out.

What is Shutterfly?

Shutterfly is an online photo service designed to help you get film-quality prints from your digital camera delivered right to your door. We'll make it easy to share your pictures with friends and family, without the expense and hassle of home printers or trips to the store.

The latest in technology to help prints last a lifetime
We use Fuji Crystal Archive paper along with Fuji chemicals and equipment to ensure that your pictures will last for years. Our exclusive VividPics® technology ensures that all your pictures are adjusted for color automatically.

Using Shutterfly is easy
Once you add your pictures to your Shutterfly account, you can enhance them as needed by reducing red eye and cropping images. You can even personalize them with a message on the back and get creative by enhancing the color, changing color pictures to black and white, or adding your choice of borders on front. And we make it simple to send prints to friends and family or to share your pictures online.

The end result
What does all this mean for you? More quality, more creativity, and more flexibility, for starters. Since you have more ways to customize your prints, your shots will look the way you want them to. Plus, you don't need to worry about trips to the local photo lab, or the expense and hassle of home printing. And we guarantee customer satisfaction.

Go to top

figure | 10-2 |

Simple, clear and concise, these headings and the associated text are easy to follow.

Use Lists and Bullets Instead of Paragraphs

Consider the two methods of describing the features and benefits of house paint in Examples 3 and 4.

EXAMPLE 3: SkinTight paint is a premium, hassle-free house paint that will give you years of excellent coverage for your house's exterior surfaces. It has been specially formulated to cover most surfaces with just one coat! It is latex based, so cleanup is a snap with just soap and water. You won't need messy turpentine or dangerous chemicals to clean your rollers and brushes. SkinTight is one of the most durable paints on the market. It resists harsh sunlight and all types of weather. It will keep your house beautiful for years to come!

EXAMPLE 4: SkinTight is the premium, hassle-free house paint!

- Covers most surfaces with just one coat

- Cleans up with soap and water—no messy turpentine or harmful chemicals

- Incredibly durable—resists harsh sunlight and rough weather

- Keeps your house beautiful for years

Example 4 contains nearly the same information as Example 3, yet it uses 56 percent fewer words! Using bullet points instead of paragraphs allows readers to access this information much more quickly than by reading the text in paragraph form. Since bullet points can be sentence fragments rather than complete sentences, we can reduce the number of words while conveying the same meaning.

Notice how the language in Example 4 supports the message. The text includes many action verbs (covers, cleans, resists) and descriptive adjectives (messy, harmful, incredibly, durable, harsh, rough, beautiful). This helps readers to conjure mental images of the positive aspects of the product and the negative aspects of its alternatives.

The formatting of the points also facilitates quick reading and understanding. Each bullet point contains just one feature. A blank line separates each bullet point. The formatting increases the visibility of the message and makes it easy for users to scan the list. The consistent way each point is structured makes it clear that here are four good reasons to buy this paint.

Include a Meaningful Tag Line

A **tag line** is a brief, one- or two-line statement that summarizes a company or organization. Tag lines are most appropriate for corporations, small companies, and organizations. They don't generally appear on an individual person's website. Tag lines are usually positioned near the logo at the top of each page.

Follow These Simple Directions

Example 4 shows how separating paragraph text into a series of points increases clarity. Look at how this same technique makes driving directions much easier to follow than writing them in paragraph form. Most directions are written in paragraph form, like this:

> Get on Route 95 South. Take this highway to exit 25, which is the Middlebury Road exit. Make a left turn at the off ramp. Continue on Middlebury Road until you have passed three traffic lights. At the third traffic light make a left turn onto Green Avenue. Continue on Green Avenue for two streets until you come to a Texaco gas station on the left. Make a right turn at this intersection onto Oak Lane. Our house is the third house on the left. It is a brown house with white shutters.

The driver or a passenger must search through the paragraph multiple times to find the next instruction to follow. Drivers should never read while operating a vehicle, but the formatting of the directions makes the situation even more dangerous. As we did in Example 4, we'll write the directions one to each line, like this:

> Route 95 South
>
> Exit 25 (Middlebury Road)
>
> At off ramp turn left
>
> At third traffic light turn left (Green Avenue)
>
> At second street (Texaco station on left) turn right (Oak Lane)
>
> Third house on left (brown with white shutters, 114 Oak Lane)

When the directions are formatted this way, it is much easier to scan the list to find the next direction. We reduced the total word count by more than half—from 93 words to 42 words. The directions are easy to understand and follow. The author of the directions could improve them further by including the approximate distance of each step of the directions.

A tag line serves several important functions:

- It communicates the site or company's purpose.
- It can provide insight into the company's philosophy and practices.
- It can evoke confidence and other positive feelings about the website or company among its visitors.

Creating a tag line that captures the spirit of the website or its company is not an easy task. Corporations and other large organizations usually hire outside advertising agencies or other consultants to help them develop their tag lines. If you are called upon to help create a tag line for a small company or organization, beware that you may find yourself in the middle of heated debates about the merits of one approach over another.

Look at the tag lines shown in Figure 10-3, and notice how they capture the essence of the company or website in just a few words.

To create a tag line you must understand a number of things about the client. First, you should know who the audience is for their products or services. Next, find out what clearly differentiates the client from its competitors. Finally, learn about the underlying philosophy that the company may want to convey. Creating a memorable tag line means weaving these considerations together into just a few words that connect with the intended audience.

figure | **10-3** |

The simplicity of these tag lines from well-known companies belies the effort required to create them.

Let Some Personality Show

As Web writer Nick Usborne suggests, Web communication, characterized by millions of people chatting with one another daily, is interactive and conversational. Typical corporation-centric writing seems overly pompous and stiffly formal when it is read on the Web. While evidence supports the need to connect emotionally with visitors, strong forces within the corporation may fight to keep its voice aloof and impersonal.

Simple techniques, such as substituting the word "we" for the name of the corporation, help to humanize the message. The idea is that *people*, not corporations, do things like release new products and services and speak to customers. Look at how Examples 5, 6, and 7 show how the choice of words can help humanize the message. Example 5 shows a paragraph written in typical corporate language.

EXAMPLE 5:

HomeProducts Corporation is pleased to announce that it is extending its highly successful Rebate program through December. HomeProducts will send a $100 rebate check to anyone who purchases a new PowerBlast 500 system from the company by December.

Example 5 makes HomeProducts Corporation sound stiff and distant. Let's apply the word "we" in place of the company name to try to humanize the message.

EXAMPLE 6: We are pleased to announce that we are extending our highly successful Rebate program through December. We will send a $100 rebate check to anyone who purchases a new PowerBlast 500 system from us by December.

The use of the words "we" and "us" in Example 6 makes HomeProducts sound more like a group of people than a faceless entity. Let's see if we can humanize the message even further.

EXAMPLE 7: Thanks so much to all of you who have made our PowerBlast 500 Rebate program so successful! We are extending the rebate offer through December to help even more people take advantage of the savings. Just buy a PowerBlast 500 from us before New Year's Day, and we'll be happy to send you a $100 rebate check! If you know someone else who might benefit from this offer, we'd appreciate your telling them, too. Thanks!

Example 7 uses an informal tone to connect with the audience. Rather than imposing its message on visitors, it starts by thanking them. Its aim is to make the reader feel like part of a community of people with a common interest.

Your goal is to convey that the people of the company are friendly, competent, trustworthy, flexible, and supportive of the customer. To win the visitor's trust, you must write truthfully without making exaggerated or unsubstantiated claims about the products or services the company provides.

The degree to which you can personalize the written message will vary according to your client's policies and goals. Even small steps, like using "we" instead of the company name, convey a feeling of humanity that will help you connect with your audience.

Don't Call Attention to the Web Medium

In the early days of the Web, writers were very conscious of the fact that they were writing for the Web. Web-conscious messages like those in Example 8 were commonplace:

EXAMPLE 8: This website is for fans of the Wilde Oates rock and roll band.

This page contains a list of authorized Bronco dealers.

Click this link to order a Spinster 1000.

You have probably noticed that very few television commercials begin by saying, "This television commercial will introduce you to the …" The writers assume you know that you are watching a television commercial.

| TIP |

Don't write in a style that is inconsistent with the organization you are representing. Attempts to make a large corporation sound like a surfer dude or hip rap artist will be seen as disingenuous and laughable. Write in a style that is true to its owner.

Similarly, you don't find magazine, radio, or newspaper ads or programs identifying themselves as such before delivering their message.

The Web is now mature enough that you can assume its viewers know they are looking at a website or Web page. Simply identify the site or page and your audience will get the idea. Include the "Wilde Oates" band's logo on each page of the site to identify it clearly. Where appropriate, include a title such as "Authorized Bronco Dealers" to identify a particular page.

Follow a similar strategy for links, although they require a little more thought. Start by keeping the following points in mind:

- Avoid mentioning the word "link" except when creating a heading for a list of links.
- Don't say "Click here to …"
- Incorporate the link in the text.

Try to think of a graceful way to incorporate the link into the text. For example, if you are providing a link to a list of authorized dealers, you might say, "Visit one of our authorized Bronco dealers." The underlined text indicates the link, of course.

| TIP |

Avoid lengthy greetings and detailed instructions how to use the website or Web page. If extensive instructions are required, chances are the site or page needs to be redesigned to be simpler and more intuitive.

Perhaps you are linking to a page containing awards that the company has won. You might say, "We at Interplay Studios are proud of the industry awards our innovative designs have won."

Whenever possible, word your links explicitly to give users clues about what is appropriate for them to do on the page. Use directives such as Pay your bills or Find a hotel. Be sure to deliver whatever it is that your links promise. Don't entice users with a clearly worded link, then force them to go through other unnecessary pages to actually get to the function.

Figure 10-4 illustrates some of the problems we have discussed so far.

Use Links to Support Your Site, Not Detract from It

As we've previously stated, links are one of the Web's most powerful tools. Use them correctly and you provide an enriching experience for your visitors while supporting the goals of your site. Include them carelessly, though, and you simply encourage visitors to leave your site, perhaps never to return.

Consider Example 9, which illustrates how links can detract from your site's message:

EXAMPLE 9: Filled with six pounds of prime Northern goose down, the Blue Cocoon sleeping bag is guaranteed to keep you warm down to -40° F. On a recent Mount Everest ascent, Skip McMurtry and his Sherpa guides found themselves removing layers of clothing at night to keep from overheating.

Worksite Benefit Plans, Inc.

> The welcome from the President is not a bad idea, but it contains mostly throwaway text. The two glaring errors in this paragraph should never have made it past the proofreaders.

Welcome to Worksite Benefit Plans, Inc.'s Homepage. We thank you for visiting our website. Our goals is to provide you an overview of our organization in a user-friendly environment. Please take your time to browse the information we have provided to give you an insight into our mission, services, products and staff. Do not hesitate to contact us if we can provide any further information about our company or if we can answer questions you may have regarding Cafeteria Plans (section 125) adminstration or in the area of Employee Benefits.

Thank you,

> Underlining the headings makes them look like clickable links, though they are not.

Employee Flex Account Information

Click here to ACCESS your Flex Account Information.

What's New

> "Click here" is unnecessary. The word ACCESS in all caps is confusing. A suggestion might be to change this line to:
>
> Access your Flex Account information.

September 28, 2000
Change of Status Categories:

Final regulations on the new change of status have been issued this year and will go into effect January 1, 2001, however they may be implemented prior to that. Worksite Benefit Plans, Inc. is in the process of compiling a new change of status matrix that should be available by November.

The new change of status regulations establishes categories of valid status change events. If an event does not fit into one of the categories listed below, it does not qualify as a status change.

For a detailed explination contact WBP at worksite_benefit_plans@msn.com

1999 IRS Form 5500 Revised

figure | **10-4** |

This page illustrates several problems we have discussed. The welcome paragraph is friendly, but poor editing sends the wrong message to visitors.

If the goal of this site is primarily to educate visitors about sleeping bags, ascending Mount Everest, and Sherpas, then perhaps you can justify including so many links in this paragraph. If your goal is to sell sleeping bags, though, then the numerous links present obstacles to making a sale. They simply provide multiple opportunities for your visitors to leave your site to explore the linked topics. The linked pages may provide further interesting links, so it is possible that your visitor will never return to your site.

There is an excellent reason to include the story of Skip and his toasty companions, however. Their experience lends credibility to the quality of the sleeping bag. Example 10 shows how we can use their experience to help convince the visitor to buy the product:

EXAMPLE 10: Filled with six pounds of prime Northern goose down, the Blue Cocoon sleeping bag is guaranteed to keep you warm down to -40° F. On a recent Mount Everest ascent, Skip McMurtry and his Sherpa guides found themselves removing layers of clothing at night to keep from overheating. Read about Skip's adventure.

A site visitor who wants justification for buying the Blue Cocoon can follow the link to Skip's adventure to get the details. Positioned at the end of the passage, the link does not interrupt the message's flow.

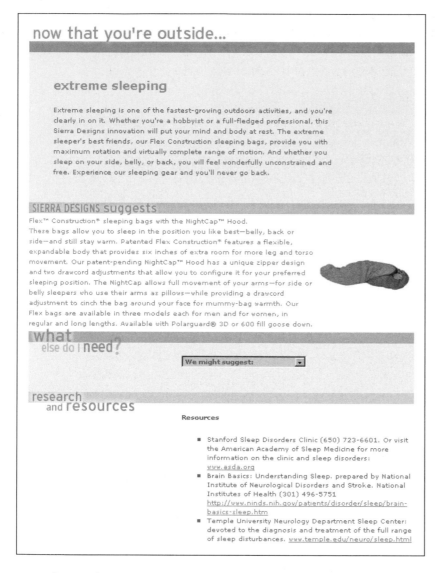

now that you're outside...

extreme sleeping

Extreme sleeping is one of the fastest-growing outdoors activities, and you're clearly in on it. Whether you're a hobbyist or a full-fledged professional, this Sierra Designs innovation will put your mind and body at rest. The extreme sleeper's best friends, our Flex Construction sleeping bags, provide you with maximum rotation and virtually complete range of motion. And whether you sleep on your side, belly, or back, you will feel wonderfully unconstrained and free. Experience our sleeping gear and you'll never go back.

SIERRA DESIGNS suggests

Flex™ Construction* sleeping bags with the NightCap™ Hood. These bags allow you to sleep in the position you like best—belly, back or side—and still stay warm. Patented Flex Construction* features a flexible, expandable body that provides six inches of extra room for more leg and torso movement. Our patent-pending NightCap™ Hood has a unique zipper design and two drawcord adjustments that allow you to configure it for your preferred sleeping position. The NightCap allows full movement of your arms—for side or belly sleepers who use their arms as pillows—while providing a drawcord adjustment to cinch the bag around your face for mummy-bag warmth. Our Flex bags are available in three models each for men and for women, in regular and long lengths. Available with Polarguard® 3D or 600 fill goose down.

what else do I need?

We might suggest: ▾

research and resources

Resources

- Stanford Sleep Disorders Clinic (650) 723-6601. Or visit the American Academy of Sleep Medicine for more information on the clinic and sleep disorders: www.asda.org
- Brain Basics: Understanding Sleep, prepared by National Institute of Neurological Disorders and Stroke. National Institutes of Health (301) 496-5751 http://www.ninds.nih.gov/patients/disorder/sleep/brain-basics-sleep.htm
- Temple University Neurology Department Sleep Center: devoted to the diagnosis and treatment of the full range of sleep disturbances. www.temple.edu/neuro/sleep.html

figure | 10-5 |

The separate "research and resources" area on this page keeps the rest of the page free of distracting links.

The linked page should be written to provide evidence of the sleeping bag's value. It should include a link to purchase the product so prospective buyers don't have to return to the original page.

Some designers create a separate area to list all of the links for a given page. The Links area is usually located near the bottom of the page. The main text of the page is kept free of links, which helps focus visitors' attention on the page. Figure 10-5 shows a page from a site that uses this technique to great advantage.

The page shown was displayed when I selected a response to the question, "What gets you outside?" I was intrigued by one of the choices—extreme sleeping—and selected it. Notice the effective use of humor in the opening paragraph. We all know that there is no sport called extreme sleeping. If there were, though, this might just be the bag to help you perform at your peak.

Bullet points may have made the product description faster and easier to scan. The writer did such a good job connecting with me in the opening paragraph, though, that I didn't mind reading the long text description. Besides, people who are researching a product for possible purchase seem perfectly willing to read and absorb a large amount of product-specific information.

WRITING FOR INSTRUCTION

Does anyone remember this classic "Saturday Night Live" skit? It's the one where the chief operator of a nuclear power plant, on his last day of work before beginning an extended vacation, gives instructions to the workers who will operate the plant in his absence. Smiling at them as he heads out the door, he pauses long enough to advise them to "Remember, you can't put too much water in a nuclear reactor!"

The rest of the skit centers on the befuddled crew's anguish as they grapple with the ambiguous meaning in those parting words. Did he mean "You mustn't put too much water in a nuclear reactor?" Or did he mean "There's no limit to the amount of water you can put in a nuclear reactor," as in "You can't get too much of Martha's home cooking"?

The vacation-bound chief operator knew what he meant, but his unfortunate choice of words failed to get that meaning across. When we converse with others, we provide meaning through much more than just the words we speak. Our facial expressions, body language, emphasis on certain words, and familiarity with one another all help us to interpret one another's meaning correctly. But instructional writers have only the words we choose to convey our meaning. For this reason, we must be especially careful in the choices we make.

Unfortunately, uncovering dual meanings in what we write is not a simple task. Like the chief operator, we usually know exactly what we mean. It never occurs to most of us that someone might misconstrue our meaning until someone actually does.

One way to help eliminate the problem is by being alert for ambiguous meanings. In some writing disciplines, selecting words with

ambiguous meanings may be acceptable or even desirable—in instructional writing it is deadly. Learners are like most people. When they come to an ambiguous word they simply apply whatever meaning suits them, assuming that you, the writer, meant it that way. And all is well until some conflicting statement makes them realize that none of what they have just read or learned makes sense.

Provide Context

I once asked a colleague to review an instructional document I had written, expecting her to heap praise on my efforts. Instead, the document was returned to me well endowed with red ink. My friend had scrawled "How come?" and "So what?" and "Who cares?" after many of the statements I had written.

It may sound silly, but now when I write, two imaginary trolls sit on my shoulders. Every time I write an instructional statement the left-side troll yells "How come?" and the right-side troll follows suit with "So what?"

For example, "Remember to give both the pink and yellow copies to the customer." (How come?) "This will enable the customer to give the pink copy to the installer, while saving the yellow copy for her records."

Or, "The SuperBee Digital Assistant is equipped with two USB ports." (So what?) "This enables you to connect two separate devices, such as your digital camera and scanner to the SuperBee at the same time.

This how come/so what technique can make your writing clearer by helping you avoid making assumptions about your learners. Providing answers to the questions "How come?" and "So what?" tells learners why the information you are giving them is important. It provides the proper context within which to apply this information. Having the proper context gives learners a more complete understanding of the subject, rather than a narrow view of just those pieces that affect them directly.

VOICE, PACE, AND SEQUENCE

Instructional writers need to pay special attention to the message carried in the words we write. This is important both for the operational instructions that tell learners how to proceed through training materials and for information about the topics themselves.

The use of voice affects the clarity of the message that our writing conveys. **Active voice** connotes directness and strength, characteristics that promote clarity. Insert tab "A" into slot "B."

Passive voice implies weakness or softness; it invites ambiguity. Slot "B" is used to receive tab "A."

To illustrate the use of voice, assume that the information presented in Example 11 accompanies a graphic drawing of a Frammis modulator valve.

EXAMPLE 11: The Frammis modulator valve is opened to drain excess fluid from the reservoir.

In this simple example, the use of passive voice hinders the learner's ability to understand exactly what is being said. Instructions worded in this fashion cause learners to ask questions such as, "Is this a picture of the Frammis modulator valve? Do I or the system open it? How do I open it?"

Because the learner is not as familiar with the topic as the writer, he may not be able to fill in the missing pieces. A better way to instruct the learner might be to change the wording of the statements as shown in Example 12:

EXAMPLE 12: This is the Frammis modulator valve. Open the Frammis modulator valve to drain excess fluid from the reservoir. To open this valve, push the toggle switch illustrated in the drawing to the "Open" position.

Besides the fact that the instructions are now written in active voice, notice that each sentence plays a specific role.

- The first sentence identifies the valve—it tells you what to look for.
- The second sentence tells you under what circumstances or when you would want to use it.
- The third sentence tells you how to use it.

This **what/when/how** construction works well in a variety of instructional circumstances. The first sentence is kept deliberately short. This control of the instruction's pace adds emphasis to the statement, possibly increasing the chances that the learner will later remember that this part is the Frammis modulator valve.

Also notice that the words Frammis modulator valve are repeated in the example. This repetition may help to further strengthen the association in the learner's mind between the part and its identifying label.

The next three examples are less effective in getting their instructional message across than Example 12. They represent some of the common problems found in instructional writing. Example 13 illustrates a problem with sequence.

EXAMPLE 13: This is the Frammis modulator valve. Open the Frammis modulator valve by pushing the toggle switch illustrated in the drawing to the "Open" position. This will drain excess fluid from the reservoir.

Notice in Example 13 that the description of what the valve does appears after the instructions that tell how to open it. The learner may not know that he wants to open the valve until after he finds out what it does. By then, of course, he must go back and reread the sentence that tells him how to open it.

Example 12 solves this problem by telling the learner how to open the valve after explaining what the valve does.

Sequence may assume an even more important role in instructional writing, as Example 14 illustrates. Imagine that Bob, a novice repairman, is using the instructions in this example to drain excess fluid from the reservoir. Approaching the live unit, Bob systematically reads and performs each of the following steps before going on to the next instruction.

EXAMPLE 14:

1. Remove the four screws from the Frammis modulator valve cover plate.

2. Remove the cover plate.

3. Open the Frammis modulator valve by pushing the toggle switch to the "Open" position.

Caution: Opening the Frammis modulator valve while the main unit is powered up will result in a violent explosion.

This is a somewhat farfetched example, but most of us can cite examples of instructions we have followed that gave us the information we needed just *after* we needed it.

Common sense dictates that any cautions or exceptions to some prescribed action need to appear before the instructions that tell the learner how to perform that action. You must assume that the learner is using the training in the field, in live circumstances, even if this is not its intended or recommended use.

The sequence of words within a sentence can also contribute to or detract from the learner's level of comfort with your training, often in subtle ways. For example, consider the method of wording the instruction in Example 15.

EXAMPLE 15: This is the Frammis modulator valve. If you wish to drain excess fluid from the reservoir, then open this valve by pushing the toggle switch illustrated in the drawing to the "Open" position.

In the second sentence, "If you wish to drain excess fluid from the reservoir, then open…," the learner must read twelve words before he can determine if draining excess fluid from the reservoir has anything to do with the Frammis modulator valve to which he has just been introduced. The student is waiting for the word "this" to tie the Frammis modulator valve to the description of that valve.

The wording in Example 12 solves the problem by effectively linking each statement to the preceding one. This linkage is accomplished by repeating identifying words such as "Frammis modulator valve" and by positioning linkage words such as "this" early in the sentence.

Writing instructional materials demands a greater attention to detail than almost any other writing form. Because the goal is to improve performance rather than to entertain or inform, the clarity of our writing is of particular importance.

By eliminating ambiguity, providing the context for information, and controlling the voice, pace, and sequence of our writing, we can help ensure that our considerable efforts bring the highest possible benefit to our audience.

As we've explored in this chapter, writing is an art all to itself. The skilled writer uses information about the intended delivery medium, audience, and message to create text that communicates clearly and efficiently. In the next chapter, we will turn our attention to designing websites and software that are accessible to people with special needs.

SUMMARY OF KEY POINTS

- Because Web visitors can access interior pages of your site without first seeing your home page, you must provide the means for visitors to quickly understand your site's identification and purpose.

- Write using an inverted pyramid structure, starting with the most important information and following with supporting details.

- Use more lists and bullets and fewer paragraphs to make it easy for users to scan information.

- To connect with your visitors, adopt an informal, friendly style that is appropriate to the organization. Using the word "we" instead of the company name is one way to reduce unnecessary formality.

- Use hypertext links to support your message, not to invite visitors to leave your site.

- Active voice, proper sequencing, and pace promote clearer instructional writing.

- Ask yourself "How come?" and "So what?" to improve the quality of your writing.

in review

1. What are three techniques that can make it easy for visitors to scan website content?

2. What is the inverted pyramid style, and why is it recommended for Web writing?

3. What are two advantages of writing text as bulleted lists over writing in paragraph form?

4. Name one of the quickest ways to humanize a dry, corporate-sounding message.

5. Put the terms *How*, *What*, and *When* in the order recommended for introducing procedures.

6. What two simple questions can improve your writing?

exercise

1. Using the inverted pyramid writing style, create some persuasive copy designed to convince site visitors to buy an actual or fictitious product or service.

designing for accessibility

objectives

Examine different types of impairments and discuss how they affect people's ability to use software and websites

Describe how assistive technologies such as screen readers and refreshable Braille displays help make websites and software more accessible

Examine how people with different types of sight impairments see the world

Examine the two major accessibility initiatives

Analyze specific techniques for assuring compliance with accessibility guidelines

Describe tools that are available to help test and ensure the accessibility of your websites and software

introduction

When most of us think about designing for accessibility, we think about creating websites that are accessible to people with disabilities. Indeed, although the Web holds nearly limitless promise for the disabled, that promise often goes unfulfilled. Many Web designers and developers unknowingly make their websites inaccessible to visitors with special needs.

Accessibility also extends beyond those with disabilities. For example, the small display size of PDAs and cell phones limits their users' ability to access the Web or software. Likewise, a worker may be driving a car, working in a noisy environment, or otherwise have their eyes, hands, or ears distracted. Designing for accessibility means considering the needs of anyone who is working under suboptimal conditions. As it turns out, optimizing websites and software for accessibility to those with disabilities also increases their accessibility to many of today's small and specialized devices.

DESIGNING FOR ACCESSIBILITY

DISABILITIES AND ASSISTIVE TECHNOLOGY

According to the Disability Law Resource Project (http://www.dlrp.org), approximately 20% of the United States population (about 40.8 million people) has some form of disability as of this writing. An estimated 10% of the population (about 27.3 million people) has a severe disability.

As the baby boom generation of the 1950s ages, the number of Americans with disabilities is likely to increase. While it is arguable that everyone, regardless of disability, deserves the opportunity to access the Web and software, the sheer size of this large and growing segment of the population makes an even stronger case for accessibility.

There are a number of disabilities that can make it difficult to access the Web or multimedia software. These impairments include:

- Vision impairments, such as blindness, low vision, and color blindness
- Hearing impairments, such as partial or total deafness
- Mobility or muscle impairments
- Cognitive impairments
- Seizure disorders

Equivalent Alternatives

Disabilities keep people from accessing certain types of Web or software content. A user may be able to see, but not hear, or hear but not see. Another may lack both sight and hearing. Still others may lack muscle function, preventing them from using a keyboard and mouse.

Enhancing accessibility for the many different types of disabilities often means providing **equivalent alternatives**. This simply means including alternate means of presenting the content of your site or software. For example, if your site includes audio or video of a person speaking, then you might provide a text transcript of the audio portions to allow a hearing impaired person to access the material.

If your site or software includes animation that cannot be captioned, then provide a text description of the animation's content. If you display graphic images that convey information rather than just providing decoration, then provide a text description of the image.

If your site or software includes interactions that cannot be made accessible, then provide an alternate means of delivering the same content.

Assistive Technologies

Assistive technologies, such as screen readers, refreshable Braille displays, screen magnifiers, and voice-recognition software help make websites and multimedia software accessible to those with certain types of disabilities. Often website designers and developers can make relatively minor adjustments to websites and software that will maximize these devices' effectiveness or otherwise increase accessibility.

Let's explore the accessibility issues associated with some common disabilities.

Vision Problems

Vision problems range from full blindness to minor difficulty differentiating certain color combinations. In between are many people with reduced or low vision, which can range from mild to severe.

Low Vision

According to the DLRP, approximately 3.5% of the U.S. population (9.2 million people) suffer **low vision**. People with low vision range from those that are nearly blind to those who retain some of their eyesight.

Figures 11-1 through 11-7 compare normal vision to various types of low-vision impairments. These images, from the National Eye Institute, simulate how a particular scene looks to people with these conditions.

| TIP |

It is generally better to create a single version of a website or multimedia software product that has been optimized for accessibility than it is to create separate accessible and non-accessible sites. Experience dictates that it is difficult to maintain two separate products, and the accessible version will ultimately lag behind the non-accessible one.

figure | 11-1 |

This is how an everyday scene looks to a person with normal vision. National Eye Institute, National Institutes of Health

figure | 11-2 |

This is how the scene looks to someone with the common condition of myopia (nearsightedness). National Eye Institute, National Institutes of Health

figure | 11-3 |

Here is how the scene might look to someone with Glaucoma. National Eye Institute, National Institutes of Health

figure | 11-4 |

Here is how the scene might look to someone with a cataract. National Eye Institute, National Institutes of Health

figure | 11-5 |

Here is how the scene might look to someone with diabetic retinopathy. National Eye Institute, National Institutes of Health

figure | 11-6 |

Here is how the scene might look to someone with age-related macular degeneration. National Eye Institute, National Institutes of Health

figure | 11-7 |

Here is how the scene might look to someone with retinitis pigmentosa. National Eye Institute, National Institutes of Health

Assistive technologies for low vision sufferers include both hardware and software devices. Hardware devices include specially designed monitors that enlarge and increase the contrast of the display. These are available in color and black and white models.

More widely used are software-based **screen magnifiers** that increase the size of what is displayed on screen and provide other accessibility functions. Examples are MAGic (by Freedom Scientific) and ZoomText (by AI Squared). Products such as these have built-in features that enable users to:

- Magnify screens up to 16 times or more
- Select different modes of operation, such as the ability to apply magnification to the full screen or to move a virtual magnifying lens over any part of the screen
- Place the cursor over on-screen text and have the software read it
- Have the software speak text as you type it, a letter or word at a time
- Select different color schemes that invert screen colors or substitute viewable colors for problem colors
- Change to an enhanced mouse pointer or text entry cursor that is easier to find and track
- Control the system's voice, personality, speed, pitch, and language

Figure 11-8 shows a simulation of how a screen magnifier looks in "lens" mode, which magnifies the part of the screen around the mouse cursor. The user can set both the magnification power and the size of the lens viewer.

Designers can help those with low vision by creating screens and page designs that enhance the contrast between the foreground and background. Since graphics tend to pixellate (their edges look like stairs) when zoomed, reduce or eliminate the use of bitmapped text.

Blindness

According to the Disability Law Resource Project (DLRP), about 4% of the U.S. population, or 10.4 million people, are visually impaired or blind. Web accessibility initiatives focus on this group, since their ability to access a Web page depends heavily on how it is coded. The blind cannot use a monitor or typical mouse. To access software or websites, they must use a software program called a **screen reader**.

figure | 11-8 |

In this simulation of a screen magnifier's lens mode, a rectangular portion of text under the mouse cursor is magnified.

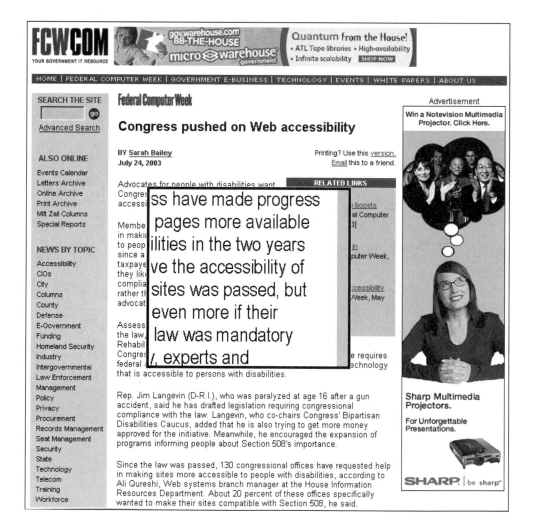

SCREEN READERS A screen reader is software that converts the text on a Web page or software program to synthesized speech. Three of the most widely used screen readers are JAWS (by Freedom Scientific), Window-Eyes (by GW Micro), and Home Page Reader (by IBM). JAWS and Window-Eyes work with browsers and any software loaded on the computer, including the operating system, while Home Page Reader works only with Web pages.

Don't confuse these screen readers with the reading capabilities of the screen magnifier products we discussed earlier. Screen readers that are intended for blind or nearly blind users offer greater flexibility and features, though they are often more complex to set up and learn.

Rather than simply reading the text that appears on a Web page, screen readers read portions of the underlying HTML code. This means that some websites may be translated into an indecipherable jumble. With just a little knowledge and effort, though, developers can tailor their HTML code to enable screen readers to present the site's content efficiently.

For example, screen readers ignore any graphic images on the page or screen. To help blind users benefit from images, Web developers can provide concise text descriptions of the images using HTML's alternative text or **alt tag**. For example, if a Web page includes a photo of Mount Rushmore, the developer can provide an alt tag that includes the text, "Photograph of Mount Rushmore showing sculpted busts of American presidents George Washington, Thomas Jefferson, Theodore Roosevelt, and Abraham Lincoln."

It is especially important to use alt tags for graphic images used as menus or individual links. Without such text descriptions, a blind user will not be able tell which links lead to which pages. Likewise, include an alt tag for each hotspot (active area) of an image map along with a **redundant text link** that matches each hotspot. You have probably seen these redundant links near the bottom of some Web pages, like the one in Figure 11-9.

figure | 11-9 |

For Web pages that include an image map, redundant text links positioned near the bottom of the page provide an accessible alternative.

Because screen readers ignore graphic images, they also ignore text that is in bitmap form, such as logos created by a paint program. This is another good reason to limit the use of bitmapped text wherever possible, even though providing the text represented by the image in an alt tag makes this text accessible.

TABLES PRESENT SPECIAL CHALLENGES Unless specially formatted for accessibility, tables present special challenges for screen readers. The problem is that some screen readers simply read the text row by row, which results in meaningless information. The example shown in Table 11-1 illustrates the problem.

table | 11-1 |

Tables Present Challenges

TEAM	COACH	WINS	LOSSES	GAME DAY	TIME
Panthers	Williams	7	3	Saturday	1:00
Wildcats	Meyer	5	5	Sunday	10:30

When this table is formatted normally, here is how a screen reader might interpret and read it to a blind user:

> "Table with six columns and three rows. Team. Coach. Wins. Losses. Game Day. Time. Panthers. Williams. Seven. Three. Saturday. One o'clock. Wildcats. Meyer. Five. Five. Sunday. Ten-thirty."

Notice that when the screen reader attempts to read the contents of this table in linear fashion, the meaning is lost. When the table is formatted for accessibility, however, here is the result:

> "Team Panthers. Coach Williams. Wins seven. Losses three. Game Day Saturday. Time one o'clock. Team Wildcats. Coach Meyer. Wins five. Losses five. Game Day Sunday. Time ten-thirty."

Notice that in this example, the column headers are read along with each cell's data. This makes the table's content meaningful to blind users. This improvement is accomplished with techniques such as using table headers to label rows or columns of data. For more information about these and other techniques, see Guideline 5 of the W3C's Web Content Accessibility Guidelines, at the URL listed earlier in this chapter.

Color Blindness

The DLRP approximates the number of people who experience some color impairment at 10% of males and .5% of females. The incidence of males with this deficiency is higher because color blindness is a genetic, sex-linked trait.

Being color blind does not mean seeing only black, white, and shades of gray. Although there is a form of color-blindness that causes the total inability to perceive color, this is a rare condition. Much more common is that individuals will have difficulty distinguishing one or more colors from each other. Colors that cause the most problems are reds, greens, oranges, and yellows.

Since there are different types of color blindness, designers cannot fix the problem by simply avoiding certain colors or color combinations. The best way to minimize color differentiation problems is to increase the contrast between foreground and background as much as possible. Use dark colors on light backgrounds or light colors on dark backgrounds.

As we discussed in the beginning of this book, avoid using color to convey meaning. For example, don't change the text color of an improperly filled-in field to red. Instead, display the word "invalid" by each improper field or use a reasonable alternative. Note that simply placing an asterisk by each improper field may make it difficult for blind users to determine the meaning of the asterisk.

Deaf-Blindness

Deaf-blind users can neither see nor hear. This condition presents special accessibility challenges, since screen readers used alone produce spoken output that is useless to a deaf-blind person.

Deaf-blind audiences can use an electronic device called a **refreshable braille display** to access the content of websites and software. Figure 11-10 shows a refreshable braille display.

Most of these braille displays are designed to fit between the computer keyboard and the user. Used in combination with a screen reader, the braille display converts the screen reader's output to braille. The braille display contains a series of cells, often 40 or 80. The number of cells

| TIP |

To test a screen design for readability to color-blind audiences, try capturing the screen and converting it to monochrome using image-editing software such as PhotoShop. The monochrome version will highlight any low-contrast problems that are likely to cause problems for color-blind users.

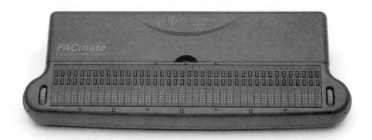

figure | **11-10** |

Refreshable Braille displays raise a series of pins to allow deaf-blind users the ability to read computerized content. Photo courtesy of Freedom Scientific.

indicates the number of characters that can be displayed at a time. 80-cell displays can carry the information stored in a full line of text. Smaller, fewer-celled models display as much of a line as possible, then require the push of a button to replace the contents of the cells with the remainder of the line.

Each cell raises or lowers a combination of pins to make the braille versions of characters. Although embossed braille characters are made up of six dots, computer braille contains eight dots. The two additional dots indicate underlined characters or numeric characters.

The same considerations that guide the design and development of websites and multimedia software for blind users applies to deaf-blind users as well, except that all information must be available in text. Simplify the design by eliminating all extraneous information to make accessing your Web pages and software as easy as possible for deaf-blind users.

Hearing Impairments

Because so much Web content consists of visual media such as text and images, hearing-impaired users have been able to experience much of what the Web has to offer. The trend, however, is toward more multimedia content such as audio files and video clips. This increases the amount of information that is inaccessible to hearing-impaired audiences.

For example, many online courses simply videotape an instructor delivering a lecture and deliver the video content online. Although many deaf people have learned the art of lip reading, it is impractical to read the lips of a person speaking in a video clip.

First, the image is usually too small to clearly see the lips form sounds. Video played back on computer may be jerky, making the task of lip reading more difficult. Finally, the instructor may look away or even turn her back to the camera in order to write on the blackboard.

As mentioned earlier in this chapter, providing a text transcript of the spoken portion of the content is an excellent solution. Technologies also exist to allow captioning of the audio portion of content, but this technology is not yet widely used.

Mobility and Muscle Impairment

Mobility impairments affect individuals' ability to move their muscles. Mild mobility problems may only slightly affect someone's ability to use a computer mouse and keyboard.

Mild mobility impairments often limit a person's fine motor control. This makes it difficult for these users to move the mouse precisely to a small target while clicking the mouse. Designing for this audience requires that we create buttons and other click targets that are relatively large in size and not too closely spaced.

Severe mobility impairments involving paralysis may require the use of special assistive technologies. There are many different types of switches designed to activate in response to a push, touch, squeeze, puff of air, muscle twitch, or other stimulus. These devices take the place of the keyboard. They allow the user to select characters for inputting to the software or Web page, and they provide a means to tab from field to field.

Certain Web page designs can be extremely fatiguing for those with mobility impairments. For example, a person without the use of his upper or lower extremities may use a device called a head wand to select and activate keyboard characters such as the tab key. If a Web page contains a long list of links above the page's content, users without disabilities can easily skip past the links by using the mouse or repeatedly pressing the down arrow or tab key.

For the severely mobility impaired, though, it may be extremely fatiguing to make the head movements necessary to repeatedly activate the tab key. For this reason, we recommend positioning lists of links near the bottom of the page, so that users do not have to skip past them to access the page's content.

Applications and Web pages that require the use of the mouse are inaccessible to these users. That is why it is important to provide some means of accessing all of the links and controls of your pages and screens via the keyboard.

Cognitive Impairments

Cognitive problems are those that affect our ability to reason and respond with appropriate actions. They range from the confusion we all feel when faced with a poorly-designed software and products to serious diseases such as Alzheimer's disease and Down's syndrome.

Following the design techniques we have discussed in this book will help those with cognitive impairments. Web pages and software should be designed as simply as possible, with concise, clearly worded text. Controls should be arranged logically and options presented when and where they are needed. The navigation should be simple and straightforward, with simple means to undo a mistake or return to a known screen, page, or state.

Seizure Disorders

Those who suffer from seizure disorders may experience seizures when subjected to rapidly flashing images. Some Web-based banner advertisements use flashing text or images to attract visitors. The frequency of such images has been identified in the range of 2 Hz to 55 Hz. To eliminate the possibility of causing such seizures, simply avoid displaying such flashing images.

WEB AND SOFTWARE ACCESSIBILITY INITIATIVES

Section 508 of the Rehabilitation Act

Section 508 of the Rehabilitation Act of 1973 requires that electronic and information technology, including websites and software, that is developed, procured, maintained, or used by the federal government be accessible to people with disabilities. On August 7, 1998, then President Clinton signed into law the **Workforce Investment Act of 1998**, which significantly expanded and strengthened the technology access requirements stated in Section 508. The full text of Section 508 is available at http://www.section508.gov/index.cfm?FuseAction=Content&ID=12.

Support for the Section 508 accessibility rules has been steadily growing. Though intended for federal government technology, some states have begun to insist that websites or software used within schools be Section 508 compliant. This means that the websites and software that publishing companies provide will have to meet the accessibility guidelines.

Although the guidelines do not apply to companies or individuals in the private sector, more and more companies are working to comply with them as well. It makes good ethical and financial sense for them to do so.

The following is a summary of the Section 508 accessibility standards for websites, with examples of passing and failing practices for each standard. These examples are used with the permission of the WebAIM (Accessibility in Mind) initiative. Although following these guidelines does not guarantee compliance with Section 508, it is an excellent step to creating accessible websites. More information about WebAIM can be found at http://www.webaim.org.

SEC. 508 STANDARD	PASS	FAIL
(a) A text equivalent for every non-text element shall be provided (e.g., via "alt", "longdesc", or in element content). [See Note 1]	Every image, Java applet, Flash file, video file, audio file, plug-in, etc. has an *alt* description.	A non-text element has no *alt* description.
	Complex graphics (graphs, charts, etc.) are accompanied by detailed text descriptions.	Complex graphics have no alternative text, or the alternative does not fully convey the meaning of the graphic.
	The *alt* descriptions succinctly describe the *purpose* of the objects, without being too verbose (for simple objects) or too vague (for complex objects).	*Alt* descriptions are verbose, vague, misleading, inaccurate or redundant to the context (e.g. the alt text is the same as the text immediately preceding or following it in the document).

	PASS	FAIL
	Alt descriptions for images used as links are descriptive of the link destination. Decorative graphics with no other function have *empty alt* descriptions (alt= ""), but they never have *missing* alt descriptions.	*Alt* descriptions for images used as links are not descriptive of the link destination. Purely decorative graphics have *alt* descriptions that say "spacer, "decorative graphic," or other titles that only increase the time that it takes to listen to a page when using a screen reader.
SEC. 508 STANDARD (b) Equivalent alternatives for any multimedia presentation shall be synchronized with the presentation.	**PASS** Multimedia files have *synchronized* captions.	**FAIL** Multimedia files do not have captions, or captions which are not synchronized.
SEC. 508 STANDARD (c) Web pages shall be designed so that all information conveyed with color is also available without color, for example from context or markup.	**PASS** If color is used to convey important information, an alternative indicator is used, such as an asterisk (*) or other symbol. Contrast is good.	**FAIL** The use of a color monitor is required. Contrast is poor.
SEC. 508 STANDARD (d) Documents shall be organized so they are readable without requiring an associated style sheet.	**PASS** Style sheets may be used for color, indentation and other presentation effects, but the document is still understandable (even if less visually appealing) when the style sheet is turned off.	**FAIL** The document is confusing or information is missing when the style sheet is turned off.
SEC. 508 STANDARD (e) Redundant text links shall be provided for each active region of a server-side image map.	**PASS** Separate text links are provided outside of the server-side image map to access the same content that the image map hot spots access.	**FAIL** The only way to access the links of a server-side image map is through the image map hot spots, which usually means that a mouse is required and that the links are unavailable to assistive technologies.
SEC. 508 STANDARD (f) Client-side image maps shall be provided instead of server-side image maps except where the regions cannot be defined with an available geometric shape.	**PASS** Standard HTML client-side image maps are used, and appropriate alt tags are provided for the image as well as the hot spots.	**FAIL** Server-side image maps are used when a client-side image map would suffice.
SEC. 508 STANDARD (g) Row and column headers shall be identified for data tables.	**PASS** Data tables have the column and row headers appropriately identified (using the \<th\> tag) Tables used strictly for <u>layout purposes</u> do NOT have header rows or columns.	**FAIL** Data tables have no header rows or columns. Tables used for layout use the header attribute when there is no true header.

SEC. 508 STANDARD	PASS	FAIL
(h) Markup shall be used to associate data cells and header cells for data tables that have two or more logical levels of row or column headers.	Table cells are associated with the appropriate headers (e.g. with the *id, headers, scope* and/or *axis* HTML attributes).	Columns and rows are not associated with column and row headers, or they are associated incorrectly.
SEC. 508 STANDARD	PASS	FAIL
(i) Frames shall be titled with text that facilitates frame identification and navigation.	Each frame is given a title that helps the user understand the frame's purpose.	Frames have no titles, or titles that are not descriptive of the frame's purpose.
SEC. 508 STANDARD	PASS	FAIL
(j) Pages shall be designed to avoid causing the screen to flicker with a frequency greater than 2 Hz and lower than 55 Hz.	No elements on the page flicker at a rate of 2 to 55 cycles per second, thus reducing the risk of optically-induced seizures.	One or more elements on the page flicker at a rate of 2 to 55 cycles per second, increasing the risk of optically-induced seizures.
SEC. 508 STANDARD	PASS	FAIL
(k) A text-only page, with equivalent information or functionality, shall be provided to make a Web site comply with the provisions of this part, when compliance cannot be accomplished in any other way. The content of the text-only page shall be updated whenever the primary page changes. [See Note 2]	A text-only version is created only when there is no other way to make the content accessible, or when it offers significant advantages over the "main" version for certain disability types. The text-only version is up-to-date with the "main" version. The text-only version provides the functionality equivalent to that of the "main" version. An alternative is provided for components (e.g. plug-ins, scripts) that are not directly accessible.	A text-only version is provided only as an excuse not to make the "main" version fully accessible. The text-only version is not up-to-date with the "main" version. The text-only version is an unequal, lesser version of the "main" version. No alternative is provided for components that are not directly accessible.
SEC. 508 STANDARD	PASS	FAIL
(l) When pages utilize scripting languages to display content, or to create interface elements, the information provided by the script shall be identified with functional text that can be read by assistive technology. [See Note 3]	Information within the scripts is text-based, or a text alternative is provided within the script itself, in accordance with (a) in these standards. All scripts (e.g. Javascript pop-up menus) are either directly accessible to assistive technologies (keyboard accessibility is a good measure of this), or an alternative method of accessing equivalent functionality is provided (e.g. a standard HTML link).	Scripts include graphics-as-text with no true text alternative. Scripts only work with a mouse, and there is no keyboard-accessible alternative either within or outside of the script.

SEC. 508 STANDARD	PASS	FAIL
(m) When a Web page requires that an applet, plug-in or other application be present on the client system to interpret page content, the page must provide a link to a plug-in or applet that complies with §1194.21(a) through (I). [See Note 4] [See Note 5] [See Note 6]	A link is provided to a disability-accessible page where the plug-in can be downloaded. All Java applets, scripts and plug-ins (including Acrobat PDF files and PowerPoint files, etc.) and the content within them are accessible to assistive technologies, or else an alternative means of accessing equivalent content is provided.	No link is provided to a page where the plug-in can be downloaded and/or the download page is not disability-accessible. Plugins, scripts and other elements are used indiscriminately, without alternatives for those who cannot access them.
SEC. 508 STANDARD (n) When electronic forms are designed to be completed on-line, the form shall allow people using assistive technology to access the information, field elements, and functionality required for completion and submission of the form, including all directions and cues.	**PASS** All form controls have text labels adjacent to them. Form elements have labels associated with them in the markup (i.e. the *id* and *for*, HTML elements). Dynamic HTML scripting of the form does not interfere with assistive technologies.	**FAIL** Form controls have no labels, or the labels are not adjacent to the controls. There is no linking of the form element and its label in the HTML. Dynamic HTML scripting makes parts of the form unavailable to assistive technologies.
SEC. 508 STANDARD (o) A method shall be provided that permits users to skip repetitive navigation links.	**PASS** A link is provided to skip over lists of navigational menus or other lengthy lists of links.	**FAIL** There is no way to skip over lists of links.
SEC. 508 STANDARD (p) When a timed response is required, the user shall be alerted and given sufficient time to indicate more time is required.	**PASS** The user has control over the timing of content changes.	**FAIL** The user is required to react quickly, within limited time restraints.

Note 1: Until the *longdesc* tag is better supported, it is impractical to use.

Note 2: "Text-only" and "accessible" are NOT synonymous. Text-only sites may help people with certain types of visual disabilities, but are not always helpful to those with cognitive, motor, or hearing disabilities.

Note 3: At this time, many elements of Dynamic HTML (client-side scripted HTML, which is usually accomplished with Javascript) cannot be made directly accessible to assistive technologies and keyboards, especially when the onMouseover command is used. If an onMouseover (or similar) element does not contain any important information (e.g., the script causes a button to "glow"), then there is no consequence for accessibility. If this scripted event reveals important information, then a keyboard-accessible alternative is required.

Note 4: When embedded into Web pages, few plug-ins are currently directly accessible. Some of them (e.g., RealPlayer) are more accessible as standalone products. It may be better to invoke the whole program rather than embed movies into pages at this point, although this may change in the future.

Note 5: Acrobat Reader 5.0 allows screen readers to access PDF documents. However, not all users have this version installed, and not all PDF documents are text-based (some are scanned in as graphics), which renders them useless to many assistive technologies. It is recommended that an accessible HTML version be made available as an alternative to PDF.

Note 6: PowerPoint files are currently not directly accessible unless the user has a full version of the PowerPoint program on the client computer (and not just the PowerPoint viewer). It is recommended that an accessible HTML version be provided as well.

Part 2: for Scripts, Plug-ins, Java, etc.

The following standards are excerpted from Section 508 of the Rehabilitation Act, §1194.21. For the full text of Section 508, please see http://www.access-board.gov/news/508-final.htm.

SEC. 508 STANDARD

(a) When software is designed to run on a system that has a keyboard, product functions shall be executable from a keyboard where the function itself or the result of performing a function can be discerned textually.

(b) Applications shall not disrupt or disable activated features of other products that are identified as accessibility features, where those features are developed and documented according to industry standards. Applications also shall not disrupt or disable activated features of any operating system that are identified as accessibility features where the application programming interface for those accessibility features has been documented by the manufacturer of the operating system and is available to the product developer.

(c) A well-defined on-screen indication of the current focus shall be provided that moves among interactive interface elements as the input focus changes. The focus shall be programmatically exposed so that assistive technology can track focus and focus changes.

(d) Sufficient information about a user interface element including the identity, operation and state of the element shall be available to assistive technology. When an image represents a program element, the information conveyed by the image must also be available in text.

(e) When bitmap images are used to identify controls, status indicators, or other programmatic elements, the meaning assigned to those images shall be consistent throughout an application's performance.

(f) Textual information shall be provided through operating system functions for displaying text. The minimum information that shall be made available is text content, text input caret location, and text attributes.

(g) Applications shall not override user selected contrast and color selections and other individual display attributes.

(h) When animation is displayed, the information shall be displayable in at least one non-animated presentation mode at the option of the user.

(i) Color coding shall not be used as the only means of conveying information, indicating an action, prompting a response, or distinguishing a visual element.

(j) When a product permits a user to adjust color and contrast settings, a variety of color selections capable of producing a range of contrast levels shall be provided.

(k) Software shall not use flashing or blinking text, objects, or other elements having a flash or blink frequency greater than 2 Hz and lower than 55 Hz.

(l) When electronic forms are used, the form shall allow people using assistive technology to access the information, field elements, and functionality required for completion and submission of the form, including all directions and cues.

The Web Content Accessibility Guidelines

The Web's primary standards organization, the **World Wide Web Consortium (W3C)**, also publishes a set of guidelines to help designers and developers create accessible websites. The W3C document, called the **Web Content Accessibility Guidelines (WCAG)**, has goals that are similar to the Section 508 guidelines. In fact, Section 508 includes a table that shows how the two sets of guidelines correlate.

The current version of the full WCAG document (as of this book's printing) is the 1.0 version. It is available at the following URL: http://www.w3.org/TR/1999/WAI-WEBCONTENT-19990505/. The 2.0 version of the document is currently under development and may be published prior to this book's release. Consult this document site for specific, up-to-date tips for making your websites accessible to the widest possible audience.

Accessibility Tools

There are resources available to help designers and developers expose and prevent accessibility problems on their websites. Some of these, such as the Bobby website, are available for free on the Web. Others are available as part of the most recent versions of Web and multimedia authoring software such as Dreamweaver and Flash.

Bobby

The Bobby site (http://bobby.watchfire.com/bobby/html/en/index.jsp) is a free service that allows website developers to check a particular URL for certain types of accessibility problems. The user specifies a URL and the site reports on any problems it finds. Sites that pass the Bobby test can display a "Bobby Approved" icon, but keep in mind that not all sites that pass the test are accessible. For that reason, Web designers and developers should use Bobby as a tool, but not the only means of determining their site's accessibility.

WAVE Web Accessibility Tool

The WAVE tool, available for free at http://wave.webaim.org/index.jsp, gives Web developers accessibility feedback in the form of icons inserted in the specified Web page. These icons show, for example, the text contained in alt text tags associated with each image on a page. Images that don't include alt text tags are marked with a red and white "error" icon.

Although WAVE does not pass or fail a page based on its accessibility, it can provide useful information that developers can use to help make their sites accessible.

Development Tools for Accessibility

Macromedia has begun adding tools and options to its Web and multimedia authoring products to help developers create accessible websites and multimedia. Products exist to add captions to Flash movies, provide accessible behaviors in Director and Shockwave modules, and help create accessible websites through Dreamweaver. Although the level of accessibility support varies by product, developers are beginning to have the tools they need to create more accessible products.

There are also third-party products, such as UsableNet's LIFT product, which works with Dreamweaver to diagnose and troubleshoot many common accessibility problems.

Accessibility is one of the hottest topics in Web and multimedia design today. As the number of users with disabilities and personal digital devices increases, the demand for designers who understand accessibility issues and can apply them to their designs will increase as well.

SUMMARY OF KEY POINTS

- As the baby boom population ages, the number of people with some sort of disability is increasing. Those creating websites and applications for U.S. government organizations are required by law to satisfy accessibility requirements.

- Creating accessible websites and software often means providing equivalent alternatives, which are alternative means of presenting information.

- When developing websites or software, ensure that they will work efficiently with assistive technologies such as screen readers, refreshable braille displays, screen magnifiers, and voice recognition software.

- Designers can help those with low vision by creating screens and page designs that enhance the contrast between the foreground and background.

- To test a screen design for readability to color-blind audiences, convert screens to monochrome using image-editing software such as PhotoShop. The monochrome version will highlight any low-contrast problems that are likely to cause problems for color-blind users.

- Applications that require the use of a mouse are inaccessible to those with certain mobility impairments. Provide keyboard control as an option whenever possible.

- Avoid rapidly flashing images to reduce the chances of seizure in susceptible users.

- There are guidelines and tools available online to help designers create accessible websites and software.

in review

1. What are equivalent alternatives, and why are they important to accessibility?

2. How can you make an audio segment accessible to a deaf audience?

3. How do screen readers work, and what types of audiences are they intended to help?

4. What is the primary purpose of a refreshable Braille display?

5. Who are the Section 508 guidelines written to serve?

6. Does it make sense to create and maintain both accessible and non-accessible versions of software and websites?

exercises

1. For sighted students, download a trial version of screen reader software, and try to access some of your favorite websites using the reader with your eyes closed. Try this experiment with several different websites to experience these sites as a blind user does.

2. For all students, select a website and submit a page of it to the Bobby website (http://bobby.watchfire.com/bobby/html/en/index.jsp) to see if it meets any of the qualification levels as an accessible page. This will also show the types of obstacles the page presents to visitors with disabilities.

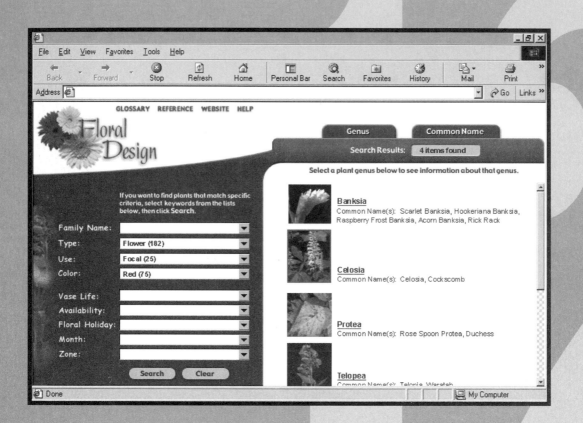

specifying the design

objectives

Describe when to create simple pencil-sketch wireframes and when it is appropriate to use draw or presentation software to create more polished wireframe documents

Identify the components of a wireframe drawing and how to successfully set up a wireframe document

Analyze how to choose software that is best suited to wireframe creation

Examine when and how to create storyboards to illustrate use cases

Describe when to use artist's concept screens to show possible graphic treatments of a website or software

Describe when and how to create functional prototypes, including useful functioning versions of wireframe documents

Identify which types of items to include in a style guide

introduction

You've done your research, analyzed your target audience, organized features and functions, and brainstormed some truly creative ideas for your website or multimedia project. Now it's time to communicate your user interface design ideas to your client, the development team, and other interested stakeholders.

Web and multimedia designers specify their designs by creating sets of paper-based drawings or electronic representations of what the finished product will be like. These specifications can range from crude pencil sketches to slide shows to highly functional prototypes. Each type of specification satisfies a particular set of goals.

What are the different methods you can use to specify your designs? How can you determine which specification method is most appropriate to a given situation? What are the advantages and disadvantages of paper-based and electronic specifications? When does it make sense to create a functional prototype and when is it a waste of your time?

The purpose of this chapter is to explore some of the most effective ways to specify a design.

WHY SPECIFY THE DESIGN?

There are several good reasons to create a specification of your design.

It Helps You Think through Important Issues

Creating a specification forces you to think through issues such as the organization of each screen or page's content and the layout of the controls you select. The process of creating the specification brings up many issues that cannot be adequately anticipated.

Creating a specification helps ensure that your design can accommodate all of the features you have planned for it, while helping you to keep from accidentally omitting any features that you intended to include.

The specification can also enable you to work on the general layout of elements on the page or screen. You may discover that you have included too many elements on a single page and need to reorganize by moving some to a different page. Sometimes you think that a particular method of accessing a function or navigating makes sense until you specify it and see how it actually looks and feels. The specification process helps you root out such problems relatively early in the design process.

It Communicates the Design to Clients, Team Members, and Users

The specification communicates the design vision to clients, members of the development team, and other stakeholders. It serves as a focal point for discussions, illustrating the design's accommodation of its intended features and indicating how readily the resulting software or website can be engineered.

As we've previously stated, making changes to specification documents is much less expensive than making them to "finished" code, artwork, or multimedia. To be effective, the specification must model the finished website or software. It need not look and operate exactly like the finished product, but like a blueprint represents a finished building, it must accurately convey the product's essence.

| TIP |

It is useful to keep your outline or list of functions handy so that you can refer to it and check off features as you accommodate them in the design.

If you are working as part of a development team, the team should review all specifications to ensure that the design being proposed is programmable and that the intended functions are represented. The specifications guide the development of the product.

Your client will review the specifications you create and recommend changes as necessary. This check ensures that the product represented by the specification meets the client's expectations. When the client approves the specification, the development team can proceed with the development of the software or website. This topic is explored further in Chapter 14, in the section "Forming and Maintaining Strong Client Relationships."

The specifications can also be used for performing early usability testing of the design on selected members of the target audience. The procedure for using specifications for this purpose is covered in Chapter 13, "Performing Usability Testing".

| TIP |

Don't cut corners by creating "quick and dirty" specifications or by only specifying part of your project. The discipline that creating the specification imposes is vital to ensuring the quality of your finished product.

TYPES OF SPECIFICATIONS

Prototypes

The word prototype can convey varying meanings to different designers and developers. Some groups use prototype to describe an electronic representation of a website or software program that includes some functionality. Other groups call their crude pencil sketches prototypes.

The word **prototype** simply means "example." Therefore, we can classify all of the types of specifications we will discuss in this chapter—from pencil sketches through functional frameworks—as prototypes.

Wireframes

Wireframes are schematic drawings that represent pages or screens of a website or software program. They are named for the simple representations of 3D drawings that look like wire mesh bent into a particular shape. In 3D drawing, the wireframe shows the basic shape of the finished object without its finished, rendered skin. Likewise, the wireframes that user interface designers create show the basic composition of elements on pages or screens, without suggesting the finished graphic look.

Wireframes can be quick pencil sketches or polished-looking drawings generated using drawing software such as ConceptDraw, Illustrator, or Visio; presentation software such as PowerPoint; or website authoring software such as Dreamweaver or FrontPage. Although it is beyond the purpose of this book to recommend a particular wireframe creation tool, later in this chapter we will describe some characteristics of good wireframe-creation software. Use wireframes to convey the overall feel of the software, including its navigation and the functional layout of its elements.

Pencil-Sketch Wireframes

Pencil-sketch wireframes are great for quickly recording ideas. Grab a pencil and paper for doing early design work—perhaps to try several possible approaches to a design problem. Figures 12-1 and 12-2 show two different approaches to organizing content on a website created for floral designers.

Designers often submit these early sketches to clients for approval or to select one of several approaches. In fact, one advantage of pencil sketches is that clients never mistake them for the finished product. A disadvantage is that clients may expect a more polished-looking deliverable than a series of crude sketches. Therefore, once the client selects or approves an overall approach, it is a good idea to switch to creating software-based wireframes (described later in this chapter) to flesh out the design.

figure | **12-1** |

A pencil-sketch wireframe is useful for quickly comparing two possible approaches to a design challenge. Approach A.

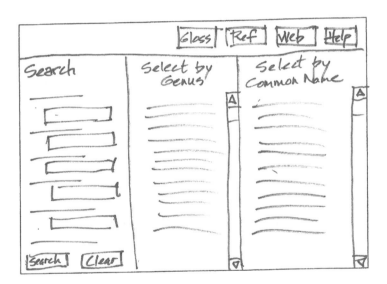

figure | **12-2** |

Approach B

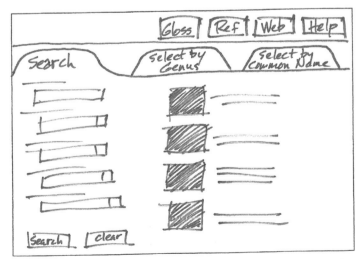

Keep template sheets handy to quickly sketch out ideas. Create each rectangle in the template sheet to the scale of 4:3, which matches the aspect ratio of today's screen resolutions. A 4:3 screen resolution simply means that there are four horizontal pixels for every three vertical ones. The common screen resolutions of 640 by 480, 800 by 600, and 1024 by 768 all reduce to 4 by 3.

Use the one-up versions (the largest rectangle) if you like plenty of room to sketch or for screens requiring lots of detail. Use the two-up template for showing two approaches side-by-side or for showing a progression. Use the four-up template when you want to try multiple approaches or sketch a longer progression of screens.

| TIP |

Create one-up, two-up, and four-up screen template sheets using draw software. A sample four-up template is shown in Figure 12-3.

figure | 12-3 |

Create simple wireframe template sheets in one-up, two-up, and four-up (shown here) versions and keep plenty on hand for making quick sketches.

Software-Based Wireframes

As mentioned above, many interface designers like to create software-based wireframes. Figures 12-4 through 12-9 show a series of wireframes that specify key screens of the floral design application we explored previously.

Software-created wireframes, such as the ones shown in Figures 12-4 through 12-9, suggest the functional layout of elements, but allow the graphic artist creativity in designing the look of the screens or pages. The software tools available today make it possible to design many screens and pages with speed, consistency, and professional-looking results that pencil sketches cannot duplicate.

Notice that the wireframes shown in Figures 12-4 through 12-9 include explanatory text. The text includes information such as:

- Under what circumstances the page or screen is displayed. For example, "This screen is displayed when the user clicks the Log On button."

- The main purpose and operation of the page or screen. For example, "This screen enables users to add or remove members to or from a distribution list."

- The effect of clicking any of the controls present on the screen. For example, "Clicking the Save button saves the user's selections and returns to the Main Menu."

- Special notes to the engineers, graphic artists, quality assurance personnel, or other members of the development team. For example, "Note to engineer: Please highlight any required fields that the user leaves blank when the user clicks Save."

- Special notes to the client. For example, "Note to client: We recommend providing a hint that suggests the next step to users."

CREATING SOFTWARE-BASED WIREFRAMES The best way to develop speed and accuracy when creating wireframes is to plan ahead. Create and save a basic template page that provides the overall elements you want to include. Our template includes an area for each screen's title, a rectangle drawn to a 4:3 aspect ratio to represent the screen or Web page area, a text description area, and a footer area for including information such as the date, name of the project, and page number.

It is a good idea to create screen captures of a Web browser window, a Windows-based application window, and a Macintosh window. Insert one of these on a background page to indicate the delivery platform for which the finished software or website is intended. Include on the background controls, such as a toolbar or menu bar, that appears on many pages. Then add controls and elements to the foreground pages that use the background.

figure | 12-4 |

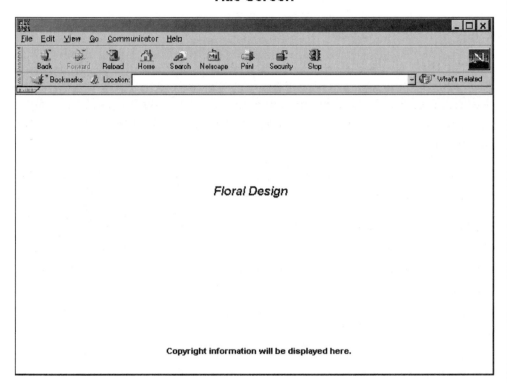

The Floral Design software will begin with a Title screen. The Title screen will include artwork that complements the subject matter. It will also include a copyright message.

The student can advance by clicking anywhere on this screen. After a set time has elapsed—e.g., 10 seconds—the software will automatically advance to the next screen.

figure | 12-5 |

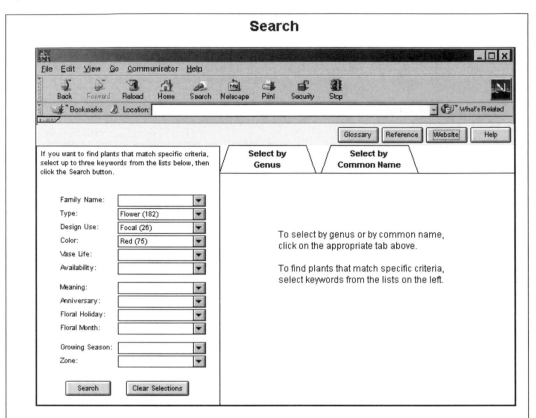

The Search page is displayed when the student advances past the Title page. The left frame contains the search area where the student can enter keywords to find genera matching particular criteria. The right frame originally contains instructions and tabs for selecting by a list of genera or common names.

Students can select up to three keywords. The number by each keyword indicates how many entries exist for that keyword. Selecting keywords and clicking the **Search** button displays results of the search in the right pane (discussed later in this document).

Clicking the **Clear Selections** button blanks all of the student's choices in the search fields.

Clicking the **Glossary** button displays the Glossary (described later in this document).

Clicking the **Reference** button displays a menu of reference information. The contents will be determined later.

Clicking the **Website** button links to the Floral Design site.

Clicking the **Help** button displays a browser window containing context-sensitive help for the current screen.

figure | 12-6 |

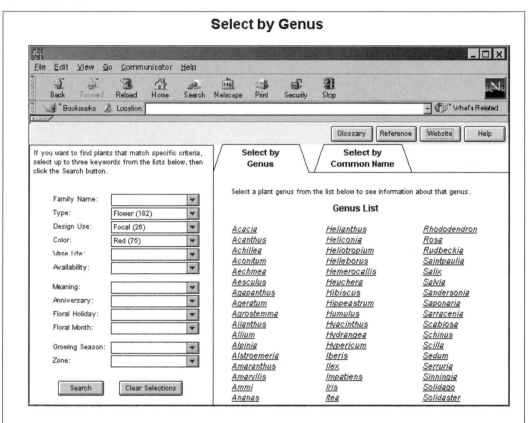

This screen is displayed when the student clicks the Select by Genus tab.

The student selects the desired genus, and the information page for that genus is displayed.

Clicking the Select by Common Name tab will produce a list similar to this one, except that the common names of the plants will be listed.

figure | 12-7 |

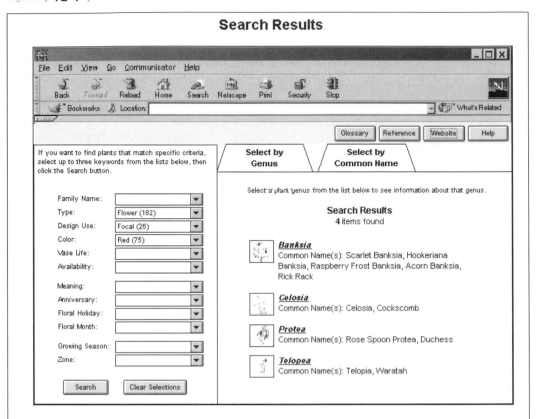

This view shows the results of the student's search. If more than one search criterion is selected, the software will display the names of plants meeting all of the selected criteria. For each plant found, the plant's genus and the common names included in that genus are listed. A thumbnail of the close-up view of the associated plant is also displayed by each plant's name. The screen will scroll vertically if necessary.

A key advantage of this page arrangement is that students can see the search criteria that resulted in the list of found plants. The student can then modify the search criteria if necessary without navigating to a different page.

Whenever the student activates a search by clicking the **Search** button, the button becomes inactivated (grayed out). It stays inactivated until the student modifies the search criteria by selecting different keywords or by clearing the existing keyword selections. This may serve as a subtle reminder to the student who has changed the search criteria to click the **Search** button to generate new results.

Clicking one of the hyperlinked plant names displays the detailed information and images for that plant (see next wireframe).

figure | 12-8 |

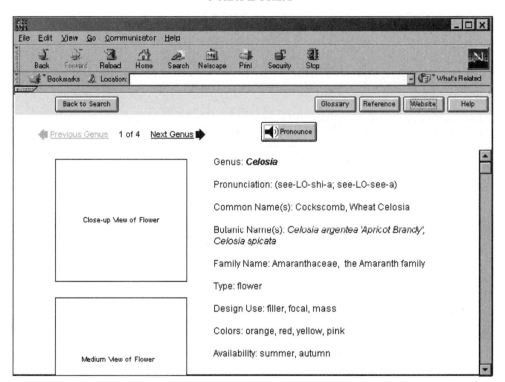

This page is displayed when the student selects a genus in the Results frame, shown on the previous wireframe.

The left side of the page contains three images of plants represented in the genus: a close-up view, a medium view, and a long-shot view of the foliage. The right side contains the text description of the genus. The entire page will vertically scroll to allow all of the information to be viewed.

Students can click the Pronounce button to hear a pronunciation of the genus.

Students can click the Previous Genus or Next Genus links to view other genera that meet the current search criteria. A counter shows the number of the current genus in relation to the total number of genera found.

Clicking the **Back to Search** button returns the student to the search/results screen, where another genus may be selected for displaying or another search may be performed.

figure | 12-9 |

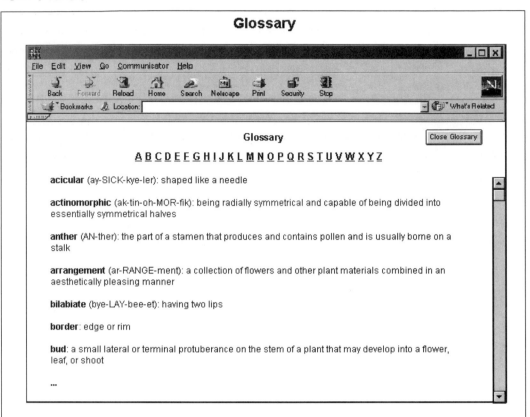

The Glossary is displayed when the student clicks the **Glossary** button on the toolbar. The Glossary is launched in its own browser window, allowing the Glossary to remain open while the student is using other parts of the software. Since the number of terms is relatively small, the entire glossary is displayed on a single page.

Clicking one of the hypertext-linked alphabetic characters at the top of the screen scrolls the list of terms so that terms beginning with the selected letter appear near the top of the display. The linked characters remain at the top of the screen when the terms and definitions are scrolled.

The Glossary displays the phonetic spelling (where applicable) and the definition of the selected term.

Here are some ideas to consider when creating electronic wireframes:

- Use realistic client data when creating wireframes of reports and other data-intensive screens. You will invariably uncover unanticipated characteristics of that data that will influence your design. Keep in mind that some clients will focus on this text to the exclusion of other aspects of the design, since it represents what they know best.

- Create elements such as text fields with the characteristics (justification, font, style, size, etc.) you want, and then copy these elements as needed to other pages. This will save you the time and effort it takes to customize each text field.

- When designing screens or pages containing text or other data, use the largest, longest, or most complex examples you are likely to encounter. This will help you avoid having to redesign later due to insufficient room to fit particular content.

- Be consistent in the creation of elements. Use the same font, font size, and style for all buttons, titles and headings, and other text areas represented in the wireframes. Copy elements from another page rather than creating new elements from scratch to ensure consistency across pages.

- Use each wireframe page's title as the name of the page. Give the wireframe file the same name as the project name. Be consistent in your naming conventions across projects.

- Create a naming convention for revisions to the wireframes and other deliverables. Including a sequence number or date in the title will help you locate the correct file later.

Almost any draw or illustration package can be used to create wireframes, but not all software does a good job of it. Some software provides functions that make the job easy, while others impose limitations that hinder the creation process. When choosing a software package to create wireframes, look for the following capabilities.

THE SOFTWARE CONTAINS A LIBRARY OF COMMON USER INTERFACE CONTROLS Look for software that contains libraries of interface controls such as radio buttons, check boxes, lists, buttons, and menus. If possible, the software should offer libraries of controls for both Windows and Macintosh operating systems. Some even offer interface elements that match the look of specific versions of the operating system.

| TIP |

The wireframe template used to create Figures 12-4 through 12-9 has accommodated a wide variety of projects, from the small to the very large, but it is by no means the only possible layout. Customize your wireframes to meet the needs of your projects, clients, and development team.

| TIP |

When beginning a large project, you may find it useful to create a "shell" wireframe document. The shell document allows you to construct the overall organization of the website or application software. To create a shell document, first create the main background page, then add empty foreground pages using that background. Specify the title of each page you know will be included in the document. Besides helping you to organize the project, creating a shell document gives you an early accomplishment that can help motivate you to dive in and accomplish more.

The packaged controls that are shipped with software often contain some intelligence that can help you create screen and page designs very quickly. Although it is possible to custom create each element, the library items often perform this task better. For example, a scrolling text box that is included in a library has the intelligence to maintain the width of its scrollbar and the size of its arrow buttons as the text box is enlarged or reduced. If you create a scrolling text box yourself, you will have to resize parts of the scrollbar manually each time you resize the box.

THE SOFTWARE MUST HANDLE MULTIPLE-PAGE DOCUMENTS WELL. Some packages facilitate creating multiple-page wireframe documents, while others claim this capability but do so poorly. Look for software with these characteristics:

- The software makes it easy to insert, delete, reorder, and rename pages. It should be easy to navigate from page to page even in large wireframe documents of greater than 100 pages. Software that provides an index of the names of all pages, which allows you to select the page to view, is especially helpful.

- The software allows you to specify one or more pages as a background. You use a background to include controls and elements that are common to many pages. If you change the background, the changes automatically affect all of the pages (sometimes called *foreground pages*) that use that background.

- Changing the zoom setting or scrolling a page affects the entire document and not just the current page. It can be frustrating to try to compare several pages in a sequence when they are all at different zoom settings and scroll positions.

- The software allows you to cut or copy elements, then paste them to a different page or document while maintaining the same horizontal and vertical location as the original.

- The software should provide the means to create a footer on each wireframe page containing information such as the date, name of the project, and page number.

THE SOFTWARE SHOULD SUPPORT EXPORTING TO COMMON FORMATS The software should enable you to save or export wireframes in a number of different common formats, including HTML, .pdf (Acrobat), .ppt (PowerPoint), and graphic formats such as .JPG, .PNG, GIF, and/or Windows metafile. This will enable you to publish your wireframes on the Web or e-mail them to clients and off-site team members.

| TIP |

It is possible to fax wireframes to clients or off-site team members. If you expect to be faxing your wireframes, reduce your use of shading and color fills as much as possible to increase the readability of the faxed documents.

THE SOFTWARE SHOULD PROVIDE COMMON SHAPE-EDITING FEATURES The software should make it simple to group and ungroup items, align selected items horizontally or vertically, distribute items evenly horizontally or vertically, and draw standard shapes such as rectangles, lines, and ellipses. Some packages also allow you to apply the settings you assigned to one shape to other shapes.

THE SOFTWARE SHOULD PROVIDE COMMON TEXT-EDITING FEATURES You should be able to check your spelling, search for a text string and replace it with another, justify text horizontally and vertically, set margins, and select fonts, styles, and colors. These functions should be accessible via toolbar buttons, menus, and shortcut keys.

THE SOFTWARE SHOULD SUPPORT WYSIWYG WYSIWYG (pronounced "wizzy-wig") is an acronym for What You See Is What You Get. It simply means that your wireframes look the same when printed on paper as they do on screen. Some software may have problems correctly representing the positioning of text within paragraph fields, especially in a printout. This may make it difficult to accurately line up a control such as a radio button with text inside the paragraph field.

THE SOFTWARE SHOULD SUPPORT MULTIPLE LAYERS Layers allow you to include elements that you can selectively display or hide. One use of layers is to provide **callouts** in your wireframes. Callouts are text boxes with directional lines that call attention and provide information specific to a particular screen element or component. You can use one layer to provide callouts for your clients and another layer for callouts to the engineers. At print or publishing time, you can specify which layers should be printed and which should be suppressed.

Another valuable feature is the scripting languages that come with some draw and illustration packages. These are programming languages that allow you more control over the actions of particular elements or the wireframe document as a whole. If you take the time to learn the syntax of the language, you can add sophisticated functionality to your wireframes and prototypes.

Storyboards

The term **storyboards** is borrowed from the animation, movie, and advertising industries. In these applications, the creative team uses a storyboard to convey key scenes and story lines. Similarly, storyboards in user interface design show sequences of screens, pages, or steps.

Although some designers use the word *storyboards* synonymously with *wireframes*, we'll define storyboards as a set of sketches or images that illustrate use cases. Remember that earlier in this book, we introduced use cases as the sequence of steps a user takes to perform some function or operation.

Storyboards are well suited to communicating use cases because they illustrate the series of screens that a user must access to perform a particular task. Each storyboard image shows the screen to be accessed and the control or controls that the user must activate to display the next screen or step in the sequence.

| **TIP** |

The helpful annotations or notes that you provide on your wireframes may mask usability problems by giving users information that won't be available in the finished software or website. Be sure to turn such annotations and notes *off* when usability testing your design using wireframes.

As with wireframes, you can create storyboards using pencil and paper, or you can create them electronically. The storyboards can include notes as necessary to help the viewer understand the steps.

Figure 12-10 shows a three-frame storyboard that conveys the steps that a user of the floral design website will take to search for flowers with particular characteristics.

A key difference between wireframes and storyboards is that wireframes indicate all of the possible functions accessible on each screen or page, while a storyboard emphasizes only those controls needed to accomplish a particular function. Stated another way, wireframes emphasize the content within a given screen or page, while storyboards stress the connections between screens or pages.

Artist-Rendered Concept Drawings

Concept drawings (or **concept screens**) give clients and the development team an example of how the finished website or software will look. Graphic designers create concept drawings for several reasons, including:

- To think through the visual challenges of a project
- To get the client's approval of the graphic look of the software before creating all of the graphic elements for the project
- To present several different visual approaches so the client can choose the preferred one
- To solicit engineering's feedback on the ease with which a particular graphic design can be implemented

| TIP |

It is usually best to deliver artist's concept screens electronically, since even expensive color laser printers can't exactly reproduce colors as they appear on screen. Since the finished website or software will be displayed on screen, that is how the concept screens should be displayed as well. If the client insists on hard copies, send them as well, but tell your client to view the screen versions for color accuracy.

Figures 12-11 through Figure 12-14 show a sequence of concept drawings created for the floral design project described earlier.

Artists usually create concept screens using their favorite image creation software, such as PhotoShop. The artist usually converts the screens to JPEG or BMP format prior to delivery to the client.

An effective way to deliver a set of concept screens is to include them in a PowerPoint presentation or Adobe Acrobat file. Both these products handle the navigation from one screen to the next and provide the means for the client to print hard copies. PowerPoint provides easy-to-use navigation, but, as of this writing, it shrinks the images slightly to display them within its viewer. If these products don't provide the features you need, consider creating a simple, reusable viewer using Director or Flash.

figure | 12-10 |

Storyboards can be used to illustrate the steps that users must take to accomplish a given task.

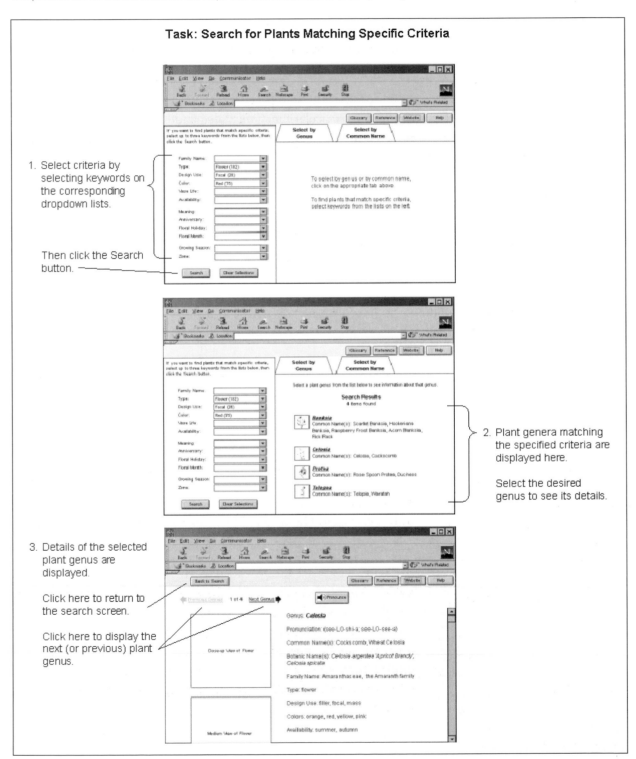

figure | 12-11 |

Concept drawing by
Derek Richards,
Dolphin Inc.

figure | 12-12 |

Concept drawing by
Derek Richards,
Dolphin Inc.

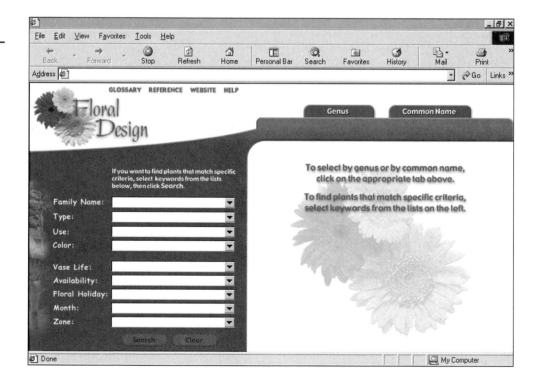

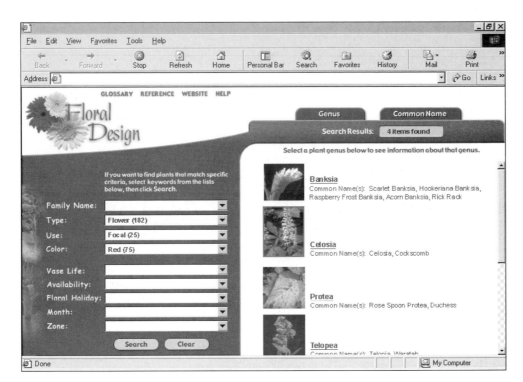

figure | 12-13 |

Concept drawing by Derek Richards, Dolphin Inc.

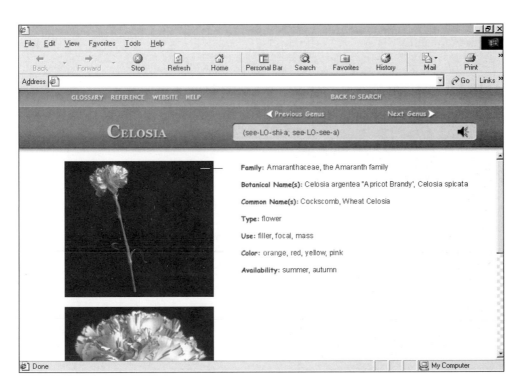

figure | 12-14 |

Concept drawings give clients and team members a sense of what the finished product will look like. Concept drawing by Derek Richards, Dolphin Inc.

| TIP |

Make your functional prototype more usable by giving your clients and team members visual cues to differentiate functional controls from nonfunctional ones. Consider including a small icon or border around "live" controls so your clients or team members won't waste time clicking inactive controls. Another approach is to allow users to click any control, and to display text explanations of those controls that are not fully functional. For example, the text might say, "Clicking this button will display a form that allows users to enter their home address and telephone number."

| TIP |

Be sure to provide a means of identifying each screen so that clients and team members can give you meaningful feedback. Use a screen title or a page or screen number for this purpose. It is much easier and useful for a client to say, "Add the account number to the Customer Profile screen" than it is to say, "Add the account number to the screen that has client information on it." Leave as little as possible to chance.

Web Frameworks and Other Functional Prototypes

Functional prototypes allow clients and team members to interact with your design. The simplest functional prototypes allow users to click buttons or controls to navigate to different pages. More complex prototypes may closely mirror the operation of finished software, even including simulations and data management.

Here are some reasons for creating a functional prototype:

- They can be used to show the operation of a particularly key, compelling, or tricky part of the design.

- A functional prototype gives users a better idea of how the finished software or website will "feel" than a static document.

- Some clients and team members aren't inclined to read all of the text included with wireframes. They can learn more from the design by clicking around.

- It may not take much longer to create a functional prototype that has clickable controls than it takes to describe in text the result of clicking each control.

- In some circumstances, the functional prototype can be used as the basis for the finished software or website.

Functional prototypes also have some disadvantages and cautions to consider:

- Clients may mistake a functional prototype for the real thing, and believe the site or software is further along than it actually is. It is important to set your client's expectations properly.

- You may waste a lot of time creating a prototype in a language or system that is different from the one that will be used to create or deliver the finished system. Using the prototype as a basis for the finished product may only work if you are both the designer and the developer.

- If the functional prototype is substituting for wireframes, it may be difficult to describe the functions of controls that are inoperative in the prototype.

- Clients and team members may prefer to write their review feedback directly on paper-based wireframes rather than having to create a separate document.

Many of today's draw and presentation software programs provide the ability to assign actions to the shapes and other elements of your drawings. This gives us a relatively easy way to create a functional prototype. You can easily specify, for example, that when a particular button is clicked, a different page of the document be displayed.

Many of these software programs provide free downloadable viewers to allow others to display the wireframes and functional prototypes you create.

Style Guides

A **style guide** is a document that specifies the design elements for a website or software program, including standards or recommendations for:

- Typography, including specifying exactly which fonts, font sizes, and styles should be used for titles, headings, body text, copyright information, and so on

- Color, including the palette and specific use of colors

- Graphics, such as the proper use of the organization's logo

- Global navigation elements, including which controls should be included on each page or screen and how to link back to a central page or function

- Other interface elements, including standards or recommendations for enabling specific types of actions

- Templates and examples of good and bad practices

Cascading style sheets (CSS) are a powerful, widely accepted means of specifying and controlling the style of a website. They have become an important component of style guides. Developers working on different parts of a site can use a common CSS to maintain a consistent style throughout the site.

A style guide can be part of a larger specification document that includes conventions for related topics such as page naming conventions, content management, and site maintenance considerations.

Functional Specifications

Functional specifications, often associated with large government projects, are like wireframes on steroids. They usually include the screen or page image portion of the wireframe, but greatly expand the text explanations. They may describe in great detail the actions that result from virtually any possible keystroke or mouse click and indicate the text of every error message and system prompt.

Most websites and multimedia software projects are not of sufficient complexity to justify the amount of time and effort it takes to develop full functional specifications. They are mentioned here because they are a type of specification that you may encounter in the workplace.

As we have seen, the specification phase of a project is one of intense personal activity for the user interface designer. It is also one of the most satisfying phases of design. After all, what is more exciting than giving life and substance to your ideas, then sharing them with the rest of the world?

Next we'll examine how to subject our work to the ultimate challenge—usability testing using live testers selected from our target audience.

SUMMARY OF KEY POINTS

- Creating specifications is important to communicate your design to the development team, your client, and end users who may be performing usability testing.

- Wireframes convey the navigation and page or screen components using a schematic style. They can be created by hand or using commercial software. They often contain text descriptions of the effect of clicking navigational controls and other elements.

- Storyboards illustrate the sequence of steps needed to accomplish a specified task.

- Concept drawings illustrate one or more possible approaches to the look of a website or software.

- Web frameworks and other functional prototypes let clients and users experience the operation of selected parts of the website or software.

- Use style guides to specify design elements for the website or software. Cascading style sheets provide control of the look of an entire website. They can be an important component of style guides.

in review

1. What are the two most important reasons for creating specifications of your designs?

2. Under what circumstances is it appropriate to create simple, pencil-based wire-frame sketches?

3. What are some features of draw or presentation software that supports the creation of multiple-page documents?

4. What is the main difference between wireframes and storyboards?

5. What are three advantages and three disadvantages of functional prototypes?

6. Why are cascading style sheets an important element of style guides?

exercise

1. A client has asked you to create a Web application that displays entries in a monthly photo contest and enables visitors to vote on their favorites. Create pencil-sketch wireframes showing at least two different design approaches to this challenge.

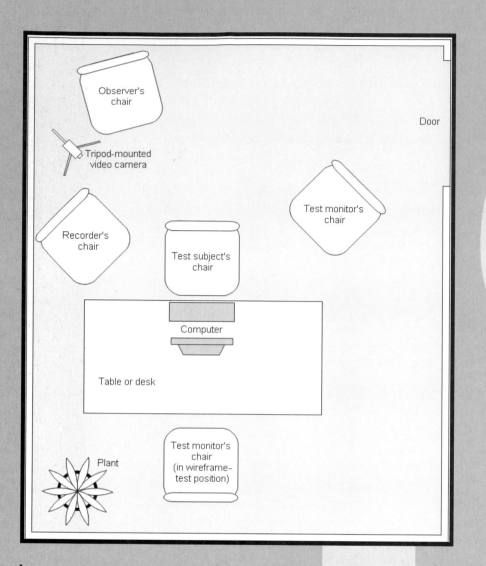

Observer's chair

Tripod-mounted video camera

Recorder's chair

Test subject's chair

Test monitor's chair

Door

Computer

Table or desk

Plant

Test monitor's chair (in wireframe-test position)

objectives

Identify the types of usability tests and be able to select the appropriate type for a given situation

Examine the six stages of usability testing

Describe the purpose of a test plan and examine how to create one

Identify the criteria for selecting participants for a usability test

Identify the components of a testing environment

Examine how to conduct a usability test

Identify the components of a usability test report

introduction

Usability tests are the only reliable way to determine if the design for a website or software application is usable by its intended audience. Some companies avoid usability testing, believing it is time-consuming, complicated, and expensive. Usability testing pioneers such as Jakob Nielsen, Jeffrey Rubin, and Rolf Molich have proven that usability testing can be accomplished quickly, easily, and inexpensively.

When most people think of usability testing, they assume that it is an actual website or software that is being tested. To be most effective, however, usability testing should begin well before any software is created. For example, exploratory usability tests can help determine which features to include in the project. Assessment usability tests are useful starting at the wireframe stage of design, through prototyping, and near the time of release or website publication.

In this chapter we will explore how to plan for, set up, and conduct basic usability testing and how to use the results to improve your designs.

USABILITY TESTING BASICS

Don't Depend on Designers to Judge Their Own Designs

The simple fact is that designers are not the best judges of their own designs. No designer ever intends to create an unusable design. We designers honestly believe that our designs are usable—after all, they are usable to *us*. Remember, though, that our orientation, background, experience, and expectations are likely to differ widely from those of our intended audience. These differences translate into usability problems that designers simply cannot anticipate.

Some designers believe that performing audience research ensures that the design will be usable by that audience. Unfortunately, this is not the case. Audience research gives us valuable insight into our users' needs, helping to ensure that the features we include are appropriate and useful. It does not guarantee that users will be able to easily find and use those features to accomplish their tasks. Only usability testing can determine this.

Another approach that some companies use is to have a usability design "expert" perform a review (often called a **heuristic** evaluation) of a website or software program. The expert then recommends design changes to improve usability. Although this strategy may improve an existing design, it is not nearly as effective as usability testing with real users. Heuristic evaluations may be based more on the reviewer's opinions than research. In fact, the reviewer may identify "problems" that don't exist for actual users. Like the designer, the reviewer does not have the same perspective or needs as the target audience. Only users behave like users.

Test Often Using Small Groups

According to research performed by Jakob Nielsen and others, it is better to conduct more tests with fewer users than to conduct a single test with a large number of users. According to Nielsen, three tests of five users yields much better results than one test of fifteen users. Five users seems to be an optimum number, although a test with as few as three or four users is sufficient to root out most significant flaws in a design.

Conducting a usability test with fewer than three users may not produce useful results. Fewer people tend to find fewer problems. Further, in every group there are some members whose software or Web usage patterns are different from the majority of the audience. By studying just one or two people, you increase the chances that someone selected as a participant does not accurately represent your audience. Selecting more testers reduces the effects of such non-representative users.

One problem with a single, large test is that all or nearly all testers will be discovering the same major problems in a design. These major problems may keep testers from delving deeper into the design to discover less-obvious usability problems. By testing with small groups and spacing tests over time, designers and developers have the opportunity to fix usability problems uncovered in the initial tests. This means that subsequent testers are free to discover new problems with the design.

Conducting multiple small tests over time also helps ensure that redesign efforts are effective, since there is no guarantee that the redesign of a troublesome component will be more usable than the original. Modified designs require user testing to ensure that they solve the existing usability problems without creating new ones.

Select the Appropriate Type of Usability Test

There is no single type of usability test that works best for all situations. Nielsen, Molich, and Rubin have identified several distinct types of tests. We will explore four usability test types: exploratory, assessment, evaluation, and comparison.

Exploratory Tests

An **exploratory test** is conducted early in the design stage. It has two main purposes. First, it helps determine if the functions chosen for a website or software are useful and appropriate. Second, it establishes how well the design fits the participant's mental model. The user's mental model is the assumptions and expectations about how things should work for the tasks being examined.

An exploratory test compares the types of functions or features the participant expects or hopes to find with those actually proposed in the design. The participant reviews the navigational structure and offers comments about the functions represented and any that the subject perceives as missing.

For example, a participant may be presented with wireframes for the home page and top-level category pages of a consumer medical information website. The monitor may ask the participant if all the types of information or capabilities he would expect or hope to find on such as site are represented. He may also be asked whether he understands the meaning of all of the choices presented.

The monitor may ask the participant to point out which control he would select to perform a particular task. The monitor then displays the wireframe representing the screen that would be displayed as a result, and the process continues. The participant points out confusing or unexpected aspects of the design. The monitor then probes the participant to find out how the feature could have been structured or presented more clearly.

| TIP |

When testing the design for a product with several distinct audience types, such as a website intended for both parents and children, be sure to include representatives of both groups. This will raise the number of total testers.

The results of an exploratory test may change the functions or tasks that a website or software includes. It may also affect the naming and ordering of navigational elements.

Assessment Tests

An **assessment test** is the most common type of usability test. It may be performed midway through the design phase or near the release date of the project. The assessment test is performed after the overall feature set and high-level navigational structure have been determined. It helps determine how well the features have been implemented in the design.

To conduct the assessment test, the monitor presents specific tasks to the participant. The monitor then observes silently while the participant attempts to perform each task. The monitor makes note of any difficulties the participant encounters with the interface while trying to complete each task.

Using our medical website as an example, the monitor may ask the participant to find information about properly treating a chemical burn. The monitor then observes whether the subject selects the proper category of information and can successfully locate the requested information.

The monitor must resist the urge to help the subject in any way, except if the participant begins to demonstrate extreme frustration or seems about to flee the test. In such a case, the monitor may abandon that task, making note of this result.

Some assessment tests include a *benchmark* (standard of performance) for each task. These tests are sometimes referred to as *validation tests*. The benchmarks, usually in the form of time durations, may be derived from previous test data, or from measurements of previous versions of the website or software, or they may be predictions about how long it should take users to accomplish these tasks.

When participants are being timed or otherwise measured, they may be given a group of related tasks to accomplish, requiring the subject to access more elements of the design. Using our medical website example, the participant may be asked to determine the likely cause of a particular set of symptoms and to find the name of a local doctor who specializes in diagnosing and treating that type of disorder. The benchmark for this set of tasks (for example, within two minutes) is included in the task list, but is not conveyed to the participant.

Evaluation Tests

Evaluation tests are similar to assessment tests, but are conducted after a website or software product has been released and is in use. Such a test may help a team determine which design changes to make to the existing product to improve its usability.

Like assessment tests, evaluation tests may include benchmarks for performance that may be compared against observed measurements and used as a basis for recommending design changes.

Comparison Tests

The **comparison test** is used to compare two or more widely different approaches to a design. The wider the difference in the two approaches, the more valuable the resulting design is likely to be. Although this type of test may be conducted at any time during design or development, it is often used near the beginning of the project to arrive at the best approach.

The participant is asked to perform tasks using each design. The monitor then probes to determine which design is easiest to use. Usually each design that is tested will have both advantages and disadvantages. The designer can use the results of this test to develop a design that incorporates the strengths of each tested approach.

Table 13-1 compares the four types of usability tests.

table | **13-1** |

As this table shows, there are different types of usability tests for different purposes. Be sure to choose the right type of test, and conduct it at the appropriate time.

USABILITY TEXT TYPE	WHEN TO PERFORM	TEST'S PURPOSE	TEST METHODOLOGY
Exploratory Test	Early in the design phase	Compare how well the functions presented match the users' mental model	The participant is asked to compare website/software features with expectations, assumptions, and hopes. The monitor probes for confusing design elements and asks for subject's recommendations.
Assessment Test	Early to midway through the design phase	Determine how well the features have been implemented in the design	As the participant completes given tasks, the monitor observes silently and records any difficulties the subject has with the interface. The monitor may time or otherwise measure the participant.
Evaluation Test	After a website or software is in use	Determine if existing website or software is achieving its design goals	Similar to the assessment test, above.
Comparison Test	Often early in the design phase, but may be performed at any time	Compare two or more widely differing design approaches	The participant is asked to perform given tasks using different designs. The findings are used to select the superior design or create a new design that combines the strongest features of all the tested designs.

SIX STAGES OF CONDUCTING A USABILITY TEST

The six main steps to conducting a usability test are:

1. Create the test plan
2. Select the participants
3. Prepare the test materials
4. Conduct the test
5. Debrief the participant
6. Convert the test results to recommendations

1. Create the Test Plan

As Jeffrey Rubin points out, you must have specific testing goals in mind, or you are likely to find whatever results you want to find. Just as wireframes serve as the blueprint for a website or software program, the **test plan** serves as the blueprint for the usability test. It summarizes the purpose, goals, audience, content, and methodology for the test, and includes the following information:

- Purpose of the usability test
- Goals of the usability test
- Test-subject profile
- List of tasks
- Test environment
- Roles of people involved in the test
- Data to collect

These points are explored in further detail below.

Purpose of the Usability Test

This section of the test plan summarizes why the test is being conducted.

Goals of the Usability Test

The goals describe what the test results are expected to accomplish. The National Cancer Institute's Usability.gov website lists questions that the usability test may help answer. Some of these questions include:

- Do users complete a task successfully?
- If so, how fast do they complete each task?
- Is that fast enough to satisfy them?
- What paths do they take in trying?
- Do those paths seem efficient enough to them?

- Where do they seem to stumble or get confused?
- What words or paths are they looking for that are not currently on the site (or in the software)

This section should also include the type of usability test (exploratory, assessment, evaluation, or comparison) that will be conducted.

Test-Subject Profile

This section lists the characteristics of the users who will be recruited to participate in the usability test and the desired number of each type of user.

List of Tasks

This section contains the list of tasks that participants will be asked to attempt to perform. In some usability tests, users may be asked to state their first impressions of a website or software screen. These probes are also included in the task list. Note that some exploratory tests may not include a task list, but instead allow the participants to explore at will. In fact, it is a good idea to include free exploration as the final task of the test. The participant is free to explore any part of the website or software, thinking out loud during the exploration, of course!

Table 13-2 shows some examples of tasks that might be used when usability testing the floral design website we discussed in the preceding chapter.

| TIP |

Don't waste time testing every feature of a website or software program. Instead, the list of included tasks should be based on the goals for the product, such as the marketing goals.

table | **13-2** |

Tasks are given to the participant one at a time to perform. The list includes both specific and open-ended tasks.

SAMPLE TASK LIST

1. What are your first impressions of this page? What do you think of the layout, colors, and other visual parts of the page?

2. Look at the options presented and tell me what you think each of the choices is for.

3. If you were exploring this site, what would you do first on this page?

4. Find a red flower that can be used as a focal point that is available year-round.

5. Perform a search that interests you.

6. List all of the available plants of the genus *Franklinia*.

7. Find the meaning of the term *anther*.

8. Display the list of flowers that are most appropriate for a Mother's Day bouquet.

9. Play the correct pronunciation of *Quercus*.

10. List all plants of the family *Asteraceae*.

11. Explore any part of the site you'd like. Please think out loud as you go.

Test Environment

This section describes where the test will take place and what equipment will be included. Although some companies and universities set up elaborate usability testing labs with major investments in equipment and architecture (see Figure 1-6), you can perform valuable usability studies with the most modest of facilities. Some groups make extensive use of a portable lab, consisting mainly of a tripod-mounted video camera and a test monitor, that enables tests to be conducted nearly anywhere—at a client site, computer lab, office, or nearly anywhere.

If your team works on many projects, you may want to set up a simple, inexpensive environment in which to conduct usability testing. Figure 13-1 shows one layout of such an environment.

The basic usability-testing environment shown in Figure 13-1 consists of the following elements:

- The room
- Furniture
- A computer
- A video camera mounted on a tripod

These elements are discussed in further detail below.

THE ROOM   To make your usability participants as comfortable as possible, the room you select for usability studies should be relatively quiet and free of clutter. If possible, refrain from trying to turn a room being used for another purpose, such as the employee lunch area, into a usability lab.

The furniture in the room is oriented relative to the door so that another worker can come to the door and get the attention of the observer(s) without disturbing or interrupting the test. A live foliage plant and soft lighting help provide a relaxing atmosphere. The plant is positioned within the participant's sight line.

THE FURNITURE   A table or desk of appropriate height is used to hold the computer system. In our sample layout, we have positioned the table or desk so that there is room to fit a chair between it and the wall. This arrangement is suitable for testing using either a computer or documents such as wireframes.

The monitor's chair is positioned in one of two possible positions, depending on the type of test. In a computer-based test, the monitor's chair is positioned slightly behind the participant's chair, but close enough to see the computer screen and the subject's face. The participant sits at the computer keyboard. In a paper-based test, the monitor or person displaying the wireframes sits across the table or desk from the participant.

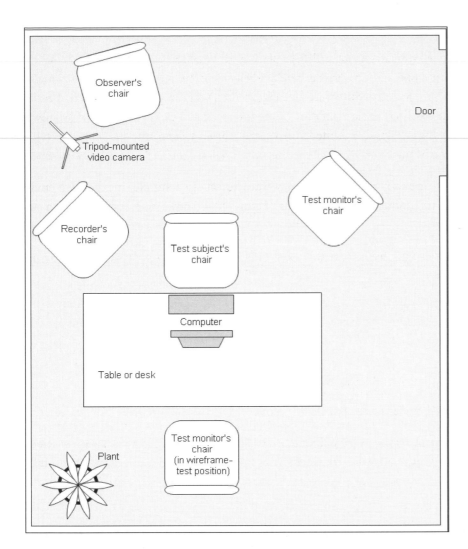

figure | **13-1** |

The various elements of the usability test room are carefully positioned to support the test goals.

There should be a chair to allow an observer to watch the test as it is conducted. The observer's chair is positioned near the back of the room. The observer should be able to see both the monitor and the subject. The monitor and observer sit behind the participant to enable the subject to focus attention on the software being tested.

If you designate someone as a recorder to time the participant's progress on each task, then include an additional chair next to the monitor or on the other side of the participant, positioned clear of the video camera and the observer's view.

In more elaborate usability lab setups, there is often a separate room for observers. In such an environment, a two-way mirror or remote monitor allows these observers to watch the test without being seen by the participant. The observers may communicate questions or comments to the monitor and subject via passed notes.

THE COMPUTER The system unit, if any, can be placed on the floor. The monitor and keyboard can be moved aside for paper-based usability tests. The computer may be loaded with recording software that captures the user's mouse clicks and keystrokes, the screens that are displayed as a result, and the voices of the subject and the test monitor.

More elaborate usability labs may include scan software that allows the computer images to be captured directly to videotape, without the need to videotape the screen.

VIDEO CAMERA MOUNTED ON TRIPOD The video is positioned to clearly capture the participant's mouse movements, keystrokes, facial expressions, the computer screen, and all spoken voices. Position the video camera in a location where it is least likely to be accidentally bumped by a test participant or someone entering the room.

As mentioned above, connecting a line from the video camera to a display monitor in a separate room allows many observers to view the results of the test without disturbing the test. More elaborate usability labs may include several cameras set to different angles and remote video controllers that allow a video technician to pan and zoom the video camera from another room.

Roles of those people involved in the test

THE MONITOR The **monitor** (sometimes called the *facilitator* or *test administrator*) acts as the host of the usability test. The person chosen to be the monitor should not have a strong personal or professional stake in the outcome of the test. The monitor may have special training in monitoring usability tests.

The designer should never serve as the monitor. The designer cannot be objective enough to run the usability test fairly. If a participant is having trouble figuring out how to navigate to or use a particular function, a designer serving as monitor might try to help the participant in subtle ways, may become defensive about the design, or may even ignore or skew observations that run counter to the designer's opinions or decisions. For these reasons, the role of designer should be observer rather than monitor.

THE PARTICIPANT The **participant** is the user who is testing the product that is the subject of the usability test. Participants' main responsibilities are to follow the monitor's instructions, to try to complete the tasks to the best of their ability, and to think out loud as they work.

THE RECORDER A person familiar with the product being tested is designated as the **recorder**. The recorder has three primary jobs. The first is to record the steps that the participant takes to try to complete each task. This is especially key when the test session is not being videotaped. The recorder may be asked to jot down any dialogue between the monitor and participant and to record relevant observations.

The recorder also measures and records the time it takes the participant to complete each task on a logging sheet, explained later in this chapter. Finally, the recorder may write down on the logging sheet the participant's rating of the ease or difficulty of completing each task.

THE OBSERVER(S) Although reading usability reports provides insight, there is nothing quite like personally watching a participant struggle with an interface. For this reason, encourage members of the development team and management to observe usability tests. Whenever possible, **observers** should be in a separate room from where the test is being conducted. As mentioned in our discussion of the testing room, two-way mirrors or remote video monitors let observers see the test as it unfolds.

If the observers must be in the same room as the test, their number should be limited to one or two. More than two observers are likely to distract and intimidate the participant. Observers in the same room as the test being conducted must be completely silent during the test. Any laughter, talking, or whispering is likely to distract the participant and the monitor and will disrupt the test. Observers in a separate but adjacent room to the test taker must be cautioned that their voices may carry to the participant.

Data to Collect

The test plan should include a summary of the type of information you will be collecting from the usability test. The types of data you collect depends on the type of study you are conducting.

Examples of the types of data that may be collected include:

- The actual steps the participant took to attempt to complete each task
- The time it took to complete each task
- The participants' rating of the ease or difficulty with which each task was completed
- Participants' comments and recorder's observations that indicate the participant's satisfaction with the product being tested
- The number of "errors," or diversions from the ideal steps outlined for each task

In assessment tests that include benchmarks, the timings for each task are compiled and compared with the benchmarks for each task. Tasks that consistently exceed the benchmark are candidates for improvements to the design.

Some studies use a five-point **Likert scale** to enable participants to rank the ease or difficulty of completing each step, with one being the most difficult and five being the easiest to complete. All participants' rankings of each step are compiled and averaged. Three is considered the lowest acceptable ranking. A task that averages lower than a three is considered a serious candidate for redesign.

2. Select the participants

The participants should reflect the target audience for the product you are testing.

Some development groups use outside usability-test recruiters or temporary employment agencies to find participants. If you plan to do your own recruiting, consider maintaining a database of possible participants. Use a *screening questionnaire* (described below) to find candidates that meet the criteria you set. Unless your participants are from your own company, you should pay or reward them for their time.

3. Prepare the Test Materials

The following list of documents will help prepare for a usability test:

- Screening questionnaire
- Orientation and administration script
- Consent form
- Post-test questionnaire

The Screening Questionnaire

Use a **screening questionnaire** to prequalify candidates for the test and to help select the final group of participants. The screening questionnaire enables you to select participants who possess the desired level of experience with the Web and, as appropriate, the application being tested. The questions you ask in your questionnaire will be specific to your needs, but Figure 13-2 shows an example.

Orientation and Administration Script

The monitor begins the session by explaining to the participant the purpose of the test and its ground rules. To ensure that each subject hears the same instructions, the monitor writes them down in advance in an **orientation script**. The monitor reads the orientation script to each subject. The following shows a sample orientation script.

Screening Questionnaire

Your occupation: _____

Your age range:
- 5 - 10 years
- 11 - 25 years
- 26 - 45 years
- 46 - 65 years
- 65 years or older

How often do you use the Internet?
- Almost every day
- About once per week
- About once per month
- Less than once per month
- I've never used it

How often do you use the [name of project]?
- Almost every day
- About once per week
- About once per month
- Less than once per month
- I've never used it

If you use the Internet, what sites do you use most often?

1. _____
2. _____
3. _____
4. _____
5. _____

figure | 13-2 |

Use a screening questionnaire to help you select participants who match the experience level or other criteria you set.

Sample Orientation Script

Thank you for coming today to help us test the design of [product name]. The test will take about one hour. We are inviting people like you to try out the product so that we can improve its design. Please remember that it is the design we are testing, not you. We want to find out how easy or difficult the product is to use. To find this out, we are going to give you a series of tasks to try to complete using the product.

As you try to complete each task, we ask that you think out loud. For example, if you can't find a way to get back to a screen you saw before, you might say, "I don't see how to get back to that other screen." This may seem a little strange, but by telling us what is going through your mind, you show us problems in the design that we might need to fix.

If we give you a task that you can't seem to do at all, don't worry. Just try whatever seems like it might work. If you get stuck, we'll give you another task to try. Remember, if you can't do something, it's not your fault; it's the design that's not working.

As you use the product, there will be some people watching. I'll introduce them to you now. [Introduce the observers and indicate whether they'll be sitting in the back of the room or in another room.]

[If the session is being videotaped] We will be taping the session so that we can review and analyze it later. We will not use the tape for any other purpose. [Give the participant the video consent form.] Please read and sign this consent form, which gives us your permission to videotape this session.

We have a total number of [x] tasks for you to try to complete. I'll read each task to you, then hand you a card that contains that task in case you want to review it. When you have completed the task, I'll give you the next task, and so on.

Do you have any questions before we begin?

Okay, I'll start the videotape now and begin with the first task. Remember to think out loud as you try to complete each task. I may occasionally ask you what you are thinking.

Task 1: [Read the first task, then hand its card to the participant]

[After each task is completed] Thank you. Here's your next task.

[When the last task is complete] Thank you. That was the last task. I am going to turn off the videotape. Before you leave, I would like you to complete a short questionnaire. We will not share or distribute the information you provide, and we won't associate your name with your answers.

[After participant has completed the questionnaire] Once again, thank you for helping us with this test today. [Pay the subject if applicable]. Do you have any additional questions or comments about today's session?

Consent Form

The **signed videotape consent** form gives your company permission to videotape the participant during the usability test. If possible, inform the participant before test day that you plan to videotape the test. In the sample orientation script, the monitor hands the participant the consent form for signing just before the test begins.

Figure 13-3 shows a sample videotape consent form.

Videotape Consent Form

I give permission for [company name] to videotape my usability testing session today. I understand that the videotape will be used only for the purposes of analyzing the results of today's test.

The videotape will only be used internally within [company name]. It will not be broadcast or used for any other purpose.

By signing below, I give my permission to conduct and videotape today's session.

Your signature: _____

Your printed name: _____

Today's date: _____

figure | **13-3** |

The signed videotape consent form gives the participant's permission to videotape the usability test.

4. Conduct the Test

The monitor conducts the test according to the orientation and administration script. Listed below are some guidelines for conducting the test. Many of these were suggested by and adapted from Rubin:

- Do not lead the participants. Let the subjects find the answer by themselves.
- Put the participants at ease.
- Be flexible. You may need to change the usability plan in response to a given situation.
- Never lose patience with a participant.

- Try playing dumb—it may lead to interesting results.

- Be a good listener.

- Keep your body language and facial expressions neutral.

- Don't jump to conclusions. Seek to discover patterns, but don't let your observations color your interaction with the participant.

The recorder uses a **logging sheet** to record the participant's results on each task. Figure 13-4 shows a sample of a logging sheet that has been pre-filled with one of the tasks. The logging sheet includes space at the bottom to record the time it takes to complete each task.

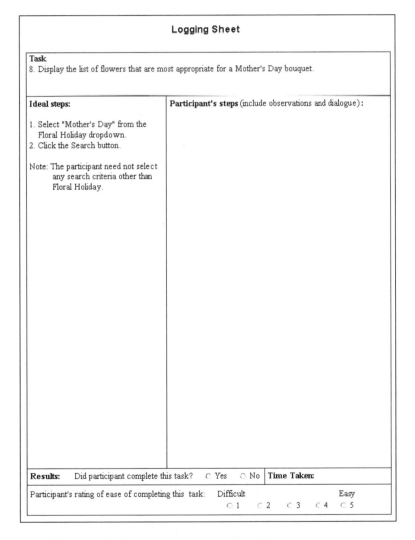

Logging Sheet

Task
8. Display the list of flowers that are most appropriate for a Mother's Day bouquet.

Ideal steps:	**Participant's steps** (include observations and dialogue):
1. Select "Mother's Day" from the Floral Holiday dropdown. 2. Click the Search button. Note: The participant need not select any search criteria other than Floral Holiday.	

Results: Did participant complete this task? ○ Yes   ○ No | **Time Taken:**

Participant's rating of ease of completing this task: Difficult   Easy
   ○ 1   ○ 2   ○ 3   ○ 4   ○ 5

figure | **13-4** |

The recorder notes the participant's progress in completing the task shown. Each task gets its own sheet, and the recorder includes the participant's spoken comments and ranking of the task's difficulty.

As previously noted, the participant may also be asked to rate the ease or difficulty of completing each task. Notice that the logging sheet in Figure 13-4 includes a Likert scale with ratings between one and five to record this information. Tasks that the participant is unable to complete receive a one, the lowest score.

You may want to designate a maximum allowable time for each task. If the time limit is reached before the participant has completed the task, the recorder notifies the monitor. The monitor instructs the participant to stop the current task and continue with the next task.

If the test becomes too intimidating or frustrating for the participant to continue, the monitor will excuse the participant from completing the remainder of the tasks. The participant may still be asked to complete the post-test questionnaire, discussed in the next section.

5. Debrief the Participant

When the tasks have all been completed, the participant is given the opportunity to express his overall opinions about the product being tested and the testing process itself. The *post-test questionnaire* is the means for gathering this useful information.

The Post-Test Questionnaire

The **post-test questionnaire** provides an opportunity for the participant to provide conclusions and recommendations about the product or design being tested. The monitor advises the subject that the information provided in the post-test questionnaire will not be shared or distributed, and the results will not be associated with the participant.

Figure 13-5 shows a sample post-test questionnaire.

| TIP |

Show respect for your participant by limiting the post-test questionnaire to just a few key questions. Ask open-ended questions—that is, questions that encourage subjects to express their opinions rather than just selecting a choice from a multiple-choice question. The participant's responses often provide useful insight.

6. Convert the Test Results to Recommendations

The goal of the usability test is to improve the product or design being tested. To achieve this goal, the test team summarizes the results of the test in a report. The report itself must be usable. Rolf Molich has analyzed reports written by many different usability-testing groups. The results of his research form a useful set of best practices for writing such reports.

KEEP IT BRIEF To be most effective, the report must be concise. Don't make management or engineering wade through pages of log sheets, descriptions of testing methodologies, and other nonessential information. Summarize the information in usable recommendations that the team can convert to design improvements.

figure | 13-5 |

When all tasks are complete, use the post-test questionnaire to record the participant's overall impressions and suggestions.

Post-Test Questionnaire

What did you think of the [product] overall?

Did you find it easy or difficult to complete the tasks we gave you?

What things did you like best about the [product]?

What things about the [product] would you most like to change, and how would you change them?

Did you enjoy the experience of participating in this usability test? What can we do to improve this experience for future subjects?

Thank you for helping us make [product] great!

INCLUDE POSITIVE FINDINGS The usability report should include positive findings as well as areas for improvement. It is just as important to know where the design is working as it is to know where it is not. If possible, try to include as many positive as negative findings.

CLASSIFY COMMENTS Organize your report by classifying your results in specific categories. Create such categories as disasters, serious problems, minor problems, positive findings, bugs, and suggestions for improving the interface. This makes the results of the test easier to find and digest.

INCLUDE AN EXECUTIVE SUMMARY Summarize the most important findings of the report in an executive summary that is placed at the front of the report. The executive summary should include the top three positive findings and the top three problems.

Rolf Molich provides a sample report that follows these recommendations at http://www.dialogdesign.dk/utestreports.html. There are many other examples of usability reports available on the Web.

Conducting usability tests at various points of a project's development, translating the results into recommendations, and following those recommendations is the only way to create a usable product. The experience of witnessing usability tests on the projects you design will make you a better designer. Now it is time to turn our attention to the business of user interface design.

SUMMARY OF KEY POINTS

- Don't wait until you have a working website or software to begin usability testing. Have users review the proposed functions list and wireframes early in the development process. Test often using small groups.

- There are different types of usability tests for different purposes, including exploratory tests, assessment tests, evaluation tests, and comparison tests. Each is unique according to its purpose, when it is performed, and its methodology.

- Create a test plan to specify the purpose, goals, audience, content, and methodology for the test.

- It is relatively simple to set up a usability testing room. Some groups use a mobile testing lab that can be brought to users or the client site.

- The people involved in usability testing include the participant, monitor, recorder, and one or more observers.

- The monitor reads an orientation script to the participant. The script is read to ensure that all participants are given the same instructions.

- It is important that the monitor not attempt to lead the participant or otherwise skew the results of the test.

- A designer should never assume the role of monitor, since it is the design that is being evaluated.

- The monitor usually creates a report that includes the results of the test. The report should be structured so that readers can easily understand its results and recommendations.

in review

1. What is a heuristic evaluation, and what are its limitations?

2. What are the major disadvantages of conducting a single usability test with many participants?

3. What type of usability test is often conducted near the release date of a product?

4. What is the role of the monitor of a usability test, and why shouldn't the interface designer play this role?

5. What elements in the testing room are designed to make the participant at ease with the surroundings?

6. Why go to the trouble of scripting what the monitor says to the participant?

7. What is a logging sheet, and what are its major components?

8. What four things can you do to make a usability test report usable?

exercise

1. Design a "nightmare" usability testing lab and describe how its operation and the roles of its participants differ from that of a well-run usability lab. If possible, form groups and create a skit that illustrates these problems. The rest of the students can observe and record problems with the way the test is being run. At the end of the skit, see how many problems the students were able to identify.

the user interface designer in professional practice

objectives

Analyze how identifying client motivators can serve both you and your clients

Examine effective strategies for dealing with common client situations

Describe two things to insist your clients do to save both them and you time and money

Examine the possible consequences of overestimating your power in a client relationship

Examine how to build your business through sales, proposal writing, and creative partnering

Identify what questions to ask to protect yourself from unethical client practices

Analyze how to set up and manage filing systems, communications, and other systems to increase the efficiency of your business

introduction

The majority of this book has been devoted to providing you with the tools and information you need to design effective, usable interfaces. In this chapter, we will explore the *business* of user interface design.

We'll start by investigating how to form and maintain the strong client relationships that are fundamental to any design business's success. Next we'll examine how to sell your services, win projects, and grow the business. Finally, we'll cover some important office procedures that can help your operation run smoothly.

FORMING AND MAINTAINING STRONG CLIENT RELATIONSHIPS

Relationships Are Essential to Business Success

When a client hires you, you provide a service that the client needs in exchange for a consideration, usually money. The client has the right to expect you to perform the work you have been hired to do with quality, according to an agreed-upon schedule, and at an agreed-upon price. The client has the responsibility to pay you for your work and to provide the information and timely reviews that you need to do your job. You have the right, although not the guarantee, to make a profit from the work you do so that you can remain in business.

Although a contract specifies many of the legal rights and responsibilities of the relationship between you and your client, the human part can be much more complex, rewarding, frustrating at times, and interesting. The legal part of the relationship is beyond the scope of this text. Our advice is to hire the best attorney and accountant you can afford to advise you on the legal and financial matters that arise in the course of doing business. We will focus our attention on the human part of the client-vendor relationship.

Your success in business hinges directly on your ability to create and maintain long-term business relationships. You, as the vendor with a service to sell, will usually take the lead in establishing the relationship, working toward gaining your client's trust, support, and eventual business.

Initially to some, this seems disingenuous or even manipulative. Aren't we just trying to gain friendship so that we can profit from it? In fact, a good business relationship is one in which each party gains something of value. Although strong business relationships can blossom into true friendships, their primary purpose is to get something useful done. That can't happen unless someone takes the initiative to create and nurture the relationship in the first place.

Win Client Trust through Performance

Trust is fundamental to any good business relationship. As a vendor, you want to perform in a way that inspires your client's trust in you. Make a client look good in the eyes of her management, and you are sure to win her trust. To build trust, do the following:

- Get to know your clients and help them get to know you.
- Anticipate and satisfy your client's business needs.
- Be responsive to your client's requests. Return telephone calls and messages the same day whenever possible.

- Take accurate notes at meetings; include the date of the meeting, the location, the participants, any decisions, and issues requiring follow-up.
- Follow through on the promises and commitments you make—deliver what you promise.
- Conduct yourself professionally and ethically.
- Send your client occasional useful articles about best practices or developments in their industry.

Take a Genuine Interest in Your Client

Clients like to deal with those they know and who know them. Take the time to learn about your client as a person. If you are genuinely interested in someone, it's not difficult to find out if they have children, what types of vacations they prefer, if they have pets, and what kinds of hobbies they enjoy.

It may be appropriate to send a small holiday gift to clients, especially if the gift bears your company's name or logo. But don't attempt to buy your way into your client's heart with expensive gifts. Such gifts smack of bribery and may violate your client's company's policies. There are plenty of other legitimate ways to show clients that you value them.

For example, pick up the telephone and ask your client's opinion on a design issue for which two more or less equally valid solutions exist. Tell her that you are considering two approaches and would like her opinion on which she prefers. Explain why you are favoring one approach over the other, and ask if she agrees or not. If she disagrees, be sure to thank her for her counsel, and implement the feature according to her wishes. In addition to building her trust, you will be learning about her preferences, which will enable you to anticipate her reactions.

Discover Your Client's Motivators

What pressures is your client facing? Is there a specific event date, such as an important presentation or rollout, which she is under pressure to meet? Knowing this information can help you make suggestions that help both you and your client.

For example, clients frequently have asked us to produce a finished website or multimedia software by an impossibly aggressive schedule. On several such occasions, we probed further and discovered that the clients needed to demonstrate the product at an important sales conference or for an important client of theirs. We suggested creating a demo version of the product instead of the full version by the required date, which satisfied our clients' needs and relieved the pressure on us.

Learn Your Client's Style

Clients come in all flavors. The best clients are those that view you as an equal partner. They do their job without trying to do yours, too. They provide the information you need in a timely manner and make only reasonable requests. They respect your expertise and recognize your time's value. They pay their bills on time and seek to cultivate a long-term business relationship with you.

Many clients fall short of this ideal. At the extremes, some clients may want as little involvement with you and your (their!) project as possible, while others may want to micromanage your every move. Some are incredibly demanding of your time, while others won't even return your telephone calls. Some require you to send them incredibly detailed specifications; while others refuse to read a single document you send them.

Succeeding in business means finding a way to do high-quality work under circumstances that are sometimes beyond your control. The key is to communicate your position clearly and directly, while keeping your emotions in check.

Table 14-1 shows some examples of types of clients you may work with and some of the advantages and disadvantages to working with them. It also includes strategies for keeping the project and relationship on track.

Recognize That Your Client Has the Upper Hand

There are examples of individuals or companies whose services are in such demand that *they* choose the clients and projects they wish to work on. Usually, though, vendors are hungry for work, so clients maintain the upper hand. If the client perceives that the vendor did not perform well on a project—because of the quality of work, the cost, the relationship, or any other reason, the client nearly always has the option to choose a different vendor next time. And vendors in search of work are easy to find.

Treat your clients with respect. You may be the interface design expert or the Web development expert, but it is still the client's project. Choose your battles carefully. When inevitable differences of opinion occur, ask yourself if this is the hill you wish to die on. In other words, is insisting on your point of view important enough to risk alienating the client or damaging the relationship? In most cases, the answer will be "no." Recognize that you cannot always protect clients from their own decisions, even when you are sure they are wrong.

Although your clients may call the shots, there are two must-haves that will help ensure the success of the projects you work on. First, insist that your client designates a single person to serve as your contact point throughout the project. All correspondence from and to the client should go through this person. Designate a single person on your end for your client to work with, as well. There is nothing worse than getting conflicting direction from different sources and having to determine which path you should follow.

table | 14-1 |

Strategies for Handling Selected Client Situations

CLIENT SITUATION	KEY ADVANTAGES	KEY DISADVANTAGES	STRATEGY
The client insists on helping you design the project.	Working closely with the client may help build a solid business relationship. The client may be more likely to be satisfied with the end product if she had a strong hand in creating it.	Heavy client involvement may increase your time and costs. The client may constantly second-guess your decisions.	If necessary, address this gently with the client. Stress that to meet budget and schedule goals, the client's role is to review work and specify revisions at key milestones.
The client can't be bothered with reviews or project details. She just wants to see the finished product.	The design process will go smoothly and quickly with few interruptions.	You may be forced to make decisions that the client should be making. This client may blame you if the finished product isn't what she expected, regardless of whether she communicated her needs to you.	Stress that to ensure that the end product is successful, it is important that she review and comment on milestones. Stress that you will do whatever you can to make this an easy process for her.
The client uses an outside consultant or group of consultants to manage the project, including reviewing your work.	The quality of the review feedback may be higher than if the client handles this herself. The consultant could be a source of leads or work in the future.	The consultant may have incentive to increase his own hours (and thus his pay) or perceived value to the client by finding many things "wrong" with your work.	If you discover this early enough, specify a fair number of revision passes (for example, 3) after which you will charge for additional passes. Stress the need to contain costs and keep the project on schedule.
Someone at the client site (other than your usual contact) seems disappointed that you were selected to do the project. He constantly finds fault with your work and makes things difficult for you.	Sometimes the presence of a critical influence encourages us to do our best work.	An adversarial business relationship can be emotionally difficult. It also costs time and money to defend yourself or your company from unjust criticism.	Acknowledge to your usual contact that you fear that this person may not want you to succeed, but stay focused on doing the job you were hired to do. Take advantage of opportunities to build support among the other members of the client team.

Second, insist that all client feedback, such as quality assurance reviews, be consolidated into a single report and sent to you at one time. Otherwise, you will be forced to resolve conflicting feedback from different sources. For example, two reviewers may each want you to change a button label, but each may suggest different text. Which reviewer's suggestion should you follow?

But Bob said that Carol told him that Jim said that Maria didn't expect the wireframes until next Thursday…

Clients may also want to "flow" the feedback to you, but this is likely to result in extra work. You may make a change in response to an early review item, just to have a later review cancel or change the first item. Requesting that feedback reviews be consolidated into a single report with duplicate items removed and conflicting items resolved will save you and your client time and money. Most clients will understand the reasoning behind this request, although it may take some a while to get used to the practice.

Finally, recognize that clients nearly always act in their own best interests, not in yours. Their goal is to do the best they can for their company while looking good in their management's eyes. This will sometimes result in decisions that may affect you adversely. Some take such actions personally, believing that the client is acting intentionally to cause them harm. This is usually not the case.

The best approach in such situations is to make carefully measured responses. Although it may seem warranted at the time, dashing off an angry e-mail or racing to call a client to express your displeasure rarely helps your cause. It could even result in you or your company being blackballed from working with that client in the future. Take time to cool off, and then think logically about the best way to proceed. In many cases you will find that a misunderstanding lies at the core of the issue.

A Vendor Learns a Costly Lesson

Here is a real-life example of a small company whose greed cost them dearly. Their story serves as a warning that situations are not always as we perceive them.

While working for a large corporation, I was asked to design and manage the development of a large series of interactive multimedia sales training programs. My responsibilities included hiring outside development companies to produce the 15 programs that comprised the series.

There was one small company in particular whose work was of good quality, and we hired them to produce two of the initial titles. After successfully completing these two titles, we put out requests for proposal (RFPs) for the

A Vendor Learns a Costly Lesson (continued)

next two projects in the series. We were surprised to find that this company's price was suddenly much higher than their original bids, although the projects were of similar scope and complexity. The company's price was also significantly higher than that of the competing groups who responded.

I thought there was a chance that they had made an error or misunderstood the project's scope, and I felt that I owed them the opportunity to review their numbers and resubmit. When I contacted them to extend this offer, they responded that there was no error, and that their bid was firm.

We had no choice but to award these projects to other vendors, whose work was also of high quality. Within a matter of weeks, the original company let go its entire multimedia development staff and closed down this part of its operations. There was almost certainly a connection to our selecting other vendors, but what had caused such an abrupt closure? It wasn't until some months later that I found out what had led to this company's odd behavior and subsequent demise.

In a conversation with one of the developers who had lost his job, I found out that the company's managers believed that doing a good job on the first two titles would greatly increase their leverage with us. In fact, they were betting that we would select their company even if their price was higher than that of competing vendors. They had interpreted my call to them as simply an effort on my part to get them to lower their price, but they did not believe we would risk selecting another vendor.

In fact, the managers had bet their company's very survival on their interpretation of the situation. Although we had no way to know this, the loss of these projects meant that they could no longer meet their payroll obligations, and they were forced into insolvency. The company's managers misjudged the strength of their position and foolishly wagered their company's future.

There is also another angle to consider in this story. Clients have a moral obligation to maintain a "level playing field" for the projects they bid out. This means simply that they should not give one group an unfair advantage over others. U.S. government agencies enforce strict rules to support this policy.

Working for a nongovernment corporation, I wasn't bound by such rules, although I believe strongly in being fair to vendors. For example, we never sent our RFPs to more than five vendors. Having been a vendor as well as a client, I know how disappointing it is to work diligently on a large proposal for a client, only to find out that you are one of 12 competitors. Such a large field greatly reduces your chances of winning.

By informing the company that their bids were inconsistent with the others', did I give this company an unfair advantage? At the time I told myself that my decision to call them did not result in their winning the business. The fact that my company did not force me to choose the lowest bidder also helped me justify calling them.

In truth, my calling the company gave them an opportunity to win a bid they otherwise would have lost outright. I doubt the other companies bidding on the project would have felt that the playing field was level at that point. If another group had also bid very high, I would have been obligated to give them the same opportunity to review their bid and submit revised pricing.

GROWING YOUR BUSINESS

Designers who work as paid consultants or contractors serve as their own salespeople. Working feverishly to complete one project while simultaneously selling the next one is a difficult part of this business. For this reason, many designers prefer to work full-time for a company if such work is available. An employer is likely to pay a proportion of health care expenses and often offers other benefits as well.

Many designers who work as consultants hope that a full-time position will emerge from a consulting assignment. There are others, however, who prefer being on their own, either by working as a consultant or by forming their own company.

For such people, generating sales is one of the most important parts of growing your business. A capable sales person helps find out about new opportunities within existing clients and with new clients. A capable sales person often serves as a client relationship manager, helping to resolve client problems.

Some clients may perceive it as an advantage to deal with you directly, without working with a sales representative. If you absolutely despise sales, however, or if you are not good at it, then consider teaming up with someone who is. For without sales, there is no business.

Finding Work

When you are working with a client, don't be afraid to ask what new projects are coming up for which you might submit a proposal. It is wise to time this request around a positive event in the project, such as an on-time, well-received deliverable. If your client is a large company, ask your contact for the names of others within the company who vend out projects and ask if you can use your contact as a reference.

Remember that contacting a client isn't bothering them. You have something of value to offer. Ask your contact if it is all right for you to touch base once a month or so to keep abreast of new opportunities.

When you are just starting out, you may have to undercharge for your work to secure business. Let prospective clients know that you are eager to establish yourself and are willing to produce excellent work at a low rate in exchange for experience. Don't overlook opportunities to do free or reduced-price work for relatives or friends in exchange for the right to list them as clients.

Your best weapon in securing new work is to leverage your successes. When you successfully complete a project, be prepared to tell the story of how the project succeeded. Metrics can be especially useful in this regard. If you are able to say, for example, that you dropped customer complaints by 25% or increased sales by 30%, these can be powerful messages to a prospective client.

Look for creative ways to market your skills and services. Consider approaching a firm that specializes in large projects to see if they might be willing to pass on smaller jobs to you. You might also develop a referral arrangement with a company in a related field, such as video production or animation. They agree to recommend you to clients of theirs who seek interactive design work, while you recommend them to clients of yours who need their services. You can also each increase the breadth of services you offer by including your partners' services as part of your own.

Do your best to build a base of different clients. Many companies do most of their work for a single client. A management change or key contact leaving can leave yourself or your company with very little business without any warning. Find at least a few different baskets in which to carry your eggs.

Exercise Fiscal Responsibility

During the boom that preceded the dot-com bust, many young companies rented lavish offices and squandered investment money on expensive furniture and equipment. Don't make the same mistake. Run your business as modestly as possible, and let sales drive your company's growth. Avoid hiring permanent staff or purchasing equipment except when absolutely necessary.

Track your time as you work on projects to determine if your business is profitable. Tracking will teach you which types of projects and clients are most and least profitable. It will help teach you where your highest costs are so that you can try to reduce them without sacrificing the quality of your work.

Writing Proposals

Most designers and design companies win projects by writing **proposals** in response to client **requests for proposal** (**RFPs**). The RFP, which states the client's requirements, may be loosely or well specified. Observe the RFP format and use as much of that format as possible when creating your proposal. If the RFP requests specific information, such as "include a section describing the staff you expect to use on the project," then be sure to include this information in your proposal.

If possible, try to set up a meeting with the client to discuss your questions and present your own work. Some clients will ask instead that you send your questions via e-mail.

Components of the Proposal

The proposals you create will be tailored to the client's RFP. In general, consider including the following in your proposals:

- **Introduction:** A restatement of the project that demonstrates your understanding of the client's needs.

- **Your solution:** How you intend to satisfy the needs of the project, including innovative ideas you might have.

- **Hardware/software:** If this project includes development as well as design, then this section includes the hardware and software required to run your solution. It may also include the languages or tools you use to create the system.

- **Methodologies:** This section includes any processes or methodologies you intend to use to satisfy the needs of the project. If methodologies are central to the client's RFP, then include them here. Otherwise, consider including them in the appendix.

- **Staff:** Include the credentials and experience of those who will work on the project.

- **Applicable project experience:** Include descriptions and/or screens from the projects you've worked on that are similar or whose experience is applicable to this project.

- **Price:** For fixed-bid projects, this is the price you are asking to perform the work specified in your proposal. Provide a detailed breakdown of costs if the client requests this. When determining your price, be sure to add the cost of travel to and from the client site. If the client will be responsible for paying any license fees for products that you use, such as installers, be sure to include this information in the proposal and/or contract.

- **Schedule:** Include a schedule that clearly shows both your and the client's responsibilities. The schedule should include a note specifying that late deliveries by the client will result in a delay of the same number of days.

- **Authorization:** Include an unsigned authorization to begin work. Your attorney can provide you with the language for the authorization.

- **Appendices:** Include your company history, design philosophy, other samples of your work, or other information that you think might help you to win the project.

EXECUTIVE SUMMARY Consider including an executive summary at the beginning of your proposal. The executive summary is a one-page synopsis of your bid, including key information needed by decision-makers on the client side. It should include a brief summary of your solution, the price, and the expected completion date.

CONCEPT SCREENS Sometimes you have to give a little to win a lot. Clients love to have something to look at that helps evaluate your skills. Sample concept screens or a prototype program help demonstrate your talent and commitment to the project and may excite your client enough to choose you.

Protect Yourself from Unethical Client Practices

Although most clients deal fairly and honestly, there are those who will take unfair advantage of you if you give them the opportunity. It is your job to watch out for such behaviors. I have personally experienced or witnessed all of the following unethical client behaviors:

- Some companies issue seemingly legitimate RFPs requesting proposals from different groups, but later change their mind and decide to build the project in-house. The completed project includes the best ideas "borrowed" from the submitted proposals.

- A fairly common practice is for companies to require three or more competing bids on a project. Some companies ask you to bid just so they can meet this requirement, although they have no intention of awarding you the project.

- Some companies don't require all proposals to be received at the same time and may share your proposal with the company they want to win the project.

- Sometimes favored bidders are invited to present their proposals in person, while the remaining vendors are asked to mail their proposals.

- Some companies hire you with no intention of ever paying you for your work. Sometimes the client company ceases to exist, but quickly reappears with the same owners under a different name.

The best way to protect yourself from such practices is by including protective language in your contracts and by asking questions up front, before you begin creating a proposal. The following questions may help root out situations that you want to avoid. They can also help determine which RFPs you choose to respond to and how much effort to put into your response. It is important that you assume clients are dealing ethically with vendors and that you not come across as distrustful. Before asking any questions of a prospective client, be sure to review the RFP and any other documents or materials the client has sent to see if they provide any of these answers.

- How many bidders are being asked to submit proposals?

- Are the proposals due from all vendors at the same time?

- Is there a vendor who is bidding on the project who worked on an earlier version of this product?

- Are vendors being asked to submit fixed-price bids or hourly rates (time and materials) for the work?

- Is there any chance that the project will not be awarded to any of the bidders?

- Who at the client company will decide which company is awarded the project?

| **TIP** |

Ask a prospective client if she is willing to give you a "ballpark" price range she is looking for. You might say that you can respond to the client's RFP with a very modest solution or with a more elaborate one, and you want to ensure you are meeting the client's needs. Many companies will candidly respond to this question. They might give you an expected range of values. This ensures that your bid is basically in line with their expectations and won't be rejected because it is far too high or even too low.

- What are the most important criteria for determining which competitor wins the project?
- Will you have the opportunity to ask questions to clarify the client's needs prior to submitting your proposal?
- Will you or any other bidders have the opportunity to present your proposal in person?

The answers to these questions should help you decide whether to create a proposal or pass on the opportunity. If you believe your chances to win are small, you might decide to respond with a brief proposal that does not require much time or effort to create. If the client is a desirable one to you, you may decide to respond with a high-quality proposal just to ensure that you remain on the list of vendors who are sent RFPs in the future.

The Winning Bidder

The winning bidder is usually the person or company who offers the best combination of the following:

- Price
- A creative solution
- An individual or company that is easy, fun, or prestigious to work with
- Someone who can be trusted to complete the work within budget and schedule

Sometimes there are other decision factors that a client may not disclose to vendors. For example, the client may prefer to work with someone who is local. Occasionally, someone who is high in the organization may express a preference for one of the bidders. In certain situations, a project is awarded to a vendor to make up for a past injustice.

If the client notifies you that you are the winning bidder, congratulations! The next step is to try to nail down the business as soon as possible by getting the client to sign your authorization letter.

You Can't Win Them All

If you lose a bid, be sure to find out why the client selected the winning bidder. Was price the issue, or was it the competitor's solution, or perhaps the client's comfort level with the other bidder? A client normally feels bad for you when you lose and may be willing to share information. Don't become defensive or negative, but wish the client success and use the opportunity to learn how to be a better bidder next time.

| TIP |

On several occasions, our company won a project we were told we lost by continuing negotiations with the client as if the project had not yet been awarded. Although such situations are relatively rare, it is possible that the client may be forced to go with a vendor due to price. In such cases, it may be worth asking if your client might accept a lower price or additional features from your company.

It Isn't Over Till It's Over

Remember that the deal isn't done until the contract is signed, and even then it isn't done. The road is littered with companies whose leaders prematurely celebrated a victory, only to find later that they actually lost or won much less than they thought. Sometimes your client contact will lead you to believe you are the favored vendor. It isn't until after the project is awarded to someone else that you realize that your contact was not the decision maker.

You may even win a project, begin work, but then be informed that the client has terminated the project for any number of reasons. You may have staffed up to handle the expected load only to be stuck with manpower and equipment you no longer need. To protect yourself in the event that a client cancels a project, include provisions in your contracts that specify that you get paid for all work you have completed and any preparation work you have performed for subsequent phases of the project.

INSTITUTE AND FOLLOW PROVEN OFFICE PRACTICES

This section contains some useful ideas to help your business run smoothly and efficiently. The ideas cover setting up filing systems and handling communications. Some benefits of instituting and following such systems include:

- They maximize efficiency. It is frustrating and costly to lose important documents or forget to bill for completed work.

- They help ensure consistency and reliability as the business grows.

- When a client asks you to update a project you worked on several years ago, it is helpful to be able to review the project's details by accessing its back file.

- An efficiently run office can be an effective selling tool when you are trying to win new business. Clients like to deal with well-organized groups and individuals. It helps projects run smoothly and shows that you are serious about being in business.

| **TIP** |

Don't look at your client through rose-colored glasses. Many vendors hear what they want to hear at client meetings or in conversations and fail to hear what the client is really saying. For many reasons, the client may not be willing to say something to you directly. Try to read between the lines, challenge your assumptions, and ask questions freely to get the true story.

| **TIP** |

When considering implementing a new office procedure, ask yourself if the new procedure is too complex or requires too much maintenance to be sustainable. The procedures you set up should serve you, not force you to be a slave to them.

| TIP |

Orient project documents such as memos and letters so that the left edge, which usually contains the document date, is facing up. This will enable you to quickly thumb through the documents to find documents of a specific date without having to remove the documents from their files.

| TIP |

It is much easier to locate a particular hanging file if all of the file labels are in a single line. This enables your eye to quickly scan the labels. Figure 14-1 illustrates this point.

Filing

Although filing ranks among the more mundane office tasks, setting up and maintaining an efficient filing system pays substantial rewards over time. In fact, being able to quickly locate a much-needed document can be downright exciting!

Create separate file drawers for projects, companies you deal with, personnel, and any other categories that fit your business. Your project files will likely expand to multiple drawers with time. To create a project file, purchase box-bottom hanging files and place brown accordion file pockets inside them. This will provide room to store many documents. For large projects, when the accordion file gets filled to capacity, simply add a new box-bottom hanging file and accordion file and continue storing.

Create a file for each new project you work on, and arrange them alphabetically by project name. Store all of the documents you send and receive for that project in date order. File the oldest documents in the back, and place newer documents in front.

Create an electronic filing system that parallels your paper files. Organize your electronic project files by project name for storing e-mail messages. Some companies print copies of all e-mail messages sent and received and store these hard copies in the project files. To save paper and to keep your paper project files from growing too quickly, consider just printing key e-mail messages for the paper project files, and storing all e-mail sent and received in the electronic files.

Create a project file for storing a CD or DVD containing each piece of software you send to a client or to contractors you are working with on

figure | 14-1 |

Lining up hanging file labels makes them easy to scan and find a specific file.

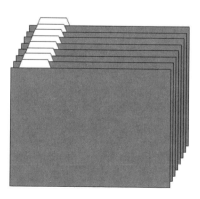

a project. Clearly label each CD with the date and identification of the software stored there. The CD or DVD should contain just those files that were sent to the client or contractor. This can help you settle disputes should they arise regarding what was sent when.

Create a separate file for storing any software the client sends you. If software is sent electronically, burn it to a CD or DVD and label and store it in this file. Buy a date stamp and stamp any undated materials you receive with today's date.

Communications

During the course of a project, there are dozens of communications that occur between you, your client, and other participants. Here are some guidelines that may help you manage the communications among the parties.

Try to set up a face-to-face meeting for holding the most important conversations, such as a project kickoff meeting. Such meetings usually take place at the client's site. Clients understand that individual contractors often work out of their homes and so are happy to hold meetings at the client's site.

A vendor who maintains offices may invite the client to meet at the vendor's site, especially if the client is a new one. This allows the vendor to show off her operation and introduce key staff that may be working on the project. This helps give the client a feeling of confidence and helps establish the relationship.

Be sure to follow up important meetings and telephone conversations with an e-mail message that summarizes any decisions that were made and action items that were assigned. E-mail is an effective means of communication because the text is searchable, allowing you to find references to a particular topic if the need arises.

When you send a deliverable through the mail, include a cover letter that indicates what is being included and the date that the client's review of the material is due according to the most recent project schedule. This will alert the client to expected deliverables on their part and will help cover you in the event that the client is late with expected deliverables.

Keep all correspondence—letters, memos, and e-mails—brief and to the point. After a friendly greeting, state the purpose of the correspondence

| **TIP** |

Consider maintaining offsite storage for your most important documents and media. If you are not sure what to store offsite, imagine a fire destroyed your office. What would it be hardest to replace?

| **TIP** |

Consider maintaining a looseleaf binder for each of your projects. The binder organizes all of the important project documents, including the RFP, proposal, feature lists, wireframes, and meeting notes. Whenever you attend a project meeting, just bring the project binder and you have access to all of the documents you might need.

right away. Write as if your reader has very little time to read your writing, and use some of the concise writing techniques discussed in Chapter 10.

Create a Company Routing Slip to Organize Mail

If you are part of a company, create a company routing slip to help you organize and keep a record of incoming and outgoing hard copy mail. Figure 14-2 shows an example of a routing slip.

Attach a completed routing slip to your office copy of each document you send or receive. Include the name of the document's sender, the date, project name, and a brief description of the contents. Check off who you wish to receive a copy of the document and, for outgoing documents, who it is being sent to and by what means (overnight mail, fax, etc.). Be sure to include the appropriate project file as one of the recipients.

figure | 14-2 |

Attach a routing slip to incoming mail and copies of outgoing mail. This creates an effective record of who received a particular mail item. Do not send the routing slip to clients or others outside your company, but include it in any copies you distribute to your coworkers.

Routing Slip

Date: _____   Project: _____   Sent by: _____

Description: _____

☐ Bob Redmond   ☐ Karen Gray   ☐

☐ Bonnie Hall   ☐ Lorenzo Thomas   ☐

☐ Chuck Wong   ☐ Monte Young   ☐

☐ Fred Schultz   ☐ Paula Rodriguez   ☐

☐ Georgia Wallace   ☐ Sally Thomas   ☐

☐ Jorge Rivera   ☐ Tory Ames   ☐

SUMMARY OF KEY POINTS

- Learn to serve your clients while protecting your own interests.

- Your client's style can determine the ease or difficulty of the relationship, the project's profitability to you, and its ultimate success or failure. You can adopt strategies to help keep the project and relationship on course.

- Take time to cool down and plan an appropriate response when a client's action affects you adversely. Don't misconstrue a business decision as a personal attack.

- Remember that clients usually can find someone else to perform work for them. The more well known the client, the more options they generally have.

- Grow your business by leveraging your successes. Develop several clients, so that a change in situation at one client doesn't leave you without business.

- Strive to develop marketing arrangements with other providers to help ensure a continuous flow of work.

- Exercise fiscal responsibility. Don't worry about creating the appearance of success; just do what it takes to create real success.

- Ask questions of a potential client to qualify an opportunity, determine if you intend to bid on it, and determine the amount of effort to put into your bid.

- Set up and maintain a dependable filing system that reflects and accommodates your need to retrieve information. Devise and incorporate new systems as necessary to streamline your operations.

in review

1. What question should you ask a client who has set an unrealistically aggressive deadline for a project?

2. What strategy should you employ to deal with a client who can't be bothered with reviews or project details?

3. What does the question, "Is this the hill I wish to die on?" have to do with client relationships?

4. Why is it important to insist that the client designate a single person to serve as your contact on a project?

5. What are some things a vendor should do to ensure that all bidders are competing on a level playing field?

6. What is an executive summary and why should you include one in your proposals?

7. What factors, in addition to price, help determine which bidder a client chooses as the winner?

8. Why is it important to set up and maintain efficient filing systems?

exercises

1. In this chapter we described how organization is key to running a successful business. We examined some simple, useful organization ideas, such as filing project documents in expandable hanging folders and creating a company routing slip to keep a record of incoming and outgoing hardcopy documents. Use the Web to find at least three other good ideas that your business could use to get and stay organized.

2. Keeping in mind the various types of clients that you may encounter, create a one-page handout to give to new clients that illustrates or describes how the client can work most effectively with you. You can use illustrations, diagrams, a table, text, or any other visual means to get your point across.

glossary

above the fold: the area of a Web page that can be seen without vertically scrolling the page. The area above the fold should contain the most important content.

active voice: method of constructing a sentence in which the one performing the action is the subject of the sentence. Active voice is preferable to passive voice for most types of writing.

adopt and adapt technique: an idea generation technique that looks to other fields for related problems and their solutions.

affordance: the function of an object. An object's perceived affordance is based on our cultural understanding of that object.

agile software development: methodologies which use a repeating (iterative) approach, where a series of prototypes are designed, developed, tested, and integrated into the software.

alpha release: an early version of a software system that includes partial functionality.

alt tag (also called *alternative text tag*): an HTML tag that is used to provide a description of an image. A screen reader reads the content of the alt tag, enabling blind and low-vision users to understand the purpose of the image.

application: a software program designed for a specific purpose or function.

assessment test: a usability test that helps determine how well features have been implemented in a design.

assistive technologies: hardware and software devices that help make websites and software accessible to those with disabilities.

audibility: the ease with which users can locate desired functions in a sound-only application.

below the fold: the area of a Web page that cannot be seen without vertically scrolling the page. The area below the fold usually includes content of lesser importance than that appearing above the fold.

beta release: a version of a software system that includes partial or full functionality but has not yet been fully tested.

breadcrumb trail: a horizontally oriented list of text links that represents the path taken through the pages of a website to get to the currently displayed page.

break the rules technique: an idea generation technique in which the least likely solutions to a problem are encouraged and explored.

callout: a text box with a directional line that calls attention and provides information specific to a particular screen element or component.

cascading menus (also called *nested menus* or *hierarchical menus*): a type of menu in which multiple menu levels are shown on the same screen or page.

cascading style sheets (CSS): collections of instructions that specify display elements such as fonts, font sizes, font colors, background colors, and images to a Web browser.

check box: a small labeled square that is clicked to indicate that a particular option is turned off or on.

combo box: a list box control that consists of a text box and a single-selection list box. The user can either select an item from the list or type the name of an item to select it.

command buttons (also called *pushbuttons*): a control containing a text and/or icon label that the user clicks to invoke the corresponding function.

comparison test: a usability test that compares two widely different approaches to a design.

computer-human interaction (CHI): a discipline concerned with the design, evaluation, and implementation of interactive computing systems for human use and with the study of major phenomena surrounding them.

concept drawings (also called *concept screens*): graphically rendered screens that show how a Web page or software screen will look.

consistency: a design principle that describes doing similar things in a similar way to promote familiarity with a system.

contextual inquiry: a method of learning about audience needs by observing workers and asking questions within the context of the tasks being performed.

disjoint: disconnected or scattered, as in a disjoint group of entries.

down state: a state of a pushbutton that is displayed when the user is clicking the pushbutton.

drop-down combo box: a list box control that the user clicks to display its entries. Once the entries are displayed, the user can select from the list or type the name of an item to select it.

drop-down list box: a list box control that only displays the selected choice until the box is opened by clicking, revealing the choices in the list.

edit control (also called a *text box*): a control for displaying text that the user can select for copying or pasting to another location.

effectiveness: the accuracy and completeness with which specified users can achieve specified goals in particular environments.

efficiency: the resources expended in relation to the accuracy and completeness of goals achieved.

equivalent alternative: an alternate means of presenting the content of a site or software to make it accessible to those with disabilities.

essential use case: a method of recording user intentions and system responses used as part of task analysis.

ethnography: studying the habits of a group of people by living among them. In user analysis, observing people while they perform their jobs to gain insights applicable to the design of a website or software system.

evaluation test: an assessment usability test that is performed after a website or software has been released and is in use.

exploratory test: a usability test that is performed early in the design phase that checks user reactions to the functions planned for a website or software system.

extended-selection list box: a list box control that enables the user to select a single entry, a continuous block of entries, or a disjoint group of entries. Multiple entries are selected by pressing a combination of keys while clicking with the mouse.

facilitator (also called the *monitor* or *test administrator*): the person who serves as the host of a usability test.

feature creep: the tendency of a software program to become laden with features over time, sacrificing usability.

feedback: information that a system provides to a user that indicates the status of his or her action.

Fitts' Law: a law stating that the time it takes a human to reach a target depends on the distance and size of that target. It takes humans longer to reach targets that are small and farther away from the current position.

flowchart: a visual representation that uses special symbols connected by arrows to illustrate the steps and flow of a process.

flow diagram: a visual representation of a website or software system that uses rectangles and lines to show the system's structure and key screens at a glance.

forgiveness: a design principle that describes systems that enable users to easily recover from mistakes or unintended actions.

functional prototype: an example of a website or software program that includes some functionality.

functional specifications: a document that includes schematic images and detailed descriptions of the effects of activating any control.

glow: a highlighting effect that is displayed when the user rolls the mouse cursor over an element such as a button.

glow state (also called the *highlighted state*): a pushbutton state in which glow is displayed when the mouse cursor is within the pushbutton's boundaries.

gold master (also called the *production master*): the final, tested version of a software system.

group brainstorming: an idea generation technique that uses a group of people to generate spontaneous ideas to solve a particular problem.

heading: a subtitle that introduces a content area of a Web page. Headings make it easy for users to scan a page's content.

heuristic: a rule of thumb or guideline.

hierarchical menus (also called *cascading menus* or *nested menus*): a type of menu in which multiple menu levels are shown on the same screen or page.

highlighted state (also called the *glow state*): a pushbutton state in which glow is displayed when the mouse cursor is within the pushbutton's boundaries.

human-computer interaction (HCI): a discipline concerned with the design, evaluation, and implementation of interactive computing systems for human use and with the study of major phenomena surrounding them.

hyperlinks: short sections of underlined text that the user clicks to display a new page, text section, image, or other element.

hypertext: a system of linking documents, images, and other elements together on the Web.

icons: symbolic pictures used to convey meaning.

image map: a graphic with a number of active areas that the user can click individually.

inactive state (also called the *unavailable state*): a pushbutton state in which the contrast of the button is lowered to make it look dim. This indicates that the pushbutton is unavailable for clicking.

incubate technique: an idea generation technique in which people set their mind to a task, then wait until a solution emerges.

information architect: a worker who specializes in the organization and design of a software application.

instructional designer: a worker who specializes in the design of systems for teaching or training.

interface: the means by which humans interact with a computer to fulfill a purpose.

intranet: a private network within an organization that enables employees to share company information and resources.

inverted L: a method of arranging Web pages in which the main content menu is aligned horizontally along the top of the page and the selected category's menu is displayed along the left side, forming an inverted L shape.

inverted pyramid: a method of structuring writing in which the most important idea is presented first, then supporting details are given. Web content is best written using the inverted pyramid structure.

lateral thinking: the process of developing new approaches by changing perspective.

Likert scale: a scale that enables users to indicate the degree of agreement or disagreement with a presented concept or statement.

list box: a control that presents a list of related options to the user.

logging sheet: a form used to record the participant's results in each task of a usability test.

low vision: subnormal vision affecting approximately 3.5% of the U.S. population. Low vision ranges from loss of some vision to near-total blindness.

mapping: the relationship between a control, the thing it affects, and the outcome that results when the control is operated.

menu: a list of choices in an application.

menu bar: a usually horizontally-oriented list of menu titles in an application.

menu items: a list of selectable items, consisting of text and sometimes icons, that are displayed beneath a menu title.

menu titles: the top-level names (e.g., File, Edit, Help) that appear on a menu bar.

metaphor: a familiar image used to make an unfamiliar idea, experience, or process understandable.

mind mapping: a technique for capturing and organizing ideas using combinations of fishbone-like lines, text, and doodles.

minimalism: a deliberate reduction in complexity for the user's benefit.

modal dialog: a box containing controls that prevents the user from selecting or activating any other controls except those within the box.

monitor (also called the *facilitator* or *test administrator*): the person who serves as the host of a usability test.

multiple-selection list box: a control that consists of a group of check boxes within a list box. It provides an intuitive means of allowing users to select multiple entries in the list.

natural mapping: a strong, positive association between a control and the resulting action.

nested menus (also called *cascading menus* or *hierarchical menus*): a type of menu in which multiple menu levels are shown on the same screen or page.

no constraints technique: an idea generation technique in which all constraints are purposely ignored.

normal state: the way a pushbutton is displayed normally, when it is available but not being pointed to or clicked.

observer: someone who watches a usability test, but who does not have a substantial role in conducting the test.

option button (also called a *radio button*): a small circular button, usually labeled and displayed in groups. Clicking one of the buttons in the group deselects the currently selected button.

orientation script: a document that is read to each participant of a usability test to ensure that all participants are given the same set of instructions.

outline control (also called a *tree control*): a control that organizes its elements in an outline format.

page title: text that summarizes the main purpose of a Web page.

participant: the person who serves as the subject of a usability test.

passive voice: method of constructing a sentence in which the receiver of the action is the subject of the sentence. Passive voice invites ambiguity, which weakens writing. Active voice is preferable to passive voice for most types of writing.

persona: imaginary people that designers create to represent the various user types of a website or software system.

post-test questionnaire: a series of questions that give a usability test participant an opportunity to provide conclusions and recommendations about the product being tested.

product gallery: a technique of grouping images and descriptions of products offered for sale on a Web page.

production master (also called the *gold master*): the final, tested version of a software system.

proposal: a document created by a vendor to try to win business from a client.

prototype: a partial implementation of a software system or website.

pushbuttons (also called *command buttons*): a control containing a text and/or icon label that the user clicks to invoke the corresponding function.

pyramid structure: a method of structuring writing in which a series of ideas is presented leading to a conclusion. Essays are often written using a pyramid structure.

radio button (also called an *option button*): a small circular button, usually labeled and displayed in groups. Clicking one of the buttons in the group deselects the currently selected button.

random word technique: an idea generation technique in which a random word is applied to a problem to enable the mind to make connections and develop possible solutions.

recorder: the person responsible for jotting down details of a usability test and often serving as timer.

redundant text links: a set of text links that mimics the function of graphic-based menus, enabling blind and low-vision users to navigate the site.

refreshable braille display: a device that is used in combination with a screen reader to convert the screen reader's output to braille. This enables deaf-blind users to access websites and software.

request for proposal (RFP): a document that a client sends to potential vendors to solicit proposals for a project.

reversal technique: an idea generation technique in which the problem is reversed.

RFP (request for proposal): a document that a client sends to potential vendors to solicit proposals for a project.

rich-text box: a control used for receiving user-provided text that can have special emphasis such as bolding, underline, and italics.

sans serif typeface: a typeface such as Arial and Helvetica that does not include tiny lines on the bases and tops of characters such as A, I, and M.

satisfaction: the comfort and acceptability of the work system to its users and other people affected by its use.

screen magnifier: software that magnifies the screen image up to 16 times or more. Screen magnifiers often include other enhancement features, such as software-based screen readers.

screen reader: software that converts the text on a Web page or software program to synthesized speech.

screening questionnaire: a set of questions given to potential participants for a usability test to select candidates whose qualifications best match the requirements of the study.

Section 508: a section of the Rehabilitation Act of 1973 that requires that electronic and information technology, including websites and software, that is developed, procured, maintained, or used by the federal government be accessible to people with disabilities.

serif typeface: a typeface such as Times New Roman that includes tiny lines on the bases and tops of characters such as A, I, and M.

shortcut key: a key sequence (such as Ctrl-S for Save) that can be invoked without the associated menu being displayed.

single-selection list box: a list box control that enables the user to select a single entry.

site/software map: a set of links that describes a large, complex site's architecture.

site/software outline: an outline that shows the structure of a website or software system.

slider: a control that enables users to select one of a range of values by dragging an indicator along a usually horizontally or vertically oriented line.

software/site outline: an outline that shows the structure of a website or software system.

spin box: a control used to enable users to select one of a range of continuous values, such as a list of contiguous numbers.

splatter vision (also called *unfocused attention*): the technique of looking with unfocused eyes to see an image or scene "all at once." Using this technique enables the viewer to quickly judge the contrast and focal points of a design.

static text field: a control used for displaying noneditable, non-selectable text, such as that used for titles, labels, and instructions.

storyboard: a set of sketches or illustrations that illustrates a specific sequence of steps, pages, or screens.

style guide: a document that defines the style conventions that guide the design and development of software or websites.

survey: an online or human-conducted series of questions designed to analyze user needs.

systems development life cycle (SDLC): the process of analyzing, planning, designing, developing, and testing software using a step-by-step methodology.

systems development method (SDM): process used to develop software.

tab control: a control that organizes pages of options or information of similar type.

tag line: a brief statement that summarizes a company or organization.

task: a specific function that a user wants or needs to accomplish.

task analysis: the process of breaking a process down into its component steps.

test administrator (also called the *monitor or facilitator*): the person who serves as the host of a usability test.

text box (also called an *edit control*): a control for displaying text that the user can select for copying or pasting to another location.

text field: one of several different controls used for displaying or allowing user input of text.

tooltip: a small text box displayed when the user rolls the mouse cursor over a specific text segment, control, or image that gives additional information about that item.

tree control (also called an *outline control*): a control that organizes its elements in an outline format.

truncate: cut off.

unavailable state (also called the *inactive state*): a pushbutton state in which the contrast of the button is lowered to make it look dim. This indicates that the pushbutton is unavailable for clicking.

unfocused attention (also called *splatter vision*): the technique of looking with unfocused eyes to see an image or scene "all at once." Using this technique enables the viewer to quickly judge the contrast and focal points of a design.

usability: the effectiveness, efficiency, and satisfaction with which specified users achieve specified goals in particular environments.

usability engineers: a group of workers who conduct testing to help ensure that a product is usable to its intended audience.

usability test: a test performed using human subjects that determines the ease or difficulty with which the subjects can complete given tasks using an existing or proposed design.

usability test plan: a document that summarizes the purpose, goals, audience, content, and methodology for a usability test.

user-centered design: the process and result of designing with the needs of the user in mind.

user experience: all facets of the interaction between a human and a company, its products, services, and systems.

user interface: the means by which humans interact with a computer to fulfill a purpose.

user stories: requirements captured in a user's own words used as input to the design process.

videotape consent form: a form that a participant in a usability test signs to give permission to videotape the test.

virtual manipulatives: computerized representations of the manipulatives, such as number cubes, spinners, math mats, etc. that are often used in schools.

visibility: a design principle that describes the ease with which users can find the functions that a website or software system offers.

W3C (World Wide Web Consortium): The Web's primary standards organization.

Waterfall model: a step-by-step method for analyzing, planning, designing, developing, and testing software in which the process always flows forward.

watermark: a faint graphic image that serves as a background for other elements on a page.

Web Content Accessibility Guidelines (WCAG): a set of guidelines published by the World Wide Web Consortium (W3C) to help designers and developers create accessible websites.

Web framework: a semi-functional prototype that is delivered in a Web browser.

what/when/how: a technique used in instructional writing in which the writer first tells the audience *what* the procedure is, then tells *when* the audience might use it, and describes *how* the method or object is used.

wireframes: schematic sketches that represent the functional layout of a Web page or software screen.

wizard: an interactive aid that guides a user through the completion of a complex task by presenting its steps one at a time.

word wrap: the automatic breaking up of long lines at word boundaries, enabling users to continue typing without pressing the Enter key at the end of each line.

Workforce Investment Act of 1998: act signed into law by President Clinton that significantly expanded and strengthened the technology access requirements stated in Section 508.

World Wide Web Consortium (W3C): the Web's primary standards organization.

WYSIWYG: an acronym for "what you see is what you get."

index